The BaGua

Science, Analysis, and Interpretation

CHARACTER MAP

THROUGH

CHINESE NUMEROLOGY

RELEASE ONE | RAKHEM SEKU

SECOND EDITION

ISBN: 978-0-9801663-0-9

PUBLISHED BY: SELF-AS-SOURCE PUBLISHING

INITIAL COVER DESIGN BY SHAWN WILSON

TABLE OF CONTENTS

How to Use This Book

This book will provide the student with a means to assess natal strengths and weakness in their character and determine when and how these traits can be utilized most efficiently. This book provides the initiate with the tools to create a complete character map of themselves or others. Relationships can be strengthened, partners more effectively selected, and project more effectively completed.

The character map will identify how each individual is viewing and interacting with the world. There are no wrong or right characteristics as even those character traits that cause conflict in our lives can be our greatest resources to accomplish our goals.

This work will also reveal how people and things should interact with one another based upon (1) their collective characters and (2) the number of people one is interacting with. There are definite laws governing how forces of personality interact with one another and these laws are represented in numbers.

Between understanding your character traits and assessing the "numbers" of people in your environment one can modify outcomes and create successful and harmonious interaction with others. For example, a husband and wife living together with no children are subject to the laws of the number two (2) or the law of complimentary relationships. Success in their relationship will demand that each person plays the proper role in the many areas of the relationship (i.e. finance, social, conflict resolution, sex, spirituality, etc.). Whereas a couple with three children are subject to the laws governing the number five which I thoroughly explain in this book.

Numbers are at the root of this book, but only in reference to the principles they represent. As a result, this book is also heavily focused on the BaGua or I Ching science utilized heavily in traditional Chinese cultures. The BaGua system utilizes numbers and maps them to trigrams which are a combination of three lines either broken (− −) or solid (-----). These trigrams can be used the same as numbers, to help persons understand various character types and how they blend or do not blend. The BaGua system is one of many systems that can be used to map a person's character; there are others. The purpose of using the BaGua is that it organizes and relates these numbers/trigrams in a way that explains them relative to the creative process governing the manifestation of all things in the world. The BaGua also represents these numbers in pictorial forms that make them easier to understand and relate to one another.

Another way to view numbers systematically is by applying the use of the Magical Square. By combining the basics of numerology, the BaGua, and the Magic Square arrangements I render in The Bagua Character Map a powerful holistic system of classification. As the reader will find, everything we do or wish to accomplish is a form of creation and as such must adhere to a strict set of laws in order to develop successfully. It is this knowledge that escapes most people and the reason why so many relationships, ventures, personal goals, and business goals fail. If we were to simply follow the necessary steps we could greatly increase our chances of success.

To gain immediate use from this work the reader can take one of two approaches: (1) to read the book from start to finish in order to understand one's personality and the fundamental concepts of the BaGua classification system or (2) target particular chapters and topics to more quickly gain an understanding of one's own personality. Approach #1 has its advantages in that the reader will become familiar with the terms, definitions and theories that comprise The Bagua classification system (i.e. names and function of trigrams, methods for analyzing people, etc.). Approach #2 will allow the reader to have immediate insight into certain characteristics of the BaGua classification system without having to understand all of its aspects.

Approach Two Key Chapters
- Chapter 2: Calculating Your Natal Trigrams – use the chapter to figure out your yearly and monthly trigrams.

- Chapter 7: Analysis of the Nine Fundamental Forces – Go to the *Trigram Analysis* section and find your trigram based on the results from Chapter 2. You can read for both your yearly and monthly trigrams.
- Chapters 10 – 19: Natal Trigram Analysis. Find your natal trigram or number obtained in Chapter 2. Each trigram has its own chapter starting with chapter 10. Read the configuration for your trigram to gain insights into the various aspects of your personality and how it's affected when superimposed against the general environment (represented by the Magic Square or Lo Shu arrangement).

The reader can also use Approach Two to do a quick analysis on friends and loved ones to get an even better idea how certain traits appear in our personalities.

That said, all you need to get started is the person's year and month of birth and we can detail some very specific character traits. The calculation could go to the day, hour, and minute level, but that is beyond the scope of this work. The reader will find plenty to work with just using the year and month of birth.

Enjoy the discovery of the BaGua and your own BaGua Character Map!!

Chapter 1: Two Principles Governing the World

A common exercise for scientists is to classify and categorize everything in the world. The same holds true for philosophers and metaphysicians. Classification is a tool to help communicate principals that govern the particular area of study. There are as many classifications as there are numbers in the world, but because this work is deeply rooted in numbers and the principles they represent, we will classify life's phenomena through them. The numbers we are focused on in this work are (1) through (9) because they are the foundation from which all others are built and from them we can acquire knowledge of the world around us.

Obviously, the number (1) contains the highest principle in physical creation, but for simplicity, let's start with the number (2) which is symbolic for the universal principle of creation/perception, or the acts of doing and interpreting; indeed, acting and experiencing. From one perspective we can categorize all of life's activities or processes into one of those two classifications.

The act of doing comes from initiating our way through the world. This includes thinking, moving, judging, and all of the verbs in our language. In other words, everything that we initiate our person's to do can be classified as an action. The act of experiencing is popularly viewed as anything coming through our five senses of seeing, smelling, touching, hearing, and tasting (actually all just one sensation of touch/feel).

Note: The five senses are really the same sensations of touch (atomic interaction), just experienced through various parts of the body.

There are two main motions in life. Humans and all other "things" are either initiating things in life or being initiated. Both have value. But this principle summarizes the importance of the number (2). As stated above a foundational number in the

BaGua and the world is two (2). This is revealed in common opposites known to man: man – woman, high – low, magnetic – electric, cold – hot, yin – yang, in – out, right – left, winter – summer, etc. Many concepts and structures of our society are based upon this principal: stop – go in traffic, House and Senate in government, etc.

The number (2) implies a creative/perceptive process. An important part of the creative and perceptive process is the knowledge that a very important part of any "thing" tends to be unseen. This invisible aspect of a thing also tends to be implemented before the seen or visible part. A good example is a building foundation which is underground versus the building itself. A natural example is a tree with branches and leaves above and roots below. This can also be seen with non-man made structures like an ant hill which above may vary in size from a centimeter to some feet depending on the part of the world, but below is always much more expansive and elaborate. This seen/unseen principle or (2) principle can also be found in the architecture of traditional cultures where the house or building utilizes the natural landscape as a foundation in support of the above ground structure. For example, the mud hut will be made of a mixture of materials originating from the ground upon which it is built; thus, making it an extension of the ground giving it a firm foundation. The (2) principle is one that most every natural process depends upon for existence.

I begin by explaining this principle of (2) because it is the number that many students are able to intuitively connect symbolic meaning to. It is important – before you calculate your natal trigram or number - that you understand how the numbers will be personified in this work. The Bagua Character Map will provide in depth treatment to each number that exists (1-9) just as we have summarized the number (2). That said, let's start with the fun stuff and calculate some natal strengths and weaknesses based upon our year and month of birth.

Chapter 2: Calculating Your Natal Trigrams

We are going to make some calculations now, but you won't necessarily be armed with the tools to understand them. That's ok. All is revealed throughout this work and you can choose to investigate your natal character traits right away or learn about them relative to the earth's natal character traits. Let's begin.

First let's familiarize ourselves with some common terms:

- **BaGua** – an ancient system perfected in traditional Chinese culture that classifies all of life's phenomena into nine categories. These nine categories are also graphically represented by a square (the Magic Square) and/or an octagon in which one can view how the phenomena, represented by trigrams, interact with one another. To view the BaGua diagram with all trigrams in place see the appendix: BaGua picture.
- **Trigram** – A three character symbol made up of broken and unbroken lines that symbolize a universal law or concept that operates in the world and within our personalities. To view all the trigrams and get a quick explanation of what they each represent go to the appendix: Trigram Quick Reference. The trigrams are actually the symbol utilized in the BaGua and the I Ching so all references in this book will be made relative to them.
- **Natal Trigram** – Also indicated by the Natal Trait in Chapters 10 – 19. A trigram that represents your dominant personality relative to your year or month of birth: Yearly Natal Trigram or Monthly Natal Trigram. The natal trigrams will give a great reference point to determine auspicious years, months, and character traits.
- **Baseline Trigram** – Also indicated by the Base House in Chapters 10 – 19. A trigram that represents the state of the earth and universe at a

given time (year or month). This trigram indicates the state of the earth consciousness during a particular year or month. We will use this baseline trigram to contrast against our natal trigram and see how our view of the world may be skewed or off center.

- **Hexagram** – A hexagram is six character symbol made up of broken (– –) and unbroken (-----) lines that symbolize a universal law or concept that operates in the world and within our personalities. A hexagram is made up of two trigrams, one sitting on top of the other. When we use a hexagram, or two trigrams, to understand our personalities or character we receive even greater insight into ourselves.

- **Number** – From a modern cultural context, a number is a commonly used symbol to designate the quantity of things at a given time. From the context of the BaGua, a number is symbol that denotes both the quantity of things at a given time and the quality of those things individually and as a group. In the BaGua system there are only nine numbers: one through nine. Numbers ten and above represent a different type of symbol used to quantify and qualify sets of things and define their interaction. This is explained in greater detail in later chapters (The Numeric Creative Unfolding).

- **Lo Shu** – Also called the Magic Square, in its modern representation. The arrangement of numerical symbols made up of nine clusters of circular markings in a square where all rows, columns, and diagonals add up to 15. This number arrangement implies the quality of each number and shows where each number falls within the creative process. See the Appendix for pictorial representations of the Lo Shu.

There are two cycles that have a major impact on your personality. One is the yearly or solar cycle and the other is the monthly or lunar. The yearly cycle is the one that dictates the seasons and how hot or cold the earth is on any given day throughout the year. It is measured by the year or 365.25 days (or just 365 days for ease of calculation).

The characteristic of the yearly cycle is that it is long, slow, and powerful relative to other cycles in our lives (lunar, weekly, daily, hourly, etc.).

The monthly cycle is often measured by the months of the year, which are originally based upon our moon's phases which recycle themselves every 28.5 days. The monthly cycle is characterized as short and fast with relative power. Each person's chart and the particular year and month we are analyzing will determine how each of these cycles will influence our lives.

Yearly Natal Trigram

Some *VERY IMPORTANT* rules to know up front:

- If the month and day of your birth is between January 1st and February 4th use the previous year. Example: If person X is born on February 1st, 1966, then use 1965 for your calculation.

- Keep adding the individual numbers in the year until you have one single digit number. 10 will be $1 + 0 = 1$.

1. Determine the year and month of birth.

Ex. 1:
Year = 1965
Month = December (so we will not have to use the previous year)

2. Determine the Yearly Natal Trigram by using ONLY the year of birth.

Add up individual numbers in the year of birth. $X + X + X + X = XY \longrightarrow X + Y = XX$ ($\rightarrow X + X = Y$)
Then add the double digits until you get a single digit even if you have to do this adding twice.

Year = 1965
$1 + 9 + 6 + 5 = 21 \rightarrow 2 + 1 = 3$

Male Formula

For males subtract the resulting number from 11. $(11 - X)$ $X =$ yearly number

$11 - 3 = 8$

So (8) is the yearly number. This person is an (8) person based on the yearly calculation!

Female Formula

For women, calculate male value $(11 - x)$ and use conversion table below.

$11 - 3 = 8$

Use conversion chart find male value and see female value to the right.

Female born in 1965 would be a (7) person.

Note: You can also check your yearly number/trigram by using the Yearly Cycle Chart found in the Appendix of this text. The separate calculation for the female yearly Gua can be found in the appendix without the need for conversion.

Table: Male Female Conversion Table

Male	Female
1	5
2	4
3	3
4	2
5	1
6	9
7	8
8	7
9	6

Monthly Natal Trigram

To determine one's monthly trigram use the Trigram Chart –
Years and Months chart in the appendix. Go through the chart
and find the table representing your year of birth. Then find
your month of birth. For males use the number in the Male
column and for females use the number in the Female column.
The number to trigram conversion table is below and is the same
for both yearly and monthly numbers.

Important points to note:
- Remember to make the yearly adjustment if born before
  February 5th of a particular year.
- For individuals born between the 1st and 4th of a month,
  use the previous month.

Table: Number to Trigram Conversion Table

Number	Trigram
1	KAN
2	KUN
3	CHEN
4	SUN
5	Et. All
6	CHIEN
7	TUI
8	KEN
9	LI

Chapter 3: The Numeric Creative Unfolding

In this chapter we will look at the manifestation of numbers through two perspectives: quantitative and qualitative. The quantitative perspective involves counting the number of specific elements throughout different levels of the creative process; whereas the qualitative perspective involves adding the number designations (or the numbers within the spheres in the diagram) to arrive at another number. These two perspectives are important as they both play a role in how the creative process works and the two primary factors of how to interact with other elements in the environment: first, by the quantity of other elements around you and secondly, by the quality of elements around you.

Figure: Number Creation

This diagram shows how the (1) becomes many and how the numbers of the BaGua get their quality and structure relative to one another. The diagram is split into two sections: 1) Quantitative (Number Origin) and 2) Qualitative (Number Origin). The Qualitative section illustrates how the one universal constant can give birth to a multitude of forms, in this case nine forms -- including itself.

The bottom row contains eight numbers that are grouped by their opposites or complimentary counterparts. All subgroups add up to (ten), which in turn add up to (1), indicating they represent two polarities of one whole. As we will see (9) and (1) are complements representing two polarities of energy. (3) and (7) are complements representing two polarities of awareness (or ways to view the world). (2) and (8) are complements representing two states of matter and (4) and (6) are compliments representing two methods of the intention. As will be illustrated later the two foursomes of (1), (9), (3), and (7) or *Heaven* and (2), (8), (4), and (6) or *Earth* make up two complimentary forces that make up the one universal whole from which all of life is derived represented by (5,5).

At this point, lets trace the unfolding process starting with (5,5) in the top row. The (5,5) sphere and row represents the totality of all that is to be created in the world. In essence it is made up of awareness, intention, energy, matter, and a fifth manifestation which is a representation of all of these elements bound in union. The (5,5) represents a level or plane of existence which exists and subsists throughout all of manifested creation. Its presence is a part of all things, yet it exists beyond time and space. This fact is inherent in its number (ten) which is a cumulative set of all elements represented by numbers (1) through (9). Its infinitude is indicated by the fact that within this (ten) set is also a (5,5) (which is split into two, as it is represented in both the yin and yang subsets). This (5,5) element also represents a complete set of nine unique elements, within which exists another (5,5) element and so on. This science is equivalent to molecular and atomic theory as modern scientists attempt to find the smallest manifestation of matter on the planet. BaGua science allows them to cease the search and know for a fact through mathematical proof that there is no smallest manifestation of matter. Trying to find the smallest or largest thing in the universe is equivalent to attempting to pinpoint the starting date of the universe and its corresponding end date. Creation is infinite by its nature; no beginning and no ending.

When (5,5) gives birth to the next set of elements: (1,9,3,7) and (2,4,6,8); it does so by releasing four of its five originating elements (consciousness, will, energy, and matter) and keeping only the conglomeration of those four (which is the fifth (5,5)) for itself. Therefore, the (5,5) element represents both an element and a plane of existence; where a plane is defined as any two dimensional space that can be confined or defined by four unique elements. Again, the fact that (5,5) can represent both a single element and a plane is a testament to its infinitude. Because the (5,5) element always exists and is the source of creation it is both the first manifestation in the world and the source of the first act of creation; thus, here the first point and plane are created.

Note: A plane is actually made up of four points, but the implication is that the two points are always in reference to their source. In math, when creating two dimensional graphs, we learned the source was the (0,0) point at the intersection of the x and y axis. Here we use the yin and yang components of each of the elements; thus, receiving four total. The (5,5) element replaces the (0,0) point and becomes the center of the plane that is ultimately formed; this is its same position in the BaGua as seen in diagram BaGua Diagram – 1 later in the text.

The elements (1,9,3,7) and (2,4,6,8) represent the second stage in the creative process as they leave no material behind in the creative process. Therefore, they do not represent points or planes, but rather energy or movement. Symbolically, this stage of creation is represented by the Will; where the first was represented by Consciousness. The (1,9,3,7) and (2,4,6,8) elements create the (1,9); (3,7); (2,8); and (4,6) elements. Again, there is no material manifestation; thus, no points or planes are created. This is the third stage in the creative process and is represented by Energy. The (1,9); (3,7); (2,8); and (4,6) elements create the individual numbers 1, 9, 3, 7, 2, 8, 4, and 6. This is the forth stage of creation as the originating (5,5) material has been differentiated qualitatively and quantitatively into its finest components.

This creative process begets a grand total of nine elements and five planes via four stages of creation wherein each stage has its yin and yang component. Thus, the four stages of creation can be further broken down into eight total stages.

The five planes are generated by grouping the eight complimentary elements (two points) into their originating four groups; thus, producing four planes plus the fifth original plane in (5,5). Diagram Plane – 1 gives additional detail on the process, but from another perspective.

Diagram: Plane – 1

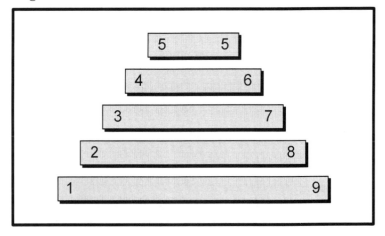

This diagram illustrates the quantitative creative process revealing how the number (5) comes into the world. The five original elements unfold in the form of planes that exist as complimentary relationships in the physical world.

Note*: We will see later that when we calculate a person's natal BaGua Configuration based upon their birth year or month, that year becomes their center or (5,5). Everything else that happens and manifests in their life will originate from that centering perspective as they will use that natal energy as the basis for their interaction, response, and reaction with the world.*

At this point, let's move into our number derivation and explore how each number in our number tree manifests and gets its quality.

A Summary of Numbers 1 through 9

One

Let's address why the first sphere or number is represented by two fives (5,5) rather than the number (1). It would seem that the number (1) would be the logical choice to represent the first number in the hierarchy. I agree. Remember the (5,5) represents the qualitative not the quantitative manifestation of the number. The (1) is implied in that there is only one (5,5) element; thus, the quantitative expression is also given. The double fives (5,5) actually represent the implication of (1)'s eventual division into two equal parts. If there are only 9 base numbers in creation then the first divides into two equal parts. It follows to ask then which number should represent the undifferentiated (1) and the differentiated (2). Five is exactly half of (ten) and (ten) is actually the representative for (1) [10 = 1 + 0]. A (ten) actually represents a set; one set. (Ten) is made up of ten elements with nine distinct qualities or, in other words, nine total elements in quality and ten in quantity. Two of the elements, the fives (5,5), share the same quality. When added together they produce (1).

$$5 + 5 = 10 \rightarrow 1 + 0 = 1$$

Thus, the double fives are two elements sharing the exact same quality. That's how we arrive at a (5,5) arrangement representing the first element of creation.

Two

We have seen from our analysis of the first spherical manifestation that each element has inherent qualities that, through deductive reasoning, can be applied. We are working with numbers (1) through (9) and that (5,5) has been allocated to represent the first manifestation, we can assume that all of the other numbers are contained or inherent within the first element. The proof for this is as follows:

$$1 + 2 + 3 + 4 + 6 + 7 + 8 + 9 = 40$$

We add 40 to the double five configuration $(5 + 5 = 10)$ as follows:

$$40 + 10 = 50 \rightarrow 5 + 0 = 5$$

When the 40 is split into two equal parts, but not the same in quality, we arrive at $40/2 = 20 \rightarrow 2 + 0 = 2$.

If we split the numbers up into two groups where each group makes up one of the two new manifested elements we have line two in figure *Number Creation*. The two groups are made up of (1,9,3,7) and (2,4,6,8). These groups represent all of the odd and even numbers, again with the exception of 5 as it is represented in the original single element. So for the purposes of explaining numerical manifestation we will focus on the remaining numbers even though five is also represented in these two groups. The unifying and original principle is never lost in the creative process. Each of these groups although equal in quantity to 20 or 2 are not the same in quality. We can represent them as the Yang and Yin elements commonly know through the Taoist system. Again, the unifying element from which the Yang and Yin are derived are implicit within both of these groupings.

The creative process of one element splitting into two is commonly seen in the world.

From a material/elemental perspective the number (2) is represented by level (row) two in figure *Number Creation*.

There are two elements at this level which have split from the one element at level one.

Three

The number two has been manifested so how do we arrive at three. Quantitatively, (3) is represented by the summation of elements (spheres) on levels one and two. One sphere on level one and two spheres on level two give us three. From a qualitative perspective the number (3) is best represented by two of the four spheres on level three (1,9; 2,8; 6,4; 7,3) and the unifying element of (5,5). This is due to the quality of (3), and all of the heavenly numbers (1, 3, 7, 9), which has deep insight into the creative process. This deep insight is rooted in the unifying element (5,5); thus, level three in the physical and level one in the mental combine to form this power.

(3), from a quantitative perspective, is simply the two spheres on level 2 plus the originating element on level 1 from which they are manifest. This originating element can be found implicit within both of the two spheres on level 2 and maintains its original quality. Without this process of manifestation we would have chaos as there would be no frame of reference from which to keep each element grounded. So in essence we have three entities: (1,3,7,9), (2,4,6,8), and the (5,5) where one (5) sits in each of the original spheres. The elemental creation of (3) can also be seen throughout the origin chart: four groups of three spheres making up the twelve total elements on levels three and four, etc.

So essentially (3) is symbolic for the "law" of the universe that has knowledge or at least proximity to the original split of the great "oneness" and contains the unseen material of understanding (keys) to how the original two spheres can function harmoniously in an evolving manifestation process.

Four

The same qualitative creative process that brought about the (2) now brings about the (4). If we take our original two spheres on level 2 and divide them per level three of figure *Number*

23

Creation we obtain: (1,9), (3,7), (2,8), and (4,6). When each of these numbers is added up within the spheres we obtain (4) as follows:

$1 + 9 = 10 \rightarrow 1 + 0 = 1$
$3 + 7 = 10 \rightarrow 1 + 0 = 1$
$2 + 8 = 10 \rightarrow 1 + 0 = 1$
$4 + 6 = 10 \rightarrow 1 + 0 = 1$

Take the sum of these:

$1 + 1 + 1 + 1 = 4$

Again, if we add the double five (5,5) we return back to originating five elements. Qualitatively speaking the number (4) has the same properties as the number (2), but with an additional level of differentiation. This is helpful as both (2) and (4) are earthly numbers and are responsible for defining all things in creation. (2) divides physical things into their male (yang) and female (yin) components while (4) further defines those gender designations.

From a quantitative perspective if we add the number of elements existing on level three we obtain four elements as well.

So individuals tied to the number (4) tend to have a mastery over the classification of physical things. These individuals can see things for what they are and don't get caught up in possibilities or what could be. In other words, the imagination or ability to visualize beyond what is presented to them is virtually non-existent.

Five
We will prove (5,5) by proving all the other numbers in creation because (5,5) is a foundational number representing an entire sub system; where a sub system is defined as one-half of a complete system. In other words, when all coupled elements in a sub system are doubled then we have a complete system.

Thus, from a qualitative and quantitative perspective we add the spheres (and numbers within them) up on level one and level three to come to five. These two levels together represent a sub system before it splits into ten elements (9 unique made up of levels four and one).

It also has to be noted that (5) is the middle number of the nine total numbers in the BaGua classification system. It is flanked by (1, 2, 3, 4) on one side and (6, 7, 8, 9) on the other side. So from one standpoint it has no affinity for any one grouping. This can also be seen when looking at numbers from their heavenly and earthly designations of (1, 3, 7, 9) and (2, 4, 6, 8), respectively. (5) is not a part of either of these groupings and serves more as an aid to both individually and in their working together.

So individuals tied to the number (5) tend to be more interested in balance and unity of all things; rather, than a self centered posture on life. Also, because their charge is to help others and unify groups, these individuals tend to be multi-talented, but not the masters of any one trade.

Six

The numbers (6) and (7) communicate a beautiful concept in the law of creation. As you can see by figure *Number Creation* both (6) and (7) are a bit less intuitive in terms of how they come into being than the other numbers. This is because in the actual creative process both (6) and (7) are hidden from physical view.

From a quantitative standpoint (6) is obtained from adding the number of elements on levels two and three together. Level one or the double five (5,5) is not required because the prerequisite for (6) is not the understanding of unity, but rather the ability to affect reality through mental processes. In other words, these individuals are able to see a complete picture of reality in their minds. They are often referred to as daydreamers and considered non attentive, but this is actually a misunderstanding. This will be covered in more detail in later chapters. Because of this fact level four is not required as this mental or metaphysical process is not yet evident on the grossest physical plane (level four).

From a qualitative standpoint (6) is created by adding the entire right or left side below (5,5) and seven is obtained by adding the (5,5) in. Again, (6) is directly connected to the physical world; thus, tying (6) to level four of the *Number Creation* diagram.

Seven

The number (7) is derived the same way as (6) except it includes level one in figure *Number Creation* as the prerequisite for wisdom and intuitive thinking which requires knowledge of oneness or unity. Thus, (7)'s nature forces it to be one with the highest principle of physical reality – unity (level one) and to be tied to the physical plane; thus, the need for level four.

From a qualitative standpoint (7) is created by adding the entire right or left side of figure *Number Creation* including the double (5,5). So to obtain the consciousness of the number (7) we use one half of levels two, three, and four and all of level one.

As result individuals tied to the number (7) have a tendency to be "religious" and judgmental in their approach to life. Religious is not saying they are in to religion, but more so dedicated to what they perceive to be the higher principles governing whatever it is they are involved with.

Eight

The nature of the number (8) is intimate interaction between things. (8) is composed two sets of four which are divided into their yin and yang natures. Thus, like (2) it involves the interaction between things and events. However (8) is an incomplete system being made up of two incomplete subsystems (four and four); thus, it lacks the inherent wisdom and unity of the first manifestation of physical reality (5,5). Thus, from a qualitative perspective we arrive at (8) through the addition of the numbers in the spheres on levels three and four in figure *Number Creation*. This makes sense as (8) is primarily interested in relationships and thus does its work on the physical realm (levels three and four primarily).

From a quantitative perspective the number of unique elements on level four of creation is eight.

Nine

The nature of the number (9) is that of completeness and maturity. It is the coming together of two sub systems (five and five) to form one complete system of manifested reality. Again, five plus five is ten, but when two of the ten elements are the same our net is (9). Thus, from a material manifestation standpoint the end of the creative process produces nine distinct and unique elements (levels one and four) to produce a total of nine.

From a qualitative perspective we receive (9) when we add up the numbers in spheres of the following three levels figure *Number Creation*: levels (1,2,3), levels (1,3,4), or levels (1,2,4). This makes sense as (9) is a multiple of (3) as well.

So individuals tied to the number (9) tend to have a sense of purpose about them and tend to be beyond superficial things. They are hard workers and tend to sacrifice themselves and others for their ultimate goal.

The 0 – 1 Relationship

The numbers (1) and zero are very similar and share many of the same qualities. Zero is a number or symbol representing a void of physical manifestation. From that perspective there is nothing to be perceived because there is nothing to do the perceiving. This is nothingness. Technically, this state is imperceptible unless it is viewed inside a controlled environment, but even in this case there is nothing to view, we are only aware it is there. It is proper that the number zero is represented by a circle which a.) has no beginning or ending and b.) shows a void inside of a perimeter. You look into it and see nothing. If you were to write a zero there is no standard starting or ending place.

The number (1) is similar in that in and of itself it cannot be perceived. If there is only one thing then there are no separate things to be perceived. It takes (2) to perceive a reality other than itself. Thus, the difference between (1) and zero is that (1) can be perceived in a controlled environment by entities other than itself. This holds true for the numbers 10, 100, 1000 and so on. They represent systems and although each system may have many parts the objective is not to view the parts of the system, but the system itself. For example, if I want to view the solar system, I would have to view it from another solar system or a place outside of this solar system. Since I am a member and part of the solar system I can never see the entire solar system as I cannot see all of myself. I can, however, view its parts, but never it as a whole and complete entity.

So zero can never be perceived and (1) can only be perceived from outside of itself. It is only the first physical differentiation that perception and thus experience comes alive and is possible. This is why the number (2) is foundational to our earthly existence and plays such a pivotal role in how we are to manage our lives. In addition, it is our inability to perceive, view, or understand this originating undifferentiated element (1) that creates many of the problems that we face in our lives.

Numbers Ten (10) and Above

So if there are only nine numbers then what do (ten) and above represent. Well as we learned in school the number (ten) represents a set, which is one thing made up of many things. What was never accurately communicated is a set of what. How many things are in that set? The answer is nine. (Ten) is therefore one set of nine unique things or physical objects. So in essence, the (tens) place denotes how many sets of nine and the ones place denotes how many things there are outside of the set.

This is a very important concept as the general perception is that ten things make up one set, but this is not the case. It's actually nine; therefore, the number (ten) is not a unique number in and of itself, but a counter of sorts representing how these nine numbers (or things) interact harmoniously together. This is true for all numbers above (9). These numbers do not hold unique properties, but actually represent how many of the original nine numbers are being represented and how.

The concept here is that when we bring nine things together and they are in the same environment and interacting with one another, they function as one unit. Each individual thing takes on one of the nine unique properties represented by a number (1) through (9). So for example, if a cat has a litter of (9) kittens, each kitten will take on a personality represented by one of the nine numbers above. We have seen this with people as well; where one siblings dominates the other or maybe they have different interests, but never the same. If five of those cats are moved to a new house; then there personalities will change as the unit is now made up of (5). This is not a complete set of nine but a subset. The interaction of the kittens will manifest as the personality type (5,5) as described above. One kitten will be the unifier (this is usually the crazy one in the bunch), two will be of varying degrees of yang, and two will be of varying degrees of yin. This is regardless of the gender. This is just how it works. When one of these kittens does not play its role for whatever reason we have serious conflict, fighting, etc. Animals in there natural habitat usually do not have this problem. Even those in captivity seem to naturally take on the roles required for harmonious interaction.

The issue more so comes in with people (human beings) as they have a "choice" of how they function and often times resist behaving in a way that would produce harmony amongst the group. That is the point and focus of this work; to show each person how they are viewing or perceiving the world so they may be empowered to make the best choices in their lives. As well to teach individuals the laws of the numbers to give insight into group interactions...

So for example, with the number (ten) we have

$10 \rightarrow 1 + 0 = 1$

1	2	3	4	5	6	7	8	9

One set of (9) and no unique numbers (or 0). For eleven we have

$11 \rightarrow 1 + 1 = 2$

One set of (9) and one unique number (in this case the number 1). This is an important concept because of how these things represented by the number interact together. This is the primary concept behind this BaGua science and numerology, etc. The question is not so much how many do you have, but what do you have and how do the things you have interact together. For the number eleven the interaction will be between the nine set and the one.

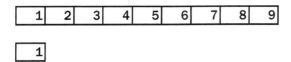

1

Thus, the set of nine will function in a unified manner in its interactions with the lone one. Because we have two things and the quality of (2) is a complimentary relationship each will play that role of yin and yang throughout the life of their interaction. These roles could change over time, but in order for there to be cooperative existence this must be the case.

NOTE: At this point we must explain the obvious. If the number ten (10) represents one set of (9) then ten (10) here does not represent ten things. That is correct! As I stated earlier there are only nine numbers. Once we move to ten and above we turn to a completely different concept and system for identifying and symbolizing reality. So let's recap. If we have nine (9) things qualitatively you have one set of things symbolized by the number ten. The symbol ten (10) means one (1) set of nine and zero (0) unique or individual things outside of that nine set.

Traditionally, we denote ten individual things with the symbol "10". That is the major difference between the traditional modern number designation and the BaGua system.

It is understandable how this mistake could be made as a complete subset is made up of five (5) individual things (2 yin, 2 yang, and 1 balancing element). So logically, when we bring two subsets (or half sets) together we think of ten (10) individual things, quantitatively, (4 yin, 4 yang, and 2 balancing elements). The issue, as mentioned in earlier chapters, is the two (2) balancing elements are the exact same things and not unique in any way other than being tied to or belonging to different subsets. Remember, numbers are symbols used to represent or denote individual unique realities. We wouldn't use the same symbol say the symbols "4" and "6" to represent the same reality; which to most people, reality is only represented in quantitative terms from a numerical standpoint rather than both quantitatively and qualitatively. The modern numerical system uses numbers only quantitatively whereas the true and more complete purpose of numbers is to use them both quantitatively and qualitatively.

This is a great point for meditation as this concept challenges the very foundation of everything we have learned in contemporary education. And again, we are not saying the modern systems are wrong, but rather the

BaGua system is foundationally different and thus can be used in ways outside the scope of a modern numerical theology.

Let's look at the example of twelve (12).

1	2	3	4	5	6	7	8	9

1		1

Here we have a total of three elements: one set of nine and two individual numbers (or just the number 2). Twelve adds up to three (3): 12 → 1 + 2 = 3

Therefore, the interaction of the things represented by the number twelve will follow the laws of the number (3). One unit will represent the yin, one the yang, and one the unifying or balancing unit between them. Again, the unifying element represents the principle that the other two units are meant to embody through their cooperative interaction.

The table *Number Sequence – 1* shows how each number maps back to one of the nine original numbers in the first row (1 – 9). So, from the examples above, the number 10 maps to 1; 11 to 2; 12 to 3, and so on. I expanded this chart to the number 360 as we will come back to that very significant number later in this work. The chart is made up of nine columns; with the first row represented by numbers one through nine. The first row is also a label representing the qualitative representation of all the numbers in that particular column. The quantitative representation of the numbers is captured in each of the cells 1 – 360; thus, each number is unique quantitatively, but not qualitatively.

Table: Number Sequence

1	2	3	4	5	6	7	8	9
10	11	12	13	14	15	16	17	18
19	20	21	22	23	24	25	26	27
28	29	30	31	32	33	34	35	36
37	38	39	40	41	42	43	44	45
46	47	48	49	50	51	52	53	54
55	56	57	58	59	60	61	62	63
64	65	66	67	68	69	70	71	72
73	74	75	76	77	78	79	80	81
82	83	84	85	86	87	88	89	90
91	92	93	94	95	96	97	98	99
100	101	102	103	104	105	106	107	108

1	2	3	4	5	6	7	8	9
109	110	111	112	113	114	115	116	117
118	119	120	121	122	123	124	125	126
127	128	129	130	131	132	133	134	135
136	137	138	139	140	141	142	143	144
145	146	147	148	149	150	151	152	153
154	155	156	157	158	159	160	161	162
163	164	165	166	167	168	169	170	171
172	173	174	175	176	177	178	179	180
181	182	183	184	185	186	187	188	189
190	191	192	193	194	195	196	197	198
199	200	201	202	203	204	205	206	207
208	209	210	211	212	213	214	215	216
217	218	219	220	221	222	223	224	225
226	227	228	229	230	231	232	233	234
235	236	237	238	239	240	241	242	243
244	245	246	247	248	249	250	251	252
253	254	255	256	257	258	259	260	261
262	263	264	265	266	267	268	269	270
271	272	273	274	275	276	277	278	279
280	281	282	283	284	285	286	287	288
289	290	291	292	293	294	295	296	297
298	299	300	301	302	303	304	305	306
307	308	309	310	311	312	313	314	315
316	317	318	319	320	321	322	323	324
325	326	327	328	329	330	331	332	333
334	335	336	337	338	339	340	341	342
343	344	345	346	347	348	349	350	351
352	353	354	355	356	357	358	359	360

Let's continue the analysis of symbols (numbers) (ten) and above to see how they manifest in both qualitative and quantitative terms. Let move to nineteen (19) which according to chart NS – 1 corresponds to the number one (1). With the number nineteen (19) we have (ten) plus (9) (quantitatively – 10 elements, although not unique [the 5s are the same from each subset] plus an additional nine elements giving us nineteen (19) total elements), which translates into a (ten) set (with two 5s that have been combined):

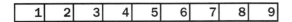

and nine individual unique numbers (or another (ten) set, but without the second 5 designation; thus, we don't have two complete subsets – only one subset and one set of four):

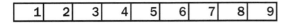

In qualitative terms we have nine symbols represented twice here; therefore, only nine unique qualities. Following the rules of algebra we can thus consolidate the like numbers (which represent the same reality) into one number giving us:

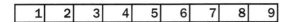

Thus, we have one complete nine set which is represented by the number (ten) or (10). A point of note here is that this set cannot be represented by the number (9). (9) is a specific symbol that represents the ninth element in this set and not each element working in unity.

Moving to twenty (20), which according to the table *Number Sequence* aligns to the number two (2) we have two complete sets of nine again. The difference here from nineteen (19) is that we have a total of twenty elements or four complete subsets made up of four 5's and two of every other number. There we have the quantitative difference where nineteen only had three 5s and two of every other number. Thus, in this case, two subsets can come together and form one complete set or independent unit and doing this twice gives us two complete units. This is how we arrive qualitatively at (2); the number of complete sets (meaning made up of four complete subsets) is (2).

Again, the point of this chapter is to help the student understand the qualitative and quantitative aspects of numbers. When we learn to look at our reality through from this perspective we understand that there are nine fundamental qualities making up our physical reality and all things can be classified into one of them; thus, giving us a frame of reference for viewing the world.

Chapter 4: The Four Fundamental Forces

There are four fundamental forces that make up the entire ever evolving and changing world: awareness, initiation, energy, and matter. Each of these forces has its active (yang) and inactive (yin) components and can be categorized as follows:

Table: Four Fundamental Forces - 1

Force	Active (Yang) State	Inactive (Yin) State
Awareness	Initiates all of creation (things)	Perceives all of creation (things)
Initiation	Physically active creative force	Mentally active perceptive force
Energy	Electric active force	Magnetic attractive force
Matter	Persisted physical reality	Subsisted metaphysical reality

Act of Creation/Perception

The following diagram indicates the four fundamental forces in their active (creative) and inactive (perceptive) states and the order of their manifestation. All things begin with invisible awareness in an inactive state and its subsequent invisible possibility to initiate energy to produce visible matter. This matter so "willed" now in physical form, through its attractive energy can affect the mental initiation and thus be perceived by awareness. This is a complete circle, or cycle, and continues on into infinity throughout the life of the world as we know it.

Diagram: *Act of Creation Simple*

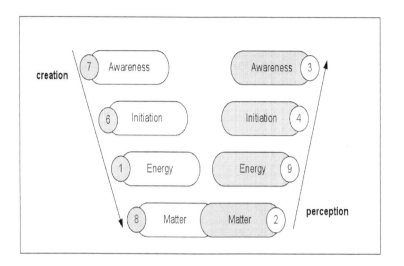

This diagram is shaped like a V, but more resembles the sin or cosine curve utilized in mathematical mapping. If we were to draw a horizontal line between the Initiation and Energy stages across both the creation and perception parts of the diagram we will notice the completion of a cycle. Again, creation begins with awareness (heaven) and descends through initiation and energy to form matter (earth). From the earth all things, especially man, struggle to live which manifests as the quest for energy, or the ability to animate, and thus gain control over themselves and their environment to ultimately realize happiness via their desires.

The Act of Creation & Perception with Numeric Designations

Here we have taken the same diagram of creation and perception but added the proper numeric symbols (numbers) to indicate the actual numerically assigned quality of each of these creative and perceptive stages. We can use this as the basis for our discussions of numbers and their matching trigrams and placement in the creative process of life.

Diagram: Act of Creation Detailed

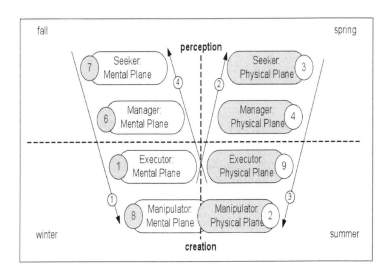

Using diagram *Act of Creation Detailed* we will begin to explain the concepts of creation and its various stages. First, let's go into some detail about the figure itself. Starting with the law of duality we will observe in the top middle of the diagram 'perception' and the bottom middle 'creation'. As mentioned in Chapter one about the law of (2), there are two complimentary forces governing everything in world as we are either creating or perceiving; initiating or being initiated. Creation is symbolized by the downward arrows labeled '1' and '3' and perception is symbolized by the upward arrows labeled '2' and '4'.

Next we have four quadrants, which are labeled as follows: fall, winter, summer, and spring; and in each quadrant are two elliptical figures (cylinders). Each cylinder represents a yin and yang element of that season; thus, we have eight cylinders in all. The purpose of using the seasons to label each of the quadrants is that they map to the seasons and to add a quality to them the student can relate to and understand. If we say KAN and KEN fall into the winter quadrant we instantly obtain a visual and a high level understanding of the qualities of these trigrams. The qualities of winter are darkness and cold.

Fall – Seeker: Mental Plane (7) and Manager: Mental Plane (6)
Winter – Executor: Magnetic (1) and Manipulator: Congregated (8)
Spring – Seeker: Physical Plane (3) and Manager: Physical Plane (4)
Summer – Executor: Electric (9) and Manipulator Segregated (2)

Note: I just wanted to acknowledge at this point that the creative process does not occur in numerical order (i.e. 1, 2, 3, 4, ...). Here the numbers are referenced based upon the quality they possess and not their chronological order.

Table: Eight Stages of Creation

Cylinder	Description
Seeker: Mental Plane (7)	It is here that the person thinks deeply about what has been accomplished in the previous cycles/years and tries to determine what strategies must be implemented to best accomplish those goals.
Manager: Mental Plane (6)	It is here that the person, once receiving the strategy to implement plays, plans, and maps the entire creative process and ultimate goal out in their minds. This is strictly a mental exercise and the more vivid and real the more effective.
Executor: Mental Plane (1)	Here the person makes all of the necessary changes within themselves and their organization to prepare for task

Cylinder	Description
	of implementing the strategic plan.
Manipulator: Mental Plane (8)	It is here that the person applies that same self preparation concept to those persons, resources, things in the general environment. Now that the organization is ready its affiliates must be prepared in a similar fashion. This is important, because we cannot succeed in life without the aid of others.
Seeker: Physical Plane (3)	Here the ideas, inventions, resources, and concepts that are in line with the overall strategic vision are identified for use in implementing the project. The person or organization is only ready for this stage once it has prepared itself (Matter: Congregated (8)) to properly use the resources it identifies.
Manager: Physical Plane (4)	Here the identified resources along with all other available resources are properly defined, allocated, and placed to execute production. It is also here that the person/organization makes sure there is no stone unturned.
Executor: Physical Plane (9)	Here the process begins of developing and manufacturing the product or thing to be utilized in the persons/organizations success. In business this could be a product for sale or from a personal standpoint it could be term paper which will be used to obtain a desired grade.
Manipulator: Physical Plane (2)	Here the product is used to ultimately achieve the measurable success metric for the person/organization. In the world of business this encompasses sales and trade. In the personal arena this encompasses exchange, barter, turning in before deadlines, etc. This is

Cylinder	Description
	the final stage of the creative process and is measured by the metric selected by the initiator. It is this metric that the person/organization uses in the Observer: Mental (7) stage to access success or failure in the previous cycle.

There is a great science indicated in these diagrams. In the BaGua the natural movement for the female (yin) is in ascending numerical order (1,2,3,4,5,6,7,8,9) and that of the male (yang) is in descending numerical order (9,8,7,6,5,4,3,2,1). We will come back to discuss this phenomena in more detail.

The force of creation is a female force and that of perception or experience is male. The creative force indicated above moves in order with the seasons and the natural flow of the BaGua (clockwise in diagram BaGua 1) which is downward in the above diagram from (7) → (8), or path (1) and from (3) →(2), or path (3); whereas the perceptive force moves against the seasons and the natural flow of the BaGua (counterclockwise in diagram BaGua 1) or upward in the above diagram from (2) → (3), or path (2) and (8) → (7), or path (4). The act of perception moves from matter to awareness while that of creation moves from consciousness to matter.

Daily Life:
Now let's take a moment to fully understand the importance and relevance of this concept to our daily lives. What is communicated here is a law that governs all things in creation, including those goals and objectives we wish to achieve in our personal and business lives. Thus, in order to create anything you must begin with awareness which is the invisible realm and follow the proper steps to manifestation. This goes for anything we are trying to accomplish in life whether it is building software, obtaining a job, having a fruitful relationship, finding a partner, learning a language, etc. By following the steps outlined in this work one will greatly increase their success rate.

What is illustrated here is the complete creation/perception cycle with the corresponding roles of each of the numbers from (1)-(9). A universal phenomenon is revealed in that the beginning of the creative process cannot be sensed (using the five senses). It is in fact invisible or imperceptible. The Creative Unfolding Process diagram indicates the natural unfolding and relationship between numbers from the universal one or (5,5) element to its eight children. All numbers are revealed with the exception of six (6) and seven (7). In the creative process these numbers are not so readily revealed or cannot be seen. This phenomena maps perfectly with the Fall season in which only the fruits of the summer's labor can be witnessed, but the creative process taking place in preparation for the winter goes unnoticed. It is implied in the apparent "decay" of life (i.e. leaves of the trees turning brown), but that activity is rarely linked to a regenerative process.

In the next chapter we will walk slowly through the meaning of each of the phases that comprise the creative process. Once this unfolding is understood and mastered we can begin to plan our lives accordingly producing success at an accelerated rate for any endeavor. Let's start from the beginning of the creative process. As well, we can map our personality to find the best station of creation or perception that is best for us in an organization, system or family.

Chapter 5: The Creative Process and the Introduction of the Eight Trigrams

In this chapter we further define the creative process as well as introduce the BaGua diagram (Diagram: BaGua – 1) which is the illustration of the eight primary trigrams in relationship to one another from the perspective of *creative un-foldment*. A trigram is a symbol made up of a combination of three broken or unbroken lines. The eight trigrams are the basis of the BaGua system perfected in ancient China. What makes the BaGua such a rich system is the creator's ability to capture the essence of life and its changes in symbols, diagrams, and mathematical equations that are meaningful, efficient, and thorough in their application.

The BaGua diagram is an octagon with each of the eight trigrams on each side and another symbol in the center representing the unification of all the trigrams. Amazingly, these symbols are also represented by the very numbers and numerical processes that are the foundation of this book. The numerical diagram illustrated in the BaGua is often displayed in a square configuration divided into nine smaller equally sized squares (like a tic-tac-toe board) with the numbers (1) – (9) in each square. This diagram is popularly referred to as the Magic Square (*Magic Square – 1*) or Lo Shu arrangement. The reason why it is "magical" is that all numbers in any row, column, or diagonal add up to fifteen. This phenomenon will be explained in greater detail in later chapters. I have combined a number of symbols in the following BaGua diagram in an attempt to capture as much meaning through one pictorial representation as possible.

Diagram: BaGua – 1

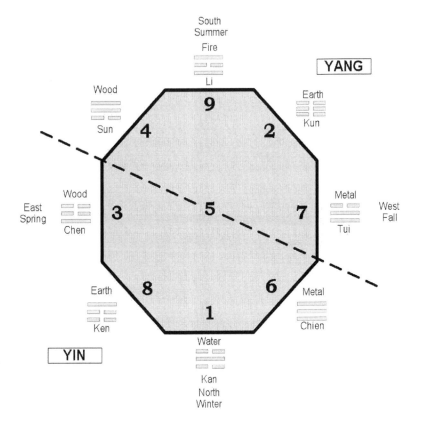

Diagram: Magic Square - 1

4	9	2
3	5	7
8	1	6

The trigrams of the BaGua can also be combined to make 64 hexagrams. A hexagram is two combined trigrams making 64 more elaborate pictorial representation of a given reality. Because of this utility, the BaGua is the basis of many Feng Shui systems, and the I Ching which is an ancient Chinese oracle system. I have added the hexagram designations in this work on numerology because the names are quite relevant to the meaning of the trigrams themselves. When we explain the hexagrams in another work we will tie the complete meaning of these symbols together.

THE CREATIVE PROCESS DEFINED

Allow me to explain each trigram in the BaGua (and the Lo Shu arrangement) from the standpoint of its roll in the creative process. This process begins with the number seven (7) also symbolized by the trigram TUI, and hexagram "The Joyous Lake".

TUI / 7 / Wisdom / The Joyous Lake / Metal / Early Fall

Objective
It is at this stage that the creative process begins. Here the person thinks very deeply (intuition) about what his or her goals should be. Once obtained, one intuits the requirements for

success in achieving these new goals. The requirement for this process is a review of the past year's projects success or failure and being able to objectively judge the final outcome -- a review of the "Harvest". Only then can one know what is required in the future. The product from this stage of the creative process – if successful – is not only a set of new goals for a new project but a specific protocol, commandments, and directives that must be followed for success in achieving the new goal. The direction coming out of this stage is not to be followed optionally. The strict adherence to the protocols that come from this intuitive process is the requirement for success in the upcoming creative cycle.

Material
From a material standpoint, one can obtain a process or protocol for the achievement of a new goal from a master at one's art or craft. A master will be able to indicate the accomplishments of the student thus far and evaluate what must be done for a student to become more proficient in the art. The master has been through the process already, trained thousands of students, and thus, has the ability to give direction to the student based on his/her intuitive judgment of their progress. These protocols, in most cases, are not understood by the student or others outside of the process, but they must be followed for success.

Spiritual
From a spiritual standpoint one queries the universal intelligence (God) for information identifying new goals for a new year and the protocols that will bring about success in the form of self mastery and wisdom in the coming year/cycle. What is received will be a set of principles with which one must live by in order to achieve specific desired and new outcomes. Living the principles means incorporating these values into one's daily living.

Note: The desired outcome at this stage is generally, success and prosperity to carry the community/family/person through the following year or cycle. The goals at this stage will be general and abstract -- the more specific the goals, the more convoluted the insight may be. There may also be a general unfamiliarity with the specific laws to be lived for success if the goals for the year are too specific at this point...

CHIEN / 6 / Prayer / The Creative / Metal / Late Fall

Objective
The objective at this phase is that the individual create a specific mental picture of everything to be achieved. This mental picture should be all inclusive: colors, sounds, faces, figures, bank account numbers, celebrations at the end once the goal is met, etc. In order to do this successfully, the information received from the TUI stage of the process must be incorporated into the vision as part of the process for achieving the goal.

Material
So the product or material deliverable from this stage of the creative process is a clear vision of the process and the end product, which are actually two polarities of the same reality, because the product doesn't exist without the process to create it. From a material standpoint the vision should be such that any part or all of it can be recalled at any time. It is best to actually draw the visual representation of the goals that have been abstractly understood in the TUI phase.

Note: *This is not a time for judgment. A seamless organization will take the information received from the TUI stage and begin the mental and visualization work immediately. The only questions should be points of clarification to further understand the principles in order to increase the effectiveness of the process.*

Note*: The previous point is actually the number one reason for organizational and personal failure in life and specific undertakings. It is the ego of the individuals involved that doesn't allow them to be receptive to the direction from others that prevents goals and objectives from succeeding in their full potential. Of course this is not a blind statement; each person must hold their respective positions based upon a unique skill set that qualifies them for that post. In addition, the organization must be properly set up from a personnel and protocol perspective to support these people/divisions and their responsibilities. But once that is complete and been tested and approved by someone who understands organizational systems/processes it must be permitted to run without question. Every person must have faith in the process. Lacking that, they must adhere to the protocol that doesn't allow them to second guess a product coming from the core competency of any group other than their own; for faith is not a quality that is easily attainable or understood. Fortunately, there are exercises that can be done to teach faith and trust, but they are outside the scope of this work.*

Spiritual
It is at this stage that the laws and principles obtained from the TUI stage are "taken to heaven" to be firmly planted in the metaphysical realm or in the person's spirit. This is done by creating or intuiting a visual image or representation of the achievement of a goal. This visual image must be crafted such that there becomes little separation between the person and the vision or mental manifestation of the physical goal; they are one.

This process is synonymous to the dragon where the actual image of one's end results, or goals, are symbolized by the dragon. The dragon – or image of completion - is the only earthly being capable of escaping the natural physical constraints (i.e. gravity, the earth's atmosphere, etc.) of the material realm to have access to heaven. Once these laws and images have been firmly planted they will undoubtedly rain down upon the earth in a course of natural unfolding. "As above, so below." They rain down with the same force and power as if that dragon suddenly reversed its direction and dove straight toward the earth/ground. With this I am trying to communicate the actual power of this process. Try and picture the dragon using all of its power and might to rise to the highest heights of heaven. Now picture that same dragon using the same power and focus to charge back to the ground. We are not just talking about gravity pulling an inert body, but rather all of the earth's forces plus those of the dragon.

A great visualization of this process is from the movie the Matrix Revolutions™ when Agent Smith, in the final battle knocked Neo nearly unconscious in their final fight in the sky. Agent Smith then grabbed Neo and drove him from the sky straight into the ground. So much so that it created a crater in the earth two or three stories deep. In other words, whatever you effectively plant during this stage will be firmly planted and rooted in your spirit and on the physical plane.

This is a powerful force. Now we see why people who skip this stage in the creative process can only create something unstable. This, by the way, is the problem with most communities, states, and nations. They are generally formed on a principle that is not intuitively gathered (TUI) and not rooted in imagery (CHIEN) and are easily destroyed/toppled. As a result the greed and incompetence of those assuming power in later administrations (not being in touch with the original goals and vision) end up making decisions that eventually destroy the nation.

The process for achieving the deliverable for this stage is ritual or ecstatic ceremony. These processes will be detailed further in another work as they are beyond our scope.

KAN / 1 / Conservative / The Abysmal / Water / Early Winter

Objective
In order to achieve a goal, especially one that hasn't been achieved before (which is every goal you account for in time and space) the person or organization must undergo fundamental changes. These changes are in essence required to effectively execute the plan and the strategy/protocol that was laid out in the TUI stage of creation. The premise behind this is simple: if a gopher wants to build a dam then he must become a beaver. In all instances the person or organization must make fundamental, structural changes in order to achieve new goals. There is no escaping this fact. Of course the degree will vary depending upon the objective and the current character, skills, and abilities of the person/organization, but there is always change.

Material
Change is effectively made up of two complimentary actions: death and birth. The material dying component involves getting rid of all of those things (thoughts, people, processes, equipment, beliefs, habits, associates, vendors, clothing, contracts, etc.) that do not directly or indirectly support the achievement of the goal. It has to be done. To add something new you must get rid of something old.

Note: I can't stress enough how important that last sentence is. So often people try to bring a person or thing into their lives, but have not made any changes to do so. They have not removed that stuff that is not supportive of the relationship. As a result two key things happen: a) people have a hard time finding a companion and thus choose options that are extreme and b) once a person is found they can't make the relationship last. The other person is eventually squeezed out because there is just no room for them with all of that unsupportive material (old stuff) taking up all of that space.

We must rise above emotional attachments here. Contracts may need to be broken which is why exit clauses must always be included at costs that will not cripple or cause hardship to the organization (and from a moral perspective not to either party involved). If there is a conflict on discarding a thing then you have to weigh the options of the goal against that thing, but keep in mind the goal of the person/organization here should be for the growth and ultimate survival of the organization. As all things that are born will surely end, we want to control how the end comes as much as possible. Would you rather the company loose its identity as a result of being bought out and absorbed into another company or filing bankruptcy? Remember every "thing" in the world moves and there are only two directions: up or down; forward or backward, increased growth or loss. There is no middle road here. Stabilization is actually stagnation, which is loss. Especially, when compared to the performance of competitors and industry/market metrics and growth factors.

Hard decisions must be made here and some serious skills are involved in many of these stages of creation. From the standpoint of the individual trying to make changes in his/her life these decisions can be tough and on top of that each person may not be able to see what needs to be discarded and/or what needs to be added. This is why family and community are so important for people, families, and nations to be successful. People individually don't achieve great things "co-operations" (or corporations, nations, and "collaboratives") do. That said one thing that most individuals must discard is the idea of individualism and the "I can do it myself mindset". Once this is discarded it opens the door for persons with knowledge and skills to help out. Even persons who achieve success always did it with support from others; whether they acknowledge it or not. That's just the way it is.

Spiritual

It is here that all physical things are internally perfected. This is the stage of time and rest; where all things may be renewed and strengthened once again. This means that the physical body and mind must be put in order so that it has the strength to carry out the upcoming tasks. One of the greatest forms of renewal is rest. We go through this stage every night when we enter deep sleep at which time the body carries out its greatest healing. An example of this is the person who works out with weights or does vigorous exercise. It is not the physical act of lifting weights that grows the muscle mass in the body. This act actually damages the body and can be seen by the immediate size increase of that targeted muscle during the workout. This is the body rushing blood and nutrients to the muscles to heal and support them during this time of stress and strain. No, it's actually the time during rest and relaxation that the body repairs the damage that was done during the work out and adds additional support in the form of muscle mass to offset possible future assaults on that same area. This is the key. Thus of greater importance to the training athlete should be the quality of rest/sleep and the richness of nutrients (fuel, raw material) in which to build up those muscles. The same is true for running and the affect it has on the heart and lungs. It's the healing process that makes them stronger not the stress and strain of the physical practice itself. This is a microcosmic example of the death and birth process; old body mass is broken down or destroyed so that it can be built anew.

The seed has been planted in heaven (CHIEN) and now the earth and its bodies must be made pure through the most natural and efficient healing processes accessible. These processes are embedded and inherent into the physiology of man and earth and when man yields to them they are able to rejuvenate and renew all that is physical.

Part of this strengthening is due to the living of the principles revealed in the west (TUI). Through these principles and the universal principles governing life all is healed for the benefit of the manifestation of the goals set forth. This is the meaning of the hexagram and why one must follow the revealed path without waiver. Additional exercises and processes for achieving this stage will be revealed in another work.

KEN / 8 / Relationships / Keeping Still (The Mountain) / Earth / Late Winter

Objective
We have made the changes that we need to make and now it is time to begin preliminary interaction with our immediate environment and the world. This interaction is two-fold: a.) to help establish relationships to fill the voids created during the KAN stage and b.) to help strengthen and improve those entities/things around us so they can support our goals and initiatives.

Material
In business this could manifest in retraining employees, teaching them the new mission and feeding them with a baby spoon the new vision. In the family this KEN phase might mean reassuring the children and the adults that everything is OK, love is still the root of the family and that change is to be welcomed. At KEN we find the form of creating new contracts with specific expectations on performance and service delivery. From an individual perspective this could include establishing relationships with individuals who can assist you along the way, mentors, coaches and other business success tools.

The key here is to lay the loving foundation for the initiation of outward expansion that will come later. This movement is not aggressive or expansive, but rather more of a natural flow or interaction with those already in our circle of influence and reach. As this stage of creation is also part of the hidden creative process nothing is to be overly advertised. This is a quiet building of relationships which ultimately strengthens the soul of the primary individual/family/corporation and its constituency.

Spiritual
KEN is a member of the *Earthly Square* and therefore its charge is to obey and support the direction of KAN its heavenly master. Thus, KEN's activity can be viewed as an extension of what KAN initiated similar to CHIEN's relationship to TUI. Once the individual/organization or any other unit/system has been redirected, given a new vision and purged of the old "stuff", it is time to find healing and strength in one another through a nurturing process that begins to rebuild the system. This is the time to heal and beautify all that is outward in the environment. This is the final stage in the unseen or hidden creative process. With the completion of this stage comes the end of the metaphysical creative process. For all that is unseen has been made perfect by the hand of natural/innate forces.

CHEN / 3 / Faith / The Arousing (Shock) / Wood / Early Spring

Objective
At this point the individual/organization is fully prepared to move forward externally with achieving its goal. It must now identify those manifested and un-manifested elements that are a part of the final solution. This is the responsibility of CHEN. What happens at this stage is that great ideas concerning project implementation are derived. From the outside this appears to be an intuitive process, but actually it involves identifying the various aspects of the original goal in its early stages of physical manifestation. It is analogous to seeing the baby blades of grass on a fully grown and mature pasture. They are there, but difficult for the average person to see.

Material
A typical CHEN statement is "Hey, I've got an idea. Let's ….." The response is usually, "That sounds nice, but there is no way

we can pull that off". The ability to "pull it off" depends upon whether the person/organization in the SUN phase has been in touch with the creative process from the TUI stage. Otherwise, CHEN'S ideas will either be ignored or implemented with usual failure due to an inability to root the idea in physical reality. So the deliverable from CHEN here is a set of "bright ideas" that gives a very strong clue or picture as to what the final goal looks like and how the final goal can be achieved.

Another point here is that CHEN is coming out of the winter and is the first part of spring. For this reason the CHEN phase is not fully awake or rooted in physical reality. This process takes place in half a dream world and half material reality. This "dual" or springtime vision allows this phase of the creative process to be fluid and moist enabling those who commit to living it's truth perception of the subtle realities of the world. At the same time these individuals need to be checked to make sure they are not making decisions based upon dreamy or lofty concepts or ideas.

Spiritual
CHEN is part of the *Heavenly Circle* and like its compliment TUI has the responsibility of having balanced sight into the physical and metaphysical planes. It is during the equinox periods of the year that we have the most balanced view of our reality; half physical and half metaphysical. It is at this stage that the physical is born from the metaphysical. That what has been created in heaven, now manifests itself on earth. Here all that has been created and will thus become manifest is identified and pieced back together into its whole. This vision, or idea, is directly related to the laws, principles, and symbols revealed in the west, TUI.

Note*: CHEN and TUI are the two trigrams that have their influence in both the physical and metaphysical realms. This is what qualifies them in their positions as initiators of the creative process for both of those realms: CHEN – physical and TUI – metaphysical. This also qualifies them as the Observers for they are balanced in their physical and metaphysical outlooks.*

SUN / 4 / Leadership / The Gentle Wind / Wood / Late Spring

Material
Once all alliances are made and all physical reality identified, including the abstract ideas and concepts offered by CHEN, the management and more importantly the leadership process is initiated. Leadership here is the talent to properly assess and define reality and move people in the right direction at the right speed and in the correct order. Leadership also includes the ability to identify and martial the required resources needed to complete a goal or project. What stands out about the SUN segment of creation is the distinct need to "see" clearly what is physically needed to earth the project. Not only must one "see", but they must understand how various resources can be used to accomplish a given goal or task.

Note: *This statement, "ability to do work", must be taken within the context of the overall creative process. Everyone has the ability to do work, but here we are discussing the roles of people based upon their dominant character traits. That said, the SUN individual is not the worker of the creative bunch. That status is reserved for LI.*

Spiritual
Now that the physical manifestation or material building blocks for success are visible, this raw material must be worked to produce the desired product and outcome. In order to accomplish this task the raw manifestation must be properly assessed and defined as to its use and value in the physical world. Included in this is who and how it must be worked to produce the desired result. It is here that all available physical resources are established and put into place (motivated) to begin the physical creative process. This is where the people, processes, and resources are properly aligned and engaged to

bring about success in the physical world. SUN thus manages, delegates and organizes, but lacks the power to carry out the work directly.

LI/ 9 / Action-Illumination / The Clinging Fire / Fire / Early Summer

Objective

The stage has been set by SUN and all things are motivated to carry out their assigned tasks and responsibilities. Now the actions can take place and the physical execution of the master plan begins. This is nothing short of flipping the switch to turn on the assembly line.

Material

Here LI takes the raw materials and fully works them producing a magnificent finished product. This is the full manifestation of physical earthly power used to shape earthly manifestation. In other words, this is where things get done. LI represents the actuality of work getting done. This characteristic is best symbolized by ants or worker bees that zealously and relentlessly carry out the tasks that have been assigned to them. We have all seen the ant who is trying to carry something twenty times its size back to the ant hill. It doesn't know fear, want, or quit. It only understands what must be done and does just that.

Spiritual

It is at the LI where all things are brought into the light and the power required to produce our greatest deeds is readily available. All obstructions are now exposed and should be removed accordingly, including our false beliefs, inhibitions, and negative emotions around our objectives. This is not the time to think, but to act. Hesitation and fear are thus destroyed and great works accordingly produced.

KUN / 2 / Trade / The Receptive / Earth / Late Summer

Objective

This stage has been set by LI and all production is complete and we now have something to offer the world. Here the proper social and business protocol must be established to fairly exchange assets with others. To accomplish the task we must display the proper "face" and demeanor and follow the established rules of conduct.

Material

At this stage we now have a finished product to work with thanks to LI. Now at KUN we must put the product to its intended use and complete the creative cycle. In business, this would manifest as trade or sale of the finished product. From a personal perspective, we may now have increased energy due to a new dietary and exercise regime, new work processes or new rules or bylaws and is now time to use that additional energy to make further improvements in our lives, families or corporations (i.e. start a side business in the evening, do more work around the house, etc.).

Generally, this phase of the creative cycle involves engaging other people who also have something to trade. As KUN is the complement to KEN, the engagement here is not for the sake of coming together, but for the sake of trade.

Spiritual

Once all earthly products have been produced their categorization and distribution now take place. It is here that all earthly needs are fairly met based upon what has been produced and the genuine need for those products. This activity is to be done without bias and based only on the true needs and goals of the community.

It is after this distribution exercise and phase that all may rejoice over the success of the "Harvest". It is in the TUI phase that now proper assessments of the level of success of the product year are made and what the needs and requirements must be for the next cycle. The ultimate success during the KUN phase is the fuel for the goals of the TUI cycle which will begin anew at this point.

B5, Balancing/Unifying

Technically, there is no ninth trigram. When we have three places to fill with only two possible symbols the maximum number of unique symbols or trigrams is eight.

The ninth trigram here is made up of any combination of the original eight trigrams. It can be any one of them, all of them, or any combination in between. From another standpoint, it is also the result of all eight trigrams working seamlessly together and from that standpoint represents the unification of the whole. In diagrams *BaGua – 1* and *Magic Square – 1*, B5 is represented by the number (placeholder/symbol) five (5,5); thus, revealing why I have given it the name B5. B is for balancing and five from its numerical representation (5,5).

B5 is interested in the balance and unity amongst those environments, people, or things that it interacts with in order to achieve its goals in life. To achieve this it tends to take on the personality or fill the void of those people/energies/character traits that are missing to help achieve its goals.

Chapter 6: The Nine Numbers as Fundamental Forces of Creation

For purposes of this work let us assume that there is only one universe. And all things in the universe are a part of its whole. With this premise in mind, we can, for the sake of convenience, categorize the many things of the universe into manageable groups. This allows us to interpret and manage our reality in small pieces which increases our chances of success. Each of these groups maps to a trigram plus a B5 placeholder.

The Nine Forces Summarized

Table: Nine Forces Summarized

Trigram	Baseline Position/ Number	Element	Brain Process	I Ching Element Image	Move	Tendency/ Talent
KAN	(1)	Water	Concentrated – inward Introverted	Abyss (Water)	Slowest	Power to achieve through magnetic energy and internalization.
KUN	(2)	Earth	Linear	Earth	fast slowing	Ability to establish working relationships with all things.
CHEN	(3)	Wood	Synthesis	Thunder	mid fasting	Ability to see subtle realities.
SUN	(4)	Wood	Reasoni	Wind	fast	Ability to

60

Trigram	Baseline Position/ Number	Element	Brain Process	I Ching Element Image	Move	Tendency/ Talent
			ng		fasting	physically see, define, and motivate all things towards the achievement of a goal.
B5	(5)	Any/All	All	N/A	inward/ outward	Ability to unify the whole through being what is required in any given situation.
CHIEN	(6)	Metal	Visual	Heaven	slow slowing	Ability to mentally see all of things (created or not).
TUI	(7)	Metal	Intuition	Lake	mid slowing	Ability to understand the laws governing the existence of things.
KEN	(8)	Earth	Circular	Mountain	slow fasting	Ability to establish intimate, communal

Trigr am	Basel ine Posit ion/ Num ber	Element	Brain Process	I Ching Element Image	Move	Tendency/ Talent
						, and cooperativ e relationshi ps with things.
LI	(9)	Fire	Focused – outward Extrove rted	Fire	Fastest	Power to achieve through electric energy and externaliz ation.

Symbolic Formation via the Nine Fundamental Forces

The symbol of Earth is a square. The symbol of Heaven is a circle. When these symbols are superimposed upon one another we are left with a figure with eight exposed sides. Four of the exposed areas (the corners or triangles) are of the square and four of the exposed areas (the segments) are of the circle. Thus, we have four representatives from each making eight in total. The exposed areas represent the individualized unique qualities of the eight energies. The area inside both the square and the circle represent relative mixtures of all the unique energies (the four unique qualities of Heaven and four unique qualities of Earth that go into the manifestation of all things). This combined area is symbolized by B5 (5,5) which is derived from two elements: circle and square.

Figure: Circle and Square Superimposed - 1

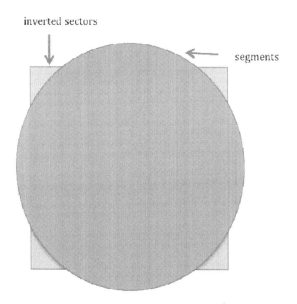

For the purposes of the BaGua and this book we will focus on the eight exposed areas and their unique qualities.

Heavenly Configuration (Circle)

Figure: Circle – 1

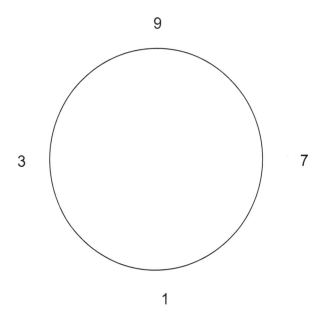

Heaven in this case refers to that which acts upon something else. In this case, Heaven acts upon the earth. The circle here is the symbol of the activity of the creative force in the world. In this case, the 3 – 7 axis (east-west axis) represents awareness and the 1 – 9 axis (north-south) represents energy. It is consciousness that acts upon the initiatory body and energy that acts upon matter to shape all things in the world. These forces follow a definite set of universal laws in how they influence and shape the world. When all the numbers from this system are added up [7 + 1 + 3 + 9 = 20 = 2 + 0 = 2] we receive the number two. The number two represents the complimentary aspects of a reality. Here we have two aspects of Heaven: awareness (mental and physical) and initiation (mental and physical). These Heavenly forces represent the first, third, fifth, and seventh stages of an eight stage creative process; thus, all originates in Heaven.

Earthly Configuration (Square)

Figure: Square – 1

4   2

8   6

The Earth here symbolizes that which is acted upon. In this example the Earth is acted upon by Heaven. The square is the symbol of the inflexibility of life as a completed product from heaven (circle). The $4 - 6$ axis represents initiation and the $2 - 8$ axis represents matter. These elements are acted upon to give shape and definition to all things out of their innate structure. When all the numbers from this system are added up $[6 + 8 + 4 + 2 = 20 = 2 + 0 = 2]$ we receive the number two. Each of the two sub systems, Heaven and Earth, adds up to two; thus, symbolizing two complimentary, but incomplete systems. This is our world of opposites and compliments: male/female, up/down, heaven/earth, etc. These compliments only form a complete whole when they are functioning properly together. When this occurs the unifying element comes into play and a balanced set or system is created. The mathematical proof is arrived by adding 5 to each of the sub systems.

Circle: $7 + 1 + 3 + 9 + 5 = 25 = 2 + 5 = 7$

Square: $6 + 8 + 4 + 2 + 5 = 25 = 2 + 5 = 7$

Combination: $7 + 7 = 14 = 1 + 4 = 5$

Five (5) being the representation of a unified system here symbolizes the coming together of two complete sub systems: circle and square (heaven and earth). To translate, when all eight of these earthly and heavenly forces are working together they produce a ninth quality represented by the number five (5,5).

When super imposed upon each other we receive the eight grossly expressed elements with the universal element five (5,5) from both systems combining into one five (5,5) element (this is due to the fact that the fives in each sub system are quantitatively and qualitatively the same).

Circle and Square Superimposed

When we take the *Heavenly Circle* and *Earthly Square* and superimpose them we end up with the skeleton for our BaGua diagram (BaGua – 1). Figure Circle and Square Superimposed – 2 captures the imposition of these elements.

Figure: Circle and Square Superimposed - 2

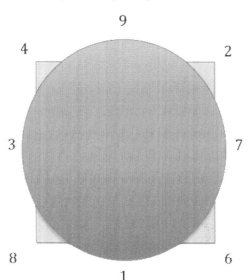

Square Numeric Designations

Square numbers are all even and circular numbers are all odd. Because the *Earthly Square* is closer to manifested reality we find even numbers easier to work with than odd which represent a more subtle reality. Thus, in general it is easier to work with even numbers than it is with odd numbers -- with the exception of the number one.

Table: Square/Circle Numbers

Square	Circle
4	1
2	3
6	9
8	7

Notice all numbers add up to 20 or 2. This is the number of sub-completion and proper placement. This indicates two complete

subsystems of the same magnitude and quality with correct
relative positions.

Table: Square/Circle Numbers Added

Square	Circle
4	1
2	3
6	9
8	7
20	20

When you add these subcomponents together you get 40 or 4
which is the number to SUN. Thus, SUN is required to balance
out the energy of these two systems and make them function
properly together.

When we add the centering component of five (5,5) to both
systems we reach a more complete state of 25 or (7) (where (7)
is the number for TUI which represents the highest state of
intuitive awareness and the beginning of the creative process) for
each subsystem. This is the second level of perfection of a
system. It is the next closest to 50 or (5).

Table: Square/Circle Subsystems Combined

Square/Circle Combined
1
2
3
4
5
5
6
7
8
9
50

When the centering elements of (5,5) are added to each subsystem we receive a balancing requirement of (5) which is B5. Thus, with the combining of two complete subsystems, with centering components, B5 is required to make them function in harmony and union with one another. B5 is also the achieved state when these subsystems are working together in a balanced state.

Chapter 7: Analysis of the Nine Fundamental Forces

Angular Analysis: The Male – Female Definition

Another way to analyze the BaGua and how the trigrams relate to each other is through mapping and examining the angles or triangles that are formed when each trigram is related to the others through the middle B5 element. This analysis utilizes three types of angles: a.) right, b.) obtuse, and c.) acute. Each of these types of angles has a dominant quality.

- **Obtuse angles** are greater than ninety degrees, but less than one hundred and eighty degrees. In general, the inside of the obtuse angles are wide, receptive, and flexible. Many things can gather into this space: people, ideas, etc. The outside of the obtuse angle has a point, but one that is not threatening and dull. The points of obtuse angles are not good for penetrating, but keeping and moving things as a whole or one unit. Obtuse angles represent the female principle. Because nine or ninety represents completeness and obtuse angles are greater than ninety degrees they represent a completely manifested or mature element in combination with additional incomplete elements. Because the obtuse angle has a sense of completeness or fulfillment, its nature is conservative, fearful of loss, nurturing of what it has, and seeking security.

- **Acute angles** are less than ninety degrees, but greater than zero degrees. In general, the inside of an acute angle is narrow and inflexible. It doesn't allow for the addition of things: people, ideas, etc.

The outside of the acute angle is sharp and pointed and is dangerous and threatening. The point of an acute angle is good for penetrating and splitting things apart into separate units. Acute angles represent the male principle. Because nine or ninety represents completeness, acute angles or the male principle represents incompleteness. The male principle lacks a fully mature system and is therefore striving to get to that point; thus, the reason for its aggressiveness in the world.

- **Right angles** are at ninety degrees ($90 \rightarrow 9 + 0 = 9$). They represent completeness and wholeness and stand between the acute and obtuse angles. These angles represent impartiality to the things of the world.

Next, we must associate the trigrams to these angles and then prove through mathematics and association the male and female principles they represent. The proof involves graphically forming and representing the angles based upon the LoMap arrangement. All angles start with a number/trigram on the circumference of the LoMap and go through the center of the LoMap or five (5) and reconnect with another number/trigram also on the circumference. So with that strategy let's begin. Let's start by building all the obtuse angles of the Bagua.

Obtuse Angle Analysis
The possible combinations for obtuse angles include: (6,3); (1,4); (8,9); (3,2); (4,7); (9,6); (2,1); and (7,8). Whenever these numbers/trigrams are connected through the center five (5) they form obtuse angles. When we add these numbers up we obtain the following numbers/trigrams:

Table: Obtuse Angle Trigrams

Number/Trigram	Quantity	Principle/Quality
(6,3) = 9	1	Male
(4,7) = 2	1	Male
(1,4) or (3,2) = 5	2	Balancing
(8,9) = 8	1	Female
(2,1) = 3	1	Female
(9,6) or (7,8) = 6	2	Female

What is interesting to note here is we have a total of eight elements represented in both the obtuse and acute angle relationships. With the obtuse angles we have four female, two male, and two balancing elements. Notice here that the obtuse or female principle is made up of male and female trigrams plus the balancing trigrams. These maps to the chromosome analysis where a woman contains two X chromosomes and the male contains an X and Y chromosome. The Y chromosome only contains only about 83 working genes where the X chromosome contains some where around 1000. Thus, the male can be said to have a deficiency relative to the female. What is not indicated in the chromosome analysis is the balancing element which has no physical form. This gives us penetrating insight into the natal nature of women and their virtuous and divisive traits.

Because women have both the male and female trigrams they are able to love and honor all things in the world. The balancing trigrams make them adaptable to almost any situation. When we look at the make up of the male we will see why this is important. History has proved this. If we look at the world today, especially in modern culture, where the natal qualities of women are not respected, women have taken on the traits of men in many cases to be recognized or become successful. Often times they show a greater aptitude in traditionally male dominated areas due to their ability to adopt both male and female character traits to be successful.

When we examine which female and male trigrams are represented we find on the female side CHIEN, KEN, and CHEN and on the male side LI and KUN. The only missing female trigram is KAN who is actually so cold her energy is more female in principle than in practicality. CHIEN, KEN, and CHEN are more recognizable female characteristics. The male trigrams are LI and KUN. LI represents pure electric energy and has the effect of enhancing any trigram it comes into contact with; in this case the three female trigrams. KUN is male, but it is the most receptive male trigram in the BaGua (really the most obedient and receptive of all the trigrams in the BaGua not just the male). So we can see that the addition of the male trigrams here do not serve to increase male dominance, but more so enhance the overall ability of the natal female traits found in the obtuse configuration.

Acute Angle Analysis

The possible combinations for acute angles include: (6,1); (1,8); (8,3); (3,4); (4,9); (9,2); (2,7); and (7,6). Whenever these numbers/trigrams are connected through the center five (5) they form acute angles. When we add these numbers up we obtain the following numbers/trigrams:

Table: Acute Angle Trigrams

Number/Trigram	Quantity	Principle/Quality
(1,8) or (2,7) = 9	2	Male
(6,1) or (3,4) = 7	2	Male
(8,3) or (9,2) = 2	2	Male
(4,9) or (7,6) = 4	2	Male

Again with the male we have eight total trigrams represented. The trigrams are all male which maps to the chromosome analysis of the male being made up of one X and one Y chromosome. Notice the lack of female and balancing representation here. Men are often depicted as cold, heartless, and fearless individuals. Men are generally not the holders of moral behavior and are usually the ones behind war and conquest at the expense of others.

Note: The male position relative to morality and spirituality has been changed in modern culture where men are the prominent members of the priesthood and clergy. But these are generally positions assigned by other men and not necessarily the indication of moral conduct. In addition, in many modern-based religious texts men are given the highest spiritual roles while women are excluded or demoted to a level of the source of evil and temptation in the world. An example of this is in the Christian religion where Eve was responsible for the fall of man from the Garden of Eden. Additionally, God's representative on earth is his son Jesus and all of his disciples were men. Lastly, the Holy Trinity is represented by the Father, the Son, and the Holy Spirit.

In this mathematical proof we use the actual conduct of men and woman throughout history and modern times to determine how their natal characteristics affect their behavior and conduct. So when we look at the source of war, killing, slavery, holocausts, dictatorships, thievery, etc. it is obvious that men are left holding the bag. Women have been primarily the victims of men's behavior throughout time.

Lastly, the goal here is not to blame one group or type of individual or another for anything that has happened throughout time. The goal here is to make an honest assessment of our natal qualities so that we are empowered to make the changes necessary in our lives. This is generally the first step when attempting to make a change. We must say this is where I am at today. Once we are clear there we can say this is where I want to be and thus the journey begins.

Right Angle Analysis ⌐
The possible combinations for right angles include: (6,8); (1,3); (8,4); (3,9); (4,2); (9,7); (2,6); and (7,1). Whenever these numbers/trigrams are connected through the center five (5) they

form right angles. When we add these numbers up we obtain the following numbers/trigrams:

Table: Right Angle Trigrams

Number/Trigram	Quantity	Principle
7	1	Male
4	1	Male
5	2	Balancing
8	2	Female
3	2	Female
6	1	Female

The right angle trigram representation, unlike the obtuse and acute angles, has nine trigrams represented instead of eight. This is because the right angle represents balance and completion. An interesting note here is the right angle configuration is the same make up as the obtuse (from a gross male-female ratio perspective) or female make up with the exception of one additional female trigram again giving an indication to the natal character of females and what a balanced character looks like.

When we examine the trigrams making up the right or balanced angle we find two male trigrams in TUI and SUN representing wisdom and leadership. Here we have the awareness and initiation coming together to provide a balanced perspective from the male gender. The female trigrams are the same as in the obtuse relationship with KEN, CHEN, and CHIEN which gives a solid foundational female influence. Again, KAN is left out of the equation as her energy is extreme and nurtures all by giving and taking as needed and without over indulgence.

Chapter 8: House Analysis

A "house", in our Bagua Character Map analysis, is a position as defined by the Lo Shu or Magic Square arrangement. LI or *(9)* in the Lo Shu is referred to as the 9th house. CHIEN or *(6)* is referred to as the 6th house in the Lo Shu arrangement and so on. There are two diagrams below illustrating the Lo Shu arrangement: 1) with the trigrams in their proper positions (used here as a reference to help the student only) and 2) with the numbers in their proper position (true Lo Shu pictorial).

Lo Shu with Trigrams

SUN	LI	KUN
CHEN	B5	TUI
KEN	KAN	CHIEN

The diagram below also illustrates the Lo Shu, but with the number designations.

Lo Shu with Numbers

4	9	2
3	5	7
8	1	6

When we calculate our individual natal trigrams they are juxtaposed against the Lo Shu and we receive two trigrams, or numbers, occupying the same position. For example, the BaGua configuration for a KAN person or Conservationist has the trigram Kan in the center position or the number 1 in the 5th house. The BaGua configuration for KAN also has the trigram KEN, or the number 8, in the 3rd house meaning that the KEN trigram occupies the position where CHEN, or the number 3, naturally resides in the Lo Shu.

Diagram: Magic Square to KAN BaGua Configuration Comparison

Lo Shu/Houses at Rest

4	9	2
3	5	7
8	1	6

KAN BaGua Configuration, 1

9	5	7
8	1	3
4	6	2

In this analytical reference we illustrate the characteristic make-up of each trigram configuration by doubling the trigrams and using the eight primary hexagrams to explain the natal energy of each character type. But before we get too far into the configuration discussion let's synchronize our understanding on an important governing principle that will put this information into context. **These configurations describe the awareness (meaning how one perceives their surroundings) of the individual and juxtapose that against the natural order and make up of the earth and general environment; or in other words, the universal consciousness.** This is important because we must realize what we are comparing here. There are many forces at play. From a purely physical perspective (meaning matter and energy) the earth and our persons (bodies) will be in a state outside of the analysis we are about to embark upon. We will add that content after we have thoroughly vetted our abilities to perceive and initiate our way through life.

These configurations describe the awareness (meaning how one perceives their surroundings) of the individual and juxtapose that against the natural order and make up of the earth and general environment; or in other words, the universal consciousness.

The physical body analysis will affect your ability to carry out your intentions regardless of its focus. The physical or material body is the fuel that will allow the person to execute or create in the world and thus will be considered at a latter point.

Baseline House Configuration (Lo Shu)

The Lo Shu is the foundation of the BaGua system. It represents the consciousness state of that living entity that we are a part of – the Earth. It is a square consisting of three rows, three columns, and two diagonals with a total of nine numbers, one in each square. These numbers are single digit numbers and thus represent all aspects of creation. The Lo Shu is a numerical representation of the Later Heaven or Inner World Arrangement. It is the second known trigram arrangement and follows the Earlier Heaven or Primal Arrangement.

These arrangements have specific meanings and purposes in representing the reality we live in. The Later Heaven Arrangement, which is the focus of this book, maps the relationships of the eight primal forces relative to the creative and perceptive process. The movements within this arrangement are circular (clockwise [female] and counter-clockwise [male]). The Earlier Heaven Arrangement is not based upon movement, but relative position to the other trigrams. One maps time and thus chronological order in the creative process and the other maps space and thus interaction of manifested reality.

The most notable fact about the Lo Shu is that when you add the numbers up in any row, column, or diagonal they add up to fifteen. Fifteen is a derivation of six (15 → 1 + 5 = 6) and thus the Lo Shu has the attribute of the number (6).

Mathematical Relevance of Six to the Magic Square (MS)

We had discussed the numbers one through nine earlier in the text, but let's expand a bit to understand the numerical relevance of six to the MS. Again, if you add any row, column, or diagonal within the MS the result is fifteen. Quantitatively, fifteen represents one complete set – ten; and one subset - five. When we add the one set plus the individual elements of the subset (5) we receive (6). (6), CHIEN, is a member of the Earthly Square, but (6) specifically as a number represents the most complete earthly knowledge available. When we expand the square into a three dimensional reality we obtain a cube which contains six sides. Each of these sides represents a step in CHIEN's process of creation. How CHIEN accesses heaven is through the receipt of wisdom and knowledge from TUI which directly precedes it in the creative process. This seventh element is the balancing and unifying element in the center of the cube. It is (6) or CHIEN's process using the wisdom of TUI along with its natal abilities that allow it to escape the gravitational pull of the earth and have access to the creative powers of heaven. This can be correlated to the saying in Genesis that God created the world in six days and rested on the seventh. The seventh is the wisdom of TUI, which is not a creation, but a manifestation of God.

From another standpoint we can also look at fifteen as being made up of three sub systems each made up of five elements. When we do this the result is the property of three – one yang/Earthly element, one yin/Heavenly element and a balancing element. From a numerical perspective and from previous proofs we have:

Yang/Earthly – CHIEN, KEN, SUN, and KUN or (6), (8), (4), and (2), respectively
Yin/Heavenly – TUI, KAN, CHEN, and LI or (7), (1), (3), and (9), respectively

Balancing – B5 or (5,5)

These three representations give the primordial forces making up all of perceived reality.

Natal House Configurations

The following table summarizes the shift in houses for each of the eight trigrams plus B5 (9 total) chart configurations. The numbers 1 – 9 on the top row (horizontal) show the correct baseline positions (fixed houses) for each of the trigrams. These positions map to the positions seen in the Lo Shu. The numbers 1 – 9 on left-most column (vertical) represent all of the possible natal trigram designations for an individual or entity. All of the remaining numbers in the diagram show the natal positions of each of the trigrams relative to the baseline numeric designations (top row of numbers). This table contains all possible configurations (81) including the standard Lo Shu B5 baseline center position (row 5).

<u>Natal Positions vs. Baseline</u>

Diagram: Net Position Difference – 1

Natal Gua	Baseline Numeric Designations									Net Position Difference
	1	2	3	4	5	6	7	8	9	
1	6	7	8	9	1	2	3	4	5	14
2	7	8	9	1	2	3	4	5	6	22
3	8	9	1	2	3	4	5	6	7	16
4	9	1	2	3	4	5	6	7	8	20
5	1	2	3	4	5	6	7	8	9	0
6	2	3	4	5	6	7	8	9	1	20
7	3	4	5	6	7	8	9	1	2	16
8	4	5	6	7	8	9	1	2	3	22
9	5	6	7	8	9	1	2	3	4	14

Color Code Key	
0	position difference
1	position difference
2	position difference
3	position difference
4	position difference

This table appears to have a multitude of things happening, but there are actually only two concepts being communicated: a) based upon a person's natal trigram or gua, which house each of their trigrams rests (represented by the top row) and b) how far all of the natal trigrams are from their proper positions as represented by the Magic Square.

Essentially this table outlines to the reader how far from the Earth's natural trigram configuration (represented by the Lo Shu and top row of the diagram) your personality vibrates. Everyone, with the exception of the B5 personality, will have a deviation from the natural order. In some of the houses we will notice a vast difference in placement. For example, the KAN (1) chart has CHEN (3) in the 7th house. Naturally, CHEN (3) sits in the 3rd house and is four places away from the 7th house; meaning, if we start in the 7th house and count the number of houses we have to cycle through to get to 3rd house we arrive at a four place difference. Going clockwise we would start with the 7th house then go to the 6th, 1st, 8th, and finally the 3rd house giving us four total houses to cycle through. The significance here is when the character attributes of CHEN are required for success the KAN person will have a tendency to respond with a CHEN consciousness heavily influenced by TUI. Being as TUI and CHEN are opposites or compliments, the outcome could be drastic depending upon the scope of the challenge. The same holds true for the SUN (4) personality type where LI (9) is found in the 1st house and is also four places from its natural position. Chapters 10 through 19 go into much more detail on the impacts for each of the trigram combinations illustrated in the above chart. The analysis goes beyond the number of positions the trigram is from its natural position, but the chart above provides a great starting point.

In general when we look at the Lo Shu diagram the 2nd house is four positions from the 8th house, the 9th house is two positions from the 7th and so on. For example, if someone receives a natal trigram of CHEN (3) where (6) or CHIEN is in the 8th house, when (8) should be in the eighth house, what is the position difference? CHIEN (6) which naturally sits in the 6th house is two houses or positions away from KEN (8) which naturally sits in the 8th house. Thus the position difference is two.

The Net Position Difference column indicates the sum total number of positions each trigram differs from the baseline or Lo Shu arrangement which has (5) in the middle. These numbers reveal a key characteristic about each of the trigrams and their relationship to the original unifying entity in (5,5). The trigrams closest to (5) are KAN (1) and LI (9) with a net 14 position difference (see last column). The next are trigrams CHEN (3) and TUI (7) with a 16 net position difference. It should be noted that (1, 9, 3 and 7) make up the Heavenly arrangement found in the circle; therefore, it is no coincidence that these trigrams would be closest to the originating element. Next comes SUN (4) and CHIEN (6) with a net position of 20 and then KUN (2) and KEN (8) with a net position of 22. These four trigrams make up the earthly arrangement of the square and are closest to physical reality. Thus, mathematically we can derive or deduce each trigrams relative function in the creative process. The *Heavenly Circle* represents the potential manifestation through awareness (3,7) and energy (1,9). The *Earthly Square* represents the kinetic manifestation through intent (4,6) and matter (2,8).

Let's do some additional quantitative analysis around the Net Position Difference diagram. KAN (1) and LI (9) represent the active state of heaven's creative energy and TUI (7) and CHEN (3) represent the inactive or passive state of heaven's creative energy. The closest numbers to the B5 center are 14 and 16 which when added together give us 30 or 3. In the Kabalistical system there are three heavenly bodies designated to carry out the primary forces represented by 14 (initiatory force) and 16 (awareness). In the Kabalistical system these heavenly bodies are Keter, Chokhmah, and Binah. The furthest numbers from B5 are represented by 20 and 22 which when added together give us 42 or 6 (God created the earth in six days). Again in the Kabalistical system the six earthly bodies governing the primary forces represented by 20 (energy) and 22 (matter) are Gevurah, Chesed, Tiferet, Netzach, Hod, and Yesod.

Baseline House and Natal Combinations

There are a number of ways to view the interaction of two trigrams. From the perspective of a person's tendency versus that of the Earth's tendency and surrounding environment we can determine what the natural tendencies will be based upon those trigrams coming together. We can also determine the following: a) personality traits we must add to the situation through a change in our own functioning, b) the addition of another person with the balancing tendency or habit, c) the balancing trigram required to help the natal and base trigram to work harmoniously together, or d) the virtuous and divisive traits produced. Here is a summary of the perspectives:

- **Challenge:** The individual's natal tendency which is dictated by how they view the world during different times of the year versus the earth's natural tendency which changes during different times of the year, months, and days. Individual v. Earth.
  Corrective Measure: a) the individual changes their own personality to that of the required balancing personality or b) another individual with the personality of the required balancing personality is added to the situation.

- **Challenge:** The individual's natal tendency which is dictated by how they view the world during different times of the year versus another person's tendency that they are interacting with at a given moment in time.
  Corrective Measure: a) the individual (one of the two involved) changes their own personality to that of the required balancing personality or b) another individual with the personality of the required balancing personality be added to the situation.

Virtues versus Vices (Divisiveness)

When we take an individual's natal chart configuration and overlay that with either the Earth's fixed chart (which is represented by the Lo Shu Arrangement) or another person's chart; we receive a two trigram combination. This two trigram combination reveals certain vices or virtues that the person may exhibit. These are laid out in the virtue and vice sections of the house configurations analysis in Chapters 10 - 19. It is up to each person to decide which vices or virtues apply to them. In some cases a person may display both the vice and the virtue.

Another way to view why certain traits are a vice versus a virtue for a particular chart is to use the quality of numbers as defined by their unfolding into the world (see chapter 5). We have numbers one through nine where (1) is the beginning of the creative process. Due to its position (1) has not gone through many experiences to get to where it is. It is the first manifestation of physical reality and very close to the original source of all creation. It therefore lacks the experience in the world and any character trait falling into the one (1), or KAN, house will generally be a deficit for the person.

Nine has gone through the most iterations and experiences to come into the world (1, 2, 3, 4, 5, 6, 7, 8, 9) and thus is experienced and battle tested. Therefore, any character trait falling into the (9) house, or LI, is our greatest virtue in life. By doing a magical square house analysis one can find one's natal talent. (5) is in the center and represents a position of completion of a sub-cycle (which is made up of five numbers including the five itself) and has thus had one complete cycle of experiences. This is valuable in that at this position the person has at least a view of the world, although usually either yin or yang based. Because it hasn't started its journey through the second sub-cycle it has a complete world view that is untainted by other experiences.

Note: This is why it is said that the B5 personality type is generally either KUN or KEN. The first experience is that of the

84

Earth and KUN and KEN, as represented by the 2ⁿᵈ and 8ᵗʰ
houses, respectively, are the two complimentary energies closest
to the Earth. KUN and KEN both belong to the Earthly Square
as do SUN and CHIEN. Therefore, the B5 person tends to be
Earth yin (KEN) or Earth yang (KUN).

Again this is primarily determined by the individual's state of
awareness which is revealed through another set of criteria.
Based upon the state of awareness we would move up the
"perceptive" chain and say the B5 individual would be one of the
compliments in the BaGua in the following order: KUN/KEN,
SUN/CHIEN, TUI/CHEN, or LI/KAN. One additional note here
is that these levels of awareness or development are not static
and can change throughout a person's life. This is usually done
either through certain difficult or "traumatic" life experiences
brought about by the person's unbalanced behavior or
intentionally through initiation. Initiation will be addressed in
detail in another work.

To further illustrate the impact of each number upon our natal
talents, I have taken the same diagram from above (diagram
NPD – 1), but changed the house numbers across the top row to
three groupings: vice, balanced, and virtue. What is revealed
here is that the three character traits that fall into the "Vice"
section tend to be areas we need to develop. The three character
traits that fall into the "Virtue" section tend to be strengths. The
three character traits that fall into the "Balanced" section tend to
be more balanced meaning not really extraordinary assets at our
disposal, but also not liabilities. The character traits in the
balanced section tend to do their job, but for the most part will
not separate themselves as being real attributes/deficits to our
character.

This Magical Square House Analysis reveals something very
significant about human characteristics in general. It would
seem that virtuous character traits would be the ultimate goal.
Well they are; and yes they are assets, but not in every sense.
Essentially they are working overtime and at a higher that
normal output. So that would mean what we call strengths or

virtues in life are still out of balance. These traits, although serving us well in many cases, are also a source of problems in our lives. There are multiple reasons for this, one being that once we find something good we tend to lean and leverage that thing way too often. As a result, we never develop other character traits and the overused strengths make us suffer in the long run. This limits our capacity to respond to life's challenges and thus cripples us over the long term. This is not to say that we cannot or should not use these talents for our benefit, but realize that we may have a tendency to not use its compliment in the process. Armed with this information we can proceed in life making conscious choices that strengthen our overall character and thus achieve success.

Diagram: *Net Position Difference – 2*

		Vice-Virtue Designations								Net Position Difference
		Vices			Balanced			Virtues		
Natal Gua	1	6	7	8	9	1	2	3	4	5	14
	2	7	8	9	1	2	3	4	5	6	22
	3	8	9	1	2	3	4	5	6	7	16
	4	9	1	2	3	4	5	6	7	8	20
	5	1	2	3	4	5	6	7	8	9	0
	6	2	3	4	5	6	7	8	9	1	20
	7	3	4	5	6	7	8	9	1	2	16
	8	4	5	6	7	8	9	1	2	3	22
	9	5	6	7	8	9	1	2	3	4	14

Color Code Key	
0	position difference
1	position difference
2	position difference
3	position difference
4	position difference

Balancing Requirement

The balancing requirement takes the mathematical sum of the two combined trigrams to come up with which trigram is required to offset, harmonize, and balance their interaction. As stated in the Corrective Measure statement above, this can come in the form of the individual changing their personality to match the required balancing trigram or by adding another person to the situation with that balancing tendency. Of course, the goal is for each person to be empowered to change their personalities as required and remove the dependency of other people for their success in any given situation.

Chapter 9: Cycle Analysis

This chapter is here to help us understand that each trigram or number can be divided into time increments. Time increments include any measure we use to define a repeatable and cyclical moment in time. This would include seconds, minutes, hours, days, weeks, months, years, etc. For the purposes of this work we will only focus on years and months and the qualities they carry. The chapters that follow will take this same quality analysis, but apply it to the unique aspects of our character.

As indicated throughout this book, the BaGua classification system and the Magical Square Analysis are based upon mathematics. As such, we can use formulas and equations to chart the cyclical nature of reality as represented by the numbers and trigrams used in the BaGua. This is the basis of analyzing and predicting the events occurring in the lives of individuals on a yearly and monthly basis. As stated earlier in this text, there are only nine numbers in the world; thus, only nine categorizations of reality. Thus, as numbers repeat so do the realities they represent. As we tend to react the same way over and over to people, events, and situations we are able to then chart a pattern of behavior and predictability in outcomes during certain years and months relative to when we were born. This is our cycle analysis.

In this text we are concerned with two cycles: one primary and one secondary. The primary cycle is the solar cycle which is equivalent to one year. The secondary cycle is the lunar cycle which is equivalent to one month. It should be noted here that these cycles are not planetary cycles, thus your fortune is not tied to the movement of the sun, moon, and stars; at least, not exactly. So from that standpoint we have to refer to the cycles as yearly and monthly cycles and not solar and lunar. To properly explain how the BaGua is tied to the motion of the stars and earth would actually require a redefining of how we measure the time from daily, monthly, and yearly basis. When we study the ancient Chinese systems and the African systems from which they were inherited we find scientific calendars that vary from what we use today, even though today's modern calendars are based upon the ancient sciences.

The good news is there are no "good" or "bad" years or cycles in our lives! Using that connotation seems to indicate a sort of uncontrollable fate bestowed upon us from the heavens above and this just isn't true. The foundational premise here is that success in all of our life's endeavors is a right bestowed upon us from the universal power that placed us here and thus we have all the tools required to ensure success. The bad news is that out of the nine available tools or talents in our personal arsenals we generally only use three or so with any effectiveness in dealing with life's challenges. There are times when we over or under use a talent, there are other times when we attempt to kill a fly with sledgehammer and wind up breaking the table or putting a hole in the floor. There are still other times when we just don't use the required talent either because we don't know it's in our toolbox or we just feel more comfortable with that sledgehammer.

So the initial part of our analysis entails understanding which tools each character type is skilled with and which ones they aren't. For this analysis we refer to diagram *Net Position Difference – 2* or *NPD – 2 (found in chapter 8)*. For each character type one through nine, as represented by our trigrams, there are innate strengths and weakness. In NPD – 2 the Natal Guas, or character types, are listed down the left hand side of the diagram. In the top middle of the diagram are three primary sections: "Vices", "Balanced", and "Virtues". The vices are those tools, or character traits, that we under utilize in a time of need; whereas, the virtues are those tools we tend to over utilize which tends to cause the same rate of failure as the under utilized tools. Lastly, the balanced character traits are those tools we tend to be most skilled with.

Let's site an example, the KAN person has the following balanced traits: LI (The Soldier), KUN (The Negotiator), and most of all KAN (The Conservationist); thus the name. In other words, when required, the Conservationist can summon these talents and resolve those required problems in and around their lives. They are excellent planners and organizers (KAN), ready and able to do work at any cost including personal harm (LI), and very skilled negotiators with the ability to mix with most crowds and people (KUN). So for one-third of their life's challenges they are adequately equipped and prepared for success. The Conservationist has the following vices: CHIEN (The Devotee), TUI (The Monk), and KEN (The Lover). The vices represent dormant talents that unless they have taken the time to cultivate will not be available in a time of need. This is the equivalent of writing in cursive with the opposite hand before the handwriting test if you have never tried to before. The Conservationist has poor mental acuity and memory (CHIEN), lacks the ability to understand the deeper underlying aspects of life (TUI), and generally cannot build strong, long lasting, and intimate relationships (KEN). The virtues represent talents that are available for use, but frequently overused; especially, during times of stress or duress. The virtues are CHEN (The Visionary), SUN (The Leader), and B5 (The Peacekeeper). These virtues also cause a problem in that when overused they become equally ineffective as the vices. The Conservationist tends to over rely on ideas and have unfounded faith (CHEN), be over bearing and dictatorial in nature (SUN), and tries to unify and balance situations unnecessarily (B5).

At this point let's take a moment to discuss what we mean by success and failure. What we find is successes and failures have the same measurement indicators: financial, health, children, relationships, career, social status, etc. How these things and others manifest in our lives determines whether they are positives or negatives in our lives. For example, a success in the health arena could be overcoming a degenerative disease or maintaining your highest level of fitness in years; whereas, a failure could be contracting a degenerative disease or falling out of shape. In the financial arena this could be coming into money versus loosing a large sum of money. So in essence what we are saying is there are certain years in which each character type will tend to have success versus failure. Why? The main reason is we are creatures of habit which means we approach the same challenges in the exact same way each and every time. And usually when we "learn" from our previous mistakes all we are really saying is now we know how to do it "my way" much better this time.

The table below lists all nine of the character types which will dominant a particular year or month and a brief summary of what is required to be successful when these energies manifest themselves during a particular year or month.

Yearly Qualities

Trigram	Comments
B5, The Peacekeeper	During these years/months the universe will demand that we unify and balance all things in our lives.
9, LI, The Soldier	Here the requirement is that we do what is right and required for success even in the face of personal loss.
1, KAN, The Conservationist	Here we must remove those things from our lives that do not serve us and our immediate circle.
4, SUN, The Leader	Here we must accurately define the reality in front of us and put it in its proper place relative to our lives.
6, CHIEN, The Devotee	Here we must have the mental and spiritual fortitude to hold on to our goals, dreams, and desires; even in the midst of adversity.
8, KEN, The Lover	Here we must join forces with others for the benefit of the overall goal. This involves being flexible.
2, KUN, The Negotiator	Here we must be willing to socialize and interact with people and things in the surrounding environment.
3, CHEN, The Visionary	Here we must be willing to go out and experience and be a part of life.
7, TUI, The Monk	Here we must be willing to live by

Trigram	Comments
	moral and spiritual principles and consult sages and experts for guidance when needed.

The trigrams that you have learned to analyze in this book reach a culmination in the following chapters as we introduce character names for each of the nine numbers/trigrams. Note that in this chapter we discuss each character/number/trigram/magic square as it pertains specifically to the actual traits persons born under each respective number will exhibit. The purpose of the next nine chapters is to apply each of the categorizations of the BaGua to our personality make-up. More specifically, these traits, represented by numbers/trigrams, will be superimposed against the houses in the Lo Shu (representing the awareness in our overall environment) to show how our personalities are affected by universal intelligence.

Chapter 10: KAN – The Conservationist

Bagua Configuration: 1

9	5	7
8	1	3
4	6	2

Summary:
The KAN (1) person or Conservationist is conservative by nature and tends to focus on themselves and those within their immediate circle first and foremost before considering others. This is not selfishness, but a strong desire to protect those in their immediate circle. The KAN (1) person possesses good communication skills and can interact well in most social and business arenas. However, they often hold mental conversations and fail to realize they have not shared certain details and information with those they are attempting to communicate with. These individuals are also hard workers with a tendency to lead and manage while working; especially, during stressful times. They also have the ability and willingness to sacrifice themselves for the goal where required, but will attempt to rationalize their way into other alternatives that do not cause bodily harm.

The extreme part of any trigram's personality shows itself most during times of stress or challenge. It is when we feel threatened that we reach for those tools which we are most comfortable with and have to most faith in. The extreme part of KAN's personality makes them talented at resolving any lack of integration or disunity in and around their lives as KAN (1) is your proactive peace keeper. Being an extreme tendency for the KAN (1) person it tends to be overused as a solution to their problems. Again, it is the overuse of these qualities that make them extreme and the source of failure in our lives. Possessing well developed leadership skills, these individuals tend to lead by forming strong relationships with others, but can tend to be overbearing and dictatorial at times. They will tend to take leadership positions in those areas they are passionate about. The KAN (1) personality will find it difficulty to have faith in things unseen and will generally lack the ability to generate solution-based ideas during challenging times.

The characteristic of a deficient personality trait is that it tends to be absent in a time of need. These are traits that rarely show themselves when needed, but when they do come to the fore they are uncontrollable and destructive. Generally, KAN (1) individuals have poor memories and don't maintain mental images very well. The KAN (1) person is not one who would pray or meditate with any effectiveness. The power of prayer and meditation requires that one hold an image in their minds over a long period of time. When emotion is added to the process simultaneously the unseen becomes the seen or that which is imagined becomes a tangible physical object. These individuals are not skilled when it comes to intimate relationships, but will have spurts of being overly expansive in this arena. Lastly, these individuals lack the ability to understand the deeper meaning to life and its laws. They will need guidance in the larger projects and endeavors in order to increase their chances of success.

Mental Acuity

Base House: 1st House -- 1 (KAN): Conservationist

Natal Trait: 6 (CHIEN): The Devotee
Balancing Agent: 7 (TUI) The Monk
Angle Analysis: Acute
I Ching Hexagram: 6, Conflict

Description:
CHIEN (6) in the KAN (1) house produces internalization of foundational principles. CHIEN (6) represents the focus of holding a mental vision of that which is to be achieved where KAN (1) has a magnetic and internalizing and conservative tendency. Although CHIEN (6) is mental and internal its functions are quite deliberate in that it is actively engaged in carrying out the orders from TUI (7) in the previous stage of the creative process. It is therefore "at one" with this vision and is not concerned about itself or other entities in the physical environment. In addition, CHIEN (6) is a part of the *Earthly Square* where KAN (1) is a part of the *Heavenly Circle*. These factors are the source of conflict between the two trigrams.

This conflict can be overcome as the CHIEN (6) and KAN (1) are only one position away from each other (net position difference = 1) and the angular analysis produces an acute angle which also indicates the close proximity to one another.

Virtuous Trait:
Although slow to get there, once these individuals are able to achieve the mental focus required to achieve their goals they can hold it for extended periods of time. Conservationists have the ability to meditate deeply upon subjects. This ultimately helps in the manifestation of their goals. They also tend to focus on the structural components of a particular subject and deeply visualize them.

Divisive Trait:
CHIEN (6) is focused on the overall goal with great intensity while KAN's slow conservative approach will delay the person's ability to achieve this internal focus. It will take these individuals some time to get their mental focus on the things they are doing. They generally cannot see things that haven't already taken physical form, have no imagination or vision of the future, and bad memories. KAN's conservative approach will add time to any mental or physical process.

From another perspective these people are very slow to turn to prayer, meditation, and internalization as a tool to address issues. They may have a tendency to look at their own personal set of circumstances and their own "reality" rather than focus on how things could or might be.

Balancing Description:
TUI (7) will provide these individuals with enough focus to make this skill useful. TUI's insight and direction are of great aid to these individuals. TUI (7) has some of its focus on manifested physical reality and can thus add some clarity to CHIEN (6) while in the house of KAN (1).

Intuitive Ability

Base House: 2nd House -- 2 (KUN): Negotiator
Natal Trait: 7 (TUI): Monk
Balancing Agent: 9 (LI): Soldier
Angle Analysis: Acute
I Ching Hexagram: 45, Gathering Together

Description:
TUI (7) in the KUN (2) house produces the effect of causing one to focus outward in the environment when it is trying to focus inward to gain insight concerning a goal. This process is possible for TUI (7) due to its remaining fire and insight into the beginning and end of the creative process. The tendencies are not too far apart where the problem cannot be corrected without some effort. TUI (7) and KUN (2) are next to each other in the creative process.

Virtuous Trait:
The Conservationist has the ability to understand the laws governing trade and commerce. This insight allows them to set plans into motion and determine the laws that must be followed in order to have success. They also have an insight into how to bring people together to achieve a goal.

Divisive Trait:
KUN (2) is a pure obedient outward tendency; whereas, TUI (7) observes the outside world to gain insight on what is to come. Here the individual will be a bit too focused on the future and inner-workings of things to meet the focus of KUN (2). However, TUI (7) and KUN (2) are only one net position away from one another and these deficiencies can generally be overcome. These individuals will be looking for insight through human interaction, rather than from going within or using intuition.

Balancing Description:
LI (9) provides the fire necessary focus to pull TUI (7) out of KUN's outward tendency.

Relationships

Base House: 3rd House -- 3 (CHEN): Visionary
Natal Trait: 8 (KEN): Lover
Balancing Agent: 2 (KUN): Negotiator
Angle Analysis: Acute
I Ching Hexagram: 27, Opening of the Mouth (Nourishment)

Description:
KEN (8) is ready to slowly expand out to develop permanent, meaningful, and long lasting relationships. CHEN (3) is ready to move into the world with speed and without regard for consequences. These two energies will conflict causing KEN (8) to be more outgoing than usual.

These two trigrams are one place from each other, but in the wrong places. KEN (8) is attempting to act while receiving influence from CHEN (3), but, according to the natural process of creation, it is CHEN (3) that turns to view the work of KEN (8) in consideration for its next moves. KEN (8) takes its orders and direction from KAN (1) not CHEN (3) so here we have a bit of confusion.

Virtuous Trait:
Here the KEN (8) person is able to act fluidly with ample foresight as to how their influence will be viewed.

Divisive Trait:
KEN (8) mixing with CHEN (3) will cause expansiveness in the area of intimate interaction. The close relationships usually generated with people within one's circle are expanded outward to those not deserving of such. This produces a dangerous situation. In addition, because CHEN (3) produces ideas and gives KEN (8) insights into things not fully materially present they invest their time and energy into the wrong places.

Thus, the Conservationists are a bit ahead of themselves in that they are not seeking their influences from the correct place. Here there is a tendency to act on impulse without seeking what is right and correct. Again these actions are toward coming together with others and could be damaging.

Balancing Description:
KUN (2) is the balancing agent. Its impersonal outward tendency based upon specific direction balances the unfocused expansive tendency of CHEN (3).

Work Ethic

Base House: 4th House -- 4 (SUN): Leader
Natal Trait: 9 (LI): Soldier
Balancing Agent: 4 (SUN): Leader
Angle Analysis: Acute
I Ching Hexagram: 50, The Cauldron

Description:
LI (9) in the SUN (4) house produces an intense focus on reasoning and rationalization as one moves towards a zealous tendency. SUN's talent is a deep penetrating insight into the

function of manifested things in the world. Along with this talent is the ability to see all things in the world and understand their functions.

However, because LI (9) is occupying the SUN (4) house, instead of vice versa, these leadership talents will only manifest under times of stress or for those things the KAN (1) person is passionate about.

Virtuous Trait:

As LI's influence on other trigrams is to intensify their natural tendencies these persons can see how physical reality fits together to create the complete picture. This sight not only includes the pieces required for assembly, but the supporting resources and elements that are required to complete it. Thus, the Conservationist has the talent to understand, define, and ultimately manipulate all of manifested reality provided they have the interest in doing such. These individuals have the potential to be very skilled leaders and managers.

Their ability to see and understand everything around them allows them to address issues quickly and effectively. This is so because they know which people or resources to use to solve or address any given situation. Essentially, they are masters of the five primary senses (look, feel, hear, taste, and touch); thus, allowing them to classify and understand reality. That is why they are labeled as having good reasoning skills. Again, passion, focus, and an interest in the subject matter in question are prerequisites for the manifestation of these talents.

Divisive Trait:

Conservationists are often labeled as dictatorial and micromanagers in their particular fields. They can be too focused on physical reality, its management, and positioning. It is quite easy for this personality type to forget that their talent is not knowledge and thus limited to what is physically available. Other talents such as intuition, planning, trade, relationship building, and a strong work ethic are not necessarily natal talents that they possess. This leaves a large void when we view overall success because they are so dependent on the work of others.

It is important to note here that the LI-SUN qualities only manifest in situations where one is passionate about the person or subject of interest. When this passion manifests as anger or enthusiasm the tendency of the Conservationist is to manage and control the situation in order to bring harmony to it. Of course the danger is in the fact that this may or may not be the approach required.

It should be noted again, that in the creative process SUN (4) is the sixth overall stage; thus putting it near the end. It is not until TUI (7), CHIEN (6), KAN (1), KEN (8), and CHEN (3) have completed their responsibilities that SUN (4) can then have something to work worth to be successful. These individuals may tend to forget they are part of a larger process or team and thus become arrogant.

Balancing Description:
SUN (4) will refocus LI (9) back on the purpose of SUN (4) tendency in the larger picture of reality.

Planning and Organizing Abilities

Base House: 5th House -- 5: Peacekeeper
Natal Trait: 1 (KAN): Conservationist
Balancing Agent: 6 (CHIEN): Devotee
Angle Analysis: N/A
I Ching Hexagram: Not Applicable

Description:
KAN (1) in the B5 house produces one whose universal balancing focus is grounded in self preparation and enhancement. These individuals believe that if their lives are structured correctly that all goes well. In addition, they tend to use their conservative tendency to bring harmony to whatever

environment they may be in.

Virtuous Trait:
These individuals have the ability to lay out the structure that all people can fit into to work together harmoniously and cooperatively. Their planning and strategizing abilities bring about harmony in their lives and in their general environment.

Divisive Trait:
These individuals will have a tendency to always use their planning ability to bring about harmony in their lives and in their general environment (i.e. work, family, etc.). As KAN (1) is only one of the nine character traits available to do this, its success will only be fully achieved just over 10% of the time. Additionally, these individuals may have a conservative approach to filling the roles required for success in a situation, especially, if it falls outside of their comfort zone.

Balancing Description:
CHIEN (6) is needed to add the mental focus that will allow KAN (1) to balance its view. CHIEN's view and focus on the whole brings KAN (1) the enlightenment required to balance out its view.

Social Skills

Base House: 6th House -- 6 (CHIEN): Devotee
Natal Trait: 2 (KUN): Negotiator
Balancing Agent: 8 (KEN): Lover
Angle Analysis: Right
I Ching Hexagram: 11, Peace

Description:
KUN (2) in the CHIEN (6) house produces an effect that moves KUN's outward tendency inward. Individuals will find a tendency to visualize and imagine their objective more so than reaching out to the people around them. In addition, CHIEN (6) is focused on goals that have not manifested on the material

plane as opposed to KUN (2) which works with fully manifested creations and completes their cycle. These two opposing tendencies create a focus issue for KUN (2) as KUN's success is dependent upon it being able to engage all peoples in any environment.

Virtuous Trait:
These individuals have the ability to communicate their (or others) thoughts and visions to others in a way they can understand. They also have the ability to see how they need to communicate and function with others to get their point across.

Divisive Trait:
KUN's ability to develop relationships and interact with others is compromised by CHIEN's inward focus. CHIEN (6) who has no interest in developing relationships will detract from KUN's ability to verbally communicate and function harmoniously with others.

Balancing Description:
KEN (8) provides enough of an outward focus to bring KUN's awareness back to its intended objective and balance the influences from CHIEN (6).

Creativity & Zest for Life

Base House: 7th House -- 7 (TUI): Monk
Natal Trait: 3 (CHEN): Visionary
Balancing Agent: 1 (KAN): Conservationist
Angle Analysis: Axis
I Ching Hexagram: 54, The Marrying Maiden

Description:
CHEN (3) in the TUI (7) house produces an axis conflict between the East and the West, respectfully. CHEN's tendency

is outward while TUI's is inward. In theory both have the same amount of heat and coolness, but in actuality this is not true due to direction of movement and inertia. TUI (7) is coming from summer where as CHEN (3) is coming from the winter. CHEN (3) is attempting to express itself in the world and further creation while TUI (7) is focused on starting the creative process which starts in the metaphysical world. So here we have a conflict of opposites or compliments.

Virtuous Trait:
When balanced the Conservationist is able to provide profound insight (ideas) to accomplish any goal that is rooted in a strong truthful principle governing the project in question. The ideas offered by these persons are thus profound and accurate. These individuals can be great inventors, because their ideas are both good and mathematically sound.

Divisive Trait:
CHEN-TUI produces a major conflict in goals and functioning. These individuals when attempting to contribute ideas or express talents will have a strong pull to seek guidance and insight. They will attempt to expand in the world and be optimistic about life and their abilities, but will be troubled with doubt concerning the validity of their actions. This can create a stalemate in their actions.

Balancing Description:
KAN (1) is the mathematical center for the East and West. Both of these trigrams are seeking movement which is why KAN (1) and not LI (9) is the balancing equivalent for the CHEN-TUI combination. The fire of LI (9) would excite these elements beyond control. The cold energy of KAN (1) slows them both down enough to see how they can coexist.

Leadership & Resourcefulness

Base House: 8th House -- 8 (KEN): Lover
Natal Trait: 4 (SUN): Leader
Balancing Agent: 3 (CHEN): Visionary
Angle Analysis: Right
I Ching Hexagram: 53, Development (Gradual Progress)

Description:
SUN (4) and KEN (8) are both part of the *Earthly Square*
arrangement and are thus accustomed to taking direction from
others. SUN (4) is the ability to see and understand all physical
reality which translates into the ability to effectively manage and
properly place things in the world. These individuals are known
as good managers and excellent business people because of their
management ability and understanding of where, when, and how
things go. KEN (8) brings seemingly unrelated things together
to work and be together via a very strong bond. So this person
will tend to manage, but keep good relationships with others.

Virtuous Trait:
The Conservationist is an excellent manager of social
relationships and working unions. These individuals although
having a general distraction in their overall management ability,
will have a strong proficiency in helping established groups or
organizations be most affective. This person can look at two
companies, families, nations, communities, etc. and explain how
they can be most effective when working collaboratively. These
individuals can also manage while keeping good relationships.

Divisive Trait:
Conversely, SUN (4) in the KEN (8) house produces one who
cannot sustain one's focus on controlling and governing the
environment and entities under its dominion. The ability to
reason and accurately define and see the reality around it is
compromised and unstable. The ability will be there for a while
then fade and then come back again. This is due to KEN's

coolness reducing SUN's rising heat. Additionally, certain decisions will be skewed by them wanting to maintain social harmony.

Balancing Description:
The balancing trigram is CHEN (3). CHEN's expansiveness will help SUN (4) move its focus away from the social arena back into the general environment and overall project.

Unifying & Balancing Abilities

Base House: 9th House -- 9 (LI): Soldier
Natal Trait: 5: Peacekeeper
Balancing Agent: 5: Peacekeeper
Angle Analysis: N/A
I Ching Hexagram: Not Applicable

Description:
B5 (5,5) in the LI (9) house creates an intense passion for balancing all environmental influences in KAN's life. The Conservationist is focused on promoting oneness, unity, and balance in their lives. These individuals manifest a moral sense that wants all things to be successful rather than any one person or thing getting more than their share of the spoils. These personalities show themselves as persons who – conservative in nature - don't want to create too many ruffles by making chaotic movements.

Virtuous Trait:
Conservationists are morally centered and balanced in their approach and outlook to life. These are you master unifiers in the world who function out of a state of fairness and balance. They quickly and readily take on whatever roll is required to bring success in their lives and the projects and communities they are associated with.

This is an enhancement of the B5 (5,5) character trait which can play any role in the "orchestra". That is their gift.

Divisive Trait:
Conservationists tend to be conservative so that the present balance of their lives is not disturbed. This is an extreme posture as one of the requirements in the creative process is that of destruction and renewal. Thus, these individuals resist change with a passion, especially when presented in radical or quick manner. In functioning this way they tend to violate their own greatest cause in maintaining oneness. The nature of the world; however, is movement and thus change in the form of destruction and creation are inevitable and required.

From another view, these individuals want to maintain unity, balance, and social order at any cost. This often will result in them acting without a plan.

Balancing Description:
B5 is needed to bring LI's fiery influence full circle and back into focus and perspective for the Conservationist character type. As the B5 tendency of taking on any role required is greatly enhanced (actually too much so) it is necessary for an additional B5 element to be added to bring the overall goals and objectives back into focus.

Chapter 11: KUN – The Negotiator

Bagua Configuration: 2

1	6	8
9	2	4
5	7	3

The Negotiator Summary:

The KUN (2) person or Negotiator has excellent communication ability. They are able to mix well in most social and professional environments and can make "friends" almost wherever they go. These individuals plan and organize well based upon what's known and available in their environment. The Negotiator has a healthy fantasy life and a passion to experience the world first hand. They have the ability to see a bit deeper into things than the average person and can generate ideas.

The Negotiator has a number of character traits that are excessive in nature. These could be characterized as talents, but tend to be overused thus making them the source of problems in their lives. The Negotiator has a great ability to hold images down to the greatest detail in their minds. They have great memories and excellent trance ability. Negotiators have a great ability to unify and harmonize with others; especially, when it comes to close relationships. This further assists them in mixing with any social group or at any function. They also exhibit well developed leadership qualities that are based upon some set of principles (often moral). The Negotiator's general outlook on life is through interaction with others.

Generally, the Negotiator lacks any sort of intuitive ability;

meaning, they can't see the deeper reasons for why things happen in their lives. It's like viewing or participating in a puppet show, but not being aware of the strings. As a result they have a hard time grasping the bigger picture. These individuals have issues forming deep, intimate relationships with others. Although they are moral in leadership positions, they have a tendency to reject the moral principles in their daily living. Lastly, these individuals tend to avoid physical labor especially if there is even a hint of personal discomfort.

Intuitive Ability

Base House: 1st House -- 1 (KAN): Conservationist
Natal Trait: 7 (TUI): Monk
Balancing Agent: 8 (KEN): Lover
Angle Analysis: Right
I Ching Hexagram: 47, Exhaustion

Description:
TUI (7) has the tendency of being expansive into the mental regions for the purpose of gaining clarity. KAN (1) has the purpose of conserving in preparation for the future by physically retreating into places of solitude. Its activity is through magnetism as it has no interest in interacting with the physical environment. TUI (7) and KAN (1) produce a net position difference of two and the angular analysis produces a right angle which indicates the potential for balanced (equal yin and yang) perspective towards life. Both trigrams are members of the *Heavenly Circle* and are thus accustomed to setting direction.

TUI (7) and KAN (1) together combine the beginning of Fall and beginning of Winter. The joyousness and intuitive ability of TUI (7) is slow to form in the heart of the Negotiator and is often only found with events needing tremendous time and planning.

Virtuous Trait:
Once the Negotiator types are able to get into a meditative state (this may take a long while) they possess the ability to intuit the underlying structure and deep meaning of the subject inquired about. These individuals will be able to hold the intuitive mind-state and see deeply into the structure of things.

Divisive Trait:
TUI (7) in KAN (1) produces in the Negotiator one who lacks intuitive ability without great effort. Once achieved, they enjoy a very deep, powerful, and insightful experience. TUI (7) and KAN (1) are both a part of the *Heavenly Circle* and are both accustomed to giving commands and setting the pace in the creative experience. This is an initial source of conflict between the two personalities.

From another perspective, KAN (1) will slow down TUI's ability to intuit. Thus, the Negotiator will have issues seeing the deep underlying laws governing reality and will thus only have success where a superficial understanding of the subject at hand is required. These are the people who must work really hard to meditate or pray and pull back meaningful symbols or information.

They tend not to understand the underlying laws governing the world around them. Absent this knowledge, only so much success can be obtained without assistance from others possessing intuitive talents.

Balancing Description:
KEN (8) will provide a balance by bringing TUI (7) and KAN (1) together harmoniously as KEN's talent is bringing together any persons for a deeper more meaningful relationship. Just the slight movement from KEN (8) is all that is needed to move this combination into productivity.

Relationships

Base House: 2nd House -- 2 (KUN): Negotiator
Natal Trait: 8 (KEN): Lover
Balancing Agent: 1 (KAN): Conservationist
Angle Analysis: Axis
I Ching Hexagram: 23, Splitting Apart

Description:
KEN (8) in the KUN (2) house produces the 23rd hexagram, Splitting Apart in the I Ching which is one of the four violently opposing tendencies. For the Negotiator, here we have a situation in which one's natal tendency is focused on intimate interaction with others but KUN (2) is looking for material exchange only. Although both trigrams are focused outward their speed and intentions are very different. KEN (8) is interested in bonding and working closely with others in hopes of creating a union; whereas, KUN (2) has no interest in intimacy which will actually interfere with its core focus.

Virtuous Trait:
There is opportunity here for the Negotiator to achieve great power and accomplishment. If one can slow the forward motion by utilizing the balancing agent of KAN (1) and realize the required tendency versus what they would naturally bring to the situation, then success and great power can be realized. Large accomplishments will not be made at this time however, but the avoidance of danger and the experienced gained by living the law in this situation will add nicely to the individuals knowledge and power base.

These individuals will have the ability to create lasting relationships with associates and partners.

Divisive Trait:
KEN (8) is the ability to mix intimately with all things in the world. KUN (2) is the ability to form superficial relationships

110

with anyone. This situation calls for an intimate relationship, but the Negotiator approaches it as a superficial opportunity and thus fails in their dealings in the situation. Both intimate and superficial relationships have their place in the world and when we mix these two – disaster is the result. For example, feel free to watch the lions in the cage, but don't try to pet them. Understanding the rules and laws governing our interactions with others is key for our success in life. The Negotiator will approach their intimate relationships (i.e. spouse, family, friends, etc.) from a business perspective. This can cause major problems; especially, once loved ones get the sense there is no love.

Balancing Description:
KAN's inward, self enhancing focus enables these outward forces of KEN (8) and KUN (2) to work harmoniously by forcing them to both look inward enough to appreciate their roles in the larger picture. KAN (1) achieves this by slowing their forward movement.

Work Ethic

Base House: 3rd House -- 3 (CHEN): Visionary
Natal Trait: 9 (LI): Soldier
Balancing Agent: 3 (CHEN): Visionary
Angle Analysis: Right
I Ching Hexagram: 21, Biting Through

Description:
LI (9) in the CHEN (3) house produces one with the ability to see the subtle physical realities of the world. As LI's influence on other trigrams is to intensify their natural tendencies, CHEN's ability to see un-manifested reality is greatly enhanced. What is also noted here is that the Negotiator will have a passion for experiencing life in all its wonderful forms. This can manifest as travel, entertainment, sex, social mixing, etc.

111

Virtuous Trait:
The Negotiator will have a healthy appetite to experience the world and will carry a strong faith that they will always be taken care of wherever their travels may take them.

When pressured, the Negotiator can see and identify things in their formative stages. For this, they are sometimes labeled as great inventors. This is because other charts (or guas) cannot see the same reality as the Negotiator can see and thus think the enticing ideas come from no where. But that couldn't be farther from the truth as these ideas are simply what was initiated in the TUI (7) and CHIEN (6) stages of creation. Negotiators are the first ones to be able to see its subtle manifestation on the physical plane. Their ideas are more readily accepted than that of the CHIEN (6) person because by the time the CHEN (3) person sees it there are traces of physical manifestation. When the CHIEN (6) person, or Devotee is visualizing the complete picture it may lack any physical construct or support mechanism. Not only that, but because the Negotiator is rooted in both the physical and mental realms they can better communicate this reality to others, especially to the SUN (4) or Leader who needs it the most.

The Negotiator can also see a bit deeper into physical and mental things than the average person. This manifests as being able to read the aura of another person. This goes beyond the five primary senses or gives them extra ability or intensity. Again, this ability only manifests during times of tension or when a deep sincere interest in the subject exists.

One note here is that the Negotiator who carries this talent must have a genuine interest in the subject or person in order to manifest this ability as opposed to the CHEN (3) person or Visionary who generates ideas naturally all of the time.

Divisive Trait:
The Negotiator often does not have the support of those around them and may try to follow through with one of the various

"ideas" that they have seen inside their minds. This is because they see these ideas as real and tangible and often act on them before they are firmly planted on the physical plane. This behavior causes failure. It is like stepping on a pond that is not fully frozen. The Negotiator sees that it will be frozen and assumes it is frozen. Additionally, during time of stress the Negotiator will attempt to cope by delving into its passion of travel, entertainment, sex, etc. This can be destructive as challenges are not met head on and dealt with directly.

These individuals end up living in a world that is partly formed. This leads to communication issues with others. The Negotiator is also labeled as a risk taker for the reasons mentioned above. Also, in times of stress these individuals have a tendency to turn to alcohol, drugs, sex, and other extreme stimuli as a coping mechanism.

Balancing Description:
The balancing factor here is an additional CHEN (3) trigram to help balance and anchor it considering the influence of LI (9).

Planning and Organizing Abilities

Base House: 4th House -- 4 (SUN): Leader
Natal Trait: 1 (KAN): Conservationist
Balancing Agent: 5: Peacekeeper
Angle Analysis: Obtuse
I Ching Hexagram: 48, The Well

Description:
KAN (1) in the SUN (4) house brings together two opposing tendencies in the Negotiator. KAN's primary focus is to strengthen itself and those it's associated with through conservative practices. SUN (4) is focused on building and creating something generally apart from itself using the resources available. SUN's interest in itself is secondary to the goal.

Virtuous Trait:
The Negotiators are able to plan and strategize effectively around resource allocation and leadership. These are your corporate planners who are responsible for determining what leadership, people, and characteristics are required to sustain and grow business. They can also plan around resource allocation and tend to be conservative in its use.

Divisive Trait:
When the Negotiator attempts to focus, concentrate, plan, and conserve he/she finds that looking outside of oneself to the things in its environment is easiest. This is in direct conflict with KAN's requirement of ignoring and "zoning out" everything in its environment so that it can focus on what is critical and essential for its continued progression – in other words – look within for the answers. Again, in order to plan effectively, one cannot interact with the outside world. Accurate and effective planning takes deep concentration.

Balancing Description:
B5 is the balancing agent as it has the ability to bring KAN (1) back to a harmonious focus.

Social Skills

Base House: 5th House -- 5: Peacekeeper
Natal Trait: 2 (KUN): Negotiator
Balancing Agent: 7 (TUI): Monk
Angle Analysis: Radial Line
I Ching Hexagram: Not Applicable

Description:
KUN (2) in the B5 house produces one who's way to harmonize life and environment is through non-committal relationships, trade, and commerce. This exchanging of resources is believed

114

to balance out the inconsistencies and unfairness in resource allocation pervading the environment. These relationships are not intimate and do not supersede the intended goal for which the relationship was formed.

Virtuous Trait:
For situations requiring harmony and balancing through bringing people together on a superficial level these individuals will have success. Many times in resolving group conflict the issue isn't so much coming up with the solution, but bringing all parties involved to the table. The Negotiator personality has the most success in accomplishing this task. This is partly due to talent, but also due to commitment.

Divisive Trait:
The Negotiator tends to address and view all issues in their lives through non-committal relationships. This is good for those situations which don't require commitment, but for the other eight situation types requiring the character of a different trigram, failure could be the result.

Balancing Description:
TUI (7) provides the insight and wisdom that KUN (2) will need to maintain its proper focus and put its outward trade focus in proper perspective.

Creativity & Zest for Life

Base House: 6th House -- 6 (CHIEN): Devotee
Natal Trait: 3 (CHEN): Visionary
Balancing Agent: 9 (LI): Soldier
Angle Analysis: Obtuse
I Ching Hexagram: 34, Power of the Great

Description:
CHEN (3) in the CHIEN (6) house produces another conflict in

movement. CHEN's tendency is outward and CHIEN's is inward. As CHEN (3) is the first outward expression in creation it is erratic and without the ability to see clearly. CHIEN (6) is well founded in its internalization and its movement and is focused on moving forward with the wisdom it inherited from TUI.

Virtuous Trait:
These individuals are able to come up with ideas and contributions based upon a mental vision of the final goal. Normally, the CHEN (3) person is viewing the physical and subtle physical realities identifying how they can be used for the overall goal. Here with the relationship of CHIEN (6) to CHEN (3), the Negotiator can pull from the mental sphere of awareness and develop ideas strictly from the vision or image in their minds. This is powerful as their tendency here will be to expand internally more so than externally.

Divisive Trait:
When the Negotiator attempts to contribute to a cause via ideas and the offering of subtle insights they find themselves going within rather than expressing themselves outwardly. The expansive energy of CHEN (3) is essentially drawn backwards into the creative process. These individuals can tend to get very "spacey" and just not be here with the rest of us.

Balancing Description:
The electric energy of LI (9) is required to break CHEN (3) from CHIEN's inward inertia. This is so because of the extreme and powerful natures of both CHEN (3) and CHIEN (6).

Leadership and Resourcefulness

Base House: 7th House -- 7 (TUI): Monk
Natal Trait: 4 (SUN): Leader
Balancing Agent: 2 (KUN): Negotiator
Angle Analysis: Obtuse

I Ching Hexagram: 61, Inner Truth

Description:
SUN (4) in the TUI (7) house produces a directional conflict where SUN's tendency is outward in that it is attempting to be present in the physical reality. TUI's tendency is inward in that it is seeking insight and guidance. SUN (4) also has increasing and greater heat where as TUI's heat is on the decline and one position from virtual elimination. TUI (7) is partly interested in the physical world, but only so it has an accurate foundation from which to gain insights. SUN (4) is ONLY interested in the physical world.

Virtuous Trait:
The Negotiators have an ability to understand universal laws as they are presented. If a law or principle is presented to them they can understand the law and how that law fits into the larger context of the reality it must address. In addition, these individuals tend to function with a moral sense about them as TUI (7) provides them the principles to govern their functioning.

Divisive Trait:
Here SUN's movement is slowed and its ability to mobilize the elements on the physical plane is hampered because it will have a tendency to go within which manifests as a "trancy" dreamy state. In order to properly manifest a SUN (4) trait the Negotiator must be completely awake and cognizant of everything around them. TUI's dreaminess is a major problem here. These individuals are constantly in and out of trance and therefore have difficulty paying attention to what is going on around them. This is the student staring off into space during the teacher's lecture.

Balancing Description:
KUN (2) will provide enough outward focus and heat to bring SUN (4) back online and produce a cooperative existence between SUN (4) and TUI (7).

Peacekeeping

Base House: 8th House -- 8 (KEN): Lover
Natal Trait: 5: Peacekeeper
Balancing Agent: 4 (SUN): Leader
Angle Analysis: Radial Line
I Ching Hexagram: Not Applicable

Description:
When B5 (5,5) is in the KEN (8) house it causes a tendency for the person to unify around social principles and interactions. As the B5 personality type tends to fill the missing influences in its life by taking on that responsibility itself, its tendency here is to do so more from a social standpoint. It will tend to look to a KEN-like energy (through relationship building, understanding of people's situations, and flexibility) first in addressing the voids in its life or situation.

Virtuous Trait:
The Negotiators are very good at restoring social harmony and befriending people for the sake of the whole.

Divisive Trait:
The Negotiator gets distracted when attempting to fill the voids in their lives. This affects their overall ability to stay focused on this objective. The distraction is on the external things that "glitter" so-to-speak.

Balancing Description:
SUN's external focus will help the B5 personality type remember and stay focused on its primary objective.

Mental Acuity

Base House: 9th House -- 9 (LI): Soldier
Natal Trait: 6 (CHIEN): Devotee
Balancing Agent: 6 (CHIEN): Devotee
Angle Analysis: Obtuse
I Ching Hexagram: 13, Fellowship with Men

Description:

CHIEN (6) in the LI (9) house enhances one's ability to go within and create mental images of what they want to manifest in their lives. CHIEN (6) individuals can clearly see their goals and various pictures and scenarios in their minds. This is a prerequisite for success in any undertaking as you first must have a mental map or picture of the goal. All of creation starts with a thought and a vision. LI's fire excites and enhances KAN's ability to mentally map its objectives.

Virtuous Trait:

The Negotiator is a master seer of un-manifested reality. These individuals can hold in their minds a complete picture with sounds, colors, and intricate details as if that thing was right in front of them (i.e. the photographic memory). No trigram combination can perform this talent better or with more focus.

This talent goes beyond just being able to see a picture in one's mind. It also involves seeing and adding in parts of that picture that could not normally be seen even if the image was manifest in front of them. The adding in of additional pieces connects the dots of what is being communicated and gives the Negotiators a complete understanding of the subject. When the Negotiators are allowed to process their reality in this way they are labeled as geniuses in their field of study or expertise. This is because they have worked out all of the inconsistencies in their minds and now have ownership of the subject. This can be seen in some children who are consistently "spacey" and often "not present" in class or a conversation. That's correct; they are not here, they are in their minds looking at a complete picture and experiencing a complete reality in even more detail than those who are "paying attention." This is the best way to own information or a lesson; to see all aspects of it in your mind. Now it is a part of you and will not be forgotten.

Note: This is the key to learning and gives us great insight into how our brains process information and thus how our educators should teach. The idea is not to continuously feed our children information, but to give them enough to create a picture in their minds. A picture is worth a thousand words. Once this picture has been created the teacher can move on with the next part of the lesson and the process repeats. As all students will not be CHIEN-LI people (or Negotiators), classes should be divided based upon how each child processes information rather than random groupings.

Divisive Trait:
The Negotiator tends to internalize and create these mental pictures in many of their daily activities. And yes this does manifest as "a spacing out" of that person. Obviously, these individuals tend not to be present in situations where they need to be, like driving a car, working with dangerous machinery, or on guard as a security worker. The possible results here are obvious.

Balancing Description:
What is required for balance is an additional CHIEN (6) element to bring LI (9) full circle and restore its path. The Negotiators will be too extreme with their inward focus and must be brought back to earth so to speak. The additional CHIEN (6) trigram will not eliminate talent, but simply put it into a right perspective relative to the whole picture.

Chapter 12: CHEN – The Visionary

Bagua Configuration: 3

2	7	9
1	3	5
6	8	4

Summary:

The CHEN (3) person, or Visionary, has a number of ideas on how to solve issues and approach life. They tend to have faith in these ideas and are willing to invest heavily in them. The CHEN (3) person has weak leadership skills and tends to have a nurturing style to leadership and management. They lead best when they have a complete visual of the task to be accomplished. The Visionary also has strong communication skills and tends to be very controlled and calculated when communicating with others.

The extreme part of the CHEN (3) personality includes their intuitive nature. The Visionary will look very deeply into problems and issues in and around their lives; especially, when under pressure. This is often times is not necessary and costs them time. CHEN (3) people also have the ability to hold complete images in their minds; especially, around relationships. Lastly, they have a strong tendency to want to unify with others around a specific set of principles. These principles can be moral or spiritual, but don't have to be.

The underdeveloped traits in the CHEN (3) person include their ability to form deep, intimate relationships with others. They generally have issues forming and maintaining these relationships as the flexibility and desire to do so just isn't there.

The Visionary also isn't your hard worker and generally is not willing to make personal sacrifices for a larger cause (unless it is their cause). When they are called to work they tend to focus more on the social and communicative side than the physical labor. Lastly, the CHEN (3) personality type has deficiencies when it comes to planning. They are either too expansive in the planning methods or it is absent all together.

Relationship Building

Base House: 1st House -- 1 (KAN): Conservationist
Natal Trait: 8 (KEN): Lover
Balancing Agent: 9 (LI): Soldier
Angle Analysis: Acute
I Ching Hexagram: 4, Youthful Folly

Description:
KEN (8) is congregative by nature and is interested in forming relationships with others as a means to strengthen its overall position in life. KAN (1) is conservative, interested in its own wellbeing, and generally has little interest in others. The net position difference between these trigrams is 1 and the angular analysis produces an acute angle indicating the possibility to resolve divergent tendencies between these trigrams.

KEN (8) in the KAN (1) house produces in the Visionary an intimacy rooted in structure and planning. These individuals tend to be intimate only with people who fit into a particular structure or pass a certain test. They can easily leave a relationship as they tend to connect with people based upon principle and structure rather than passion and superficial characteristics. They may connect with individuals based upon looks, but these physical characteristics will be the same from person to person; variety within structure only.

In addition, their dress and clothing selections follows a similar pattern and lack "pizzazz" or social risk taking. Their homes are decorated using square formations and no roundness or loud mixing of colors.

Virtuous Trait:
Once these Visionaries connect with a person or situation they exhibit strong intimacy and closeness to them. There is very little to separate these individuals from that to which they are attached. This is the typical mother's love of the son. The drawback here is the effort and probability to get to that point far exceeds the norm. The positive coming from this is the ability to react in a more rational and logical manner towards loved ones instead of out of emotion or strong feelings.

They have strong caring for the virtues and principles governing compassion and relating to others and the environment.

Divisive Trait:
The cool energy of KEN (8) and the cold energy of KAN (1) produce in the Visionary a tendency to be dispassionate towards others initially. The result is the Visionary will tend to be more introverted and conservative when attempting to create meaningful and intimate relationships. These individuals generally lack the ability to care deeply for others or to share a true meaningful bond with other people. Visionaries do not "fall in love" in the popular modern sense which involves emotional attachment and behaving in a way beyond logic or reason.

Once they do create relationships with people or grow attachments to things there is little to be done to break them. This is the person insisting on staying in an abusive relationship scenario.

Balancing Description:
Addition of LI's passion and light in this area will help balance these frigid behavioral tendencies. This will help bring compassion towards others and the surrounding environment and help break out of strong attachments.

Work Ethic

Base House: 2nd House -- 2 (KUN): Negotiator
Natal Trait: 9 (LI): Soldier
Balancing Agent: 2 (KUN): Negotiator
Angle Analysis: Acute
I Ching Hexagram: 35, Progress

Description:
LI (9) in the KUN (2) house produces one intensely focused on interacting with and exchanging with the surrounding environment. This manifests in trade, commerce, social interactions, and business. The Visionaries have the ability to enter any environment and a) fit in and b) bring social harmony. They have a chameleon-like ability to blend in, but can also direct and change the mood of the interaction through witty words and actions.

Virtuous Trait:
When passionate or energized towards a subject or goal, the Visionary is masterful at interacting with people and the surrounding environment. They can in essence make friends with all people and in any situation. They are trusted and liked by all and have success in arenas where social interaction is a requirement. This is especially true in new and unfamiliar environments as the excitement and/or stress brings out this talent to the fullest.

Divisive Trait:
The Visionary interacts well with others, but tends to lean too heavily on this talent. As a result, the substance required to complete tasks, which often times is the purpose of the social interaction, is lacking.

In another sense, because these individuals are focused on social harmony, they tend to say and do things to promote that harmonious state at the expense of the truth. As they would rather see everyone happy and getting along, they tend to compromise principles to achieve it. This can obviously lead to tragedy if not dealt with accordingly.

In addition, individuals whom they interact with may get the wrong impression from these Visionary types and false attachments or expectations are created. This could lead to the opposite effect taking place and social disorder. It is important to note that there is not much substance behind these Visionary individuals as they are interacting to bring social harmony or "stasis". Once that goal is achieved they no longer have an interest in hanging around or exploring other aspects of the relationship. This manifests in relationships where the Visionary individual may have a tendency to "use" a person to achieve self fulfillment (i.e. via sex, money, talent, etc.).

Balancing Description:
KUN (2) is the balancing agent here as LI (9) serves to increase the energy of any trigram it influences. The addition of another KUN (2) element will offset LI's influence and bring balance and harmony.

Planning and Organizing Abilities

Base House: 3rd House -- 3 (CHEN): Visionary
Natal Trait: 1 (KAN): Conservationist
Balancing Agent: 4 (SUN): Leader
Angle Analysis: Right
I Ching Hexagram: 3, Difficulty at the Beginning

Description:
KAN (1) in the CHEN (3) house causes the Visionary personality type to look outward and expand into the world. KAN (1) wants to achieve success through a conservative approach to life; while CHEN (3) is eager to flex its cultivated power and contribute to the world. From this perspective there is conflict between these hexagrams. In addition, KAN's tendency

125

is towards seriousness and its focus is intensely inward. KAN's intensity is partly brought about by its association to one of the two highest energy points in the cycle. CHEN (3) also intense and also focused has nothing (at least initially) to focus on. Even when it finds something to focus on it cannot maintain that focus for very long before it has to move on to other things. That is its inherent tendency.

KAN (1) in the CHEN (3) house brings out in the Visionary a conservative tendency with an inquisitive and curious nature. These energies are in conflict from a directional standpoint. KAN's natural tendency is to not move or at least not be a trail blazer. CHEN (3) is not so much concerned with which direction so long as a direction is chosen and CHEN (3) can contribute.

Virtuous Trait:
These individuals will generate ideas as they concentrate on their goals. This will come in the form of dreams and instant images on the subject of focus. This ability will allow them to have a larger view and deeper insight into their goals and objectives and these insights can be incorporated into concentration exercises.

Divisive Trait:
The Visionary will lack the ability to maintain concentration and focus on a particular subject. KAN (1) is usually able to concentrate without issue. CHEN (3) will cause KAN (1) to dream and look away from its focus. This will adversely affect the Visionary's ability to plan effectively. It will also adversely impact their ability to properly nourish and take care of themselves.

Balancing Description:
SUN's focus on physical reality will balance the inward and partial inward focus on KAN (1) and CHEN (3) respectfully. SUN's addition will generate 1.5 parts internal focus and 1.5 parts external to bring balance between CHEN (3) and KAN (1).

Social Skills

Base House: 4th House -- 4 (SUN): Leader
Natal Trait: 2 (KUN): Negotiator
Balancing Agent: 6 (CHIEN): Devotee
Angle Analysis: Right
I Ching Hexagram: 46, Pushing Upward

Description:
KUN (2) and SUN (4) are both members of the *Earthly Square* and are therefore in a position of servitude. Here SUN (4) is attempting to influence KUN (2), but has nothing substantial to offer KUN (2). Thus, when these individuals are attempting to interact with the world and other persons SUN (4) acts as a distraction that has KUN (2) focused on the items of trade rather than the people it is to trade with.

KUN's goal is to achieve a level of interaction amongst people such that particular goals and objectives can be met. These goals are unrelated to the interaction itself; thus, KUN (2) types generally don't have a sincere interest in the people they interact with. SUN's focus is strictly on defining the role and value of resources (people, assets, things, etc.) and doesn't know how to create or maintain relationships. SUN (4) does understand that people must come together to achieve a goal.

The Visionary will have the ability to bring leaders and people in authoritative positions together to achieve a common goal. These individuals are best suited for working with leaders of nations, big corporations, heads of families, etc. In this case KUN (2) has a great insight into leadership and the way rational people view the world and is able to leverage that knowledge to achieve a working union.

Divisive Trait:
When the Visionary individual attempts to create relationships and communicate with others they find themselves trying to

force or manage people into working together. Unfortunately, individuals cannot be managed into working together and have true, comprehensive success. Forced relationships just are not as effective. SUN's talent is being able to bring people to work together without them realizing it.

Balancing Description:
CHIEN (6) is the balancing agent here as its inward focus will counter SUN's intense outward focus.

Creativity and Zest for Life

Base House: 5th House -- 5: Peacekeeper
Natal Trait: 3 (CHEN): Visionary
Balancing Agent: 8 (KEN): Lover
Angle Analysis: Radial Line
I Ching Hexagram: Not Applicable

Description:
Any trigram in the B5 house will have a universal view based on its inherent tendency. CHEN (3) is focused on coming into the light and bringing forth and identifying new manifestation. Therefore the effect of CHEN (3) in the B5 house produces one who views balancing the world through the discovery of unique ideas that once implemented will solve a number of the problems of focus. This is effective only if the idea (subtle physical manifestation) originates from TUI. As B5 has the tendency to become the missing personality needed to address situations and issues, these individuals will want to fill those voids using a CHEN (3) talent and perspective.

Virtuous Trait:
These individuals are able to bring harmony to their lives and the environment through generating ideas.

Divisive Trait:
As these persons have a CHEN (3) perspective on everything in

the world they will tend to view the world from that perspective first and most frequently. Obviously the proper view or foundation would be from a B5 perspective which then allows the individual to flow into whichever trigram is required to bring about harmony in the situation. The deficit here comes from the fact that only one ninth of all situations can be viewed or addressed from any particular perspective; thus, these individuals will only bat just over 10% correct in their perceptions of reality.

Balancing Description:
KEN (8) will allow CHEN (3) to put its expansiveness in proper boundary as KEN (8) is not as aggressively outward, but looks for quality interaction with those around it. This slowing in outward movement will bring the proper balance to CHEN (3) when in this position.

Leadership and Resourcefulness

Base House: 6th House -- 6 (CHIEN): Devotee
Natal Trait: 4 (SUN): Leader
Balancing Agent: 1 (KAN): Conservationist
Angle Analysis: Axis
I Ching Hexagram: 9, The Taming Power of the Small

Description:
SUN (4) in the CHIEN (6) house produces an axis conflict in which two opposing complimentary trigrams are forced to interact. SUN's tendency is outward while CHIEN's tendency is inward. Additionally, SUN (4) has a high amount of increasing heat where as CHIEN (6) is almost completely cooled off.

Virtuous Trait:
These individuals have the ability to see and understand the visions put forth by CHIEN (6) individuals. Most people will not understand CHIEN (6) as they try to communicate the reality they see in their minds, but the Visionary can. They can see how a mental or visual image can be manifest in the world and relate those mental images and components to physical reality.

A weakness of SUN-CHIEN is that it has a tendency to visualize images when it should be focusing its work. The positive here is that when those things are visualized the Visionary knows how they can be made into reality. Depending on the task this can be of great benefit as it gives 360 degrees of knowledge surrounding a particular subject.

Divisive Trait:
For the CHEN (3) person, this is the trigram combination causing the most problems in their lives. These individuals will have an inability to stay focused on physical reality. Thus, a very compromised ability to reason and make sound decisions. The focus here is to lead and manage one's situation and environment, but CHIEN's inward focus causes a major distraction in SUN's ability to see, lead, and manage. These individuals may focus on a project or objective and find themselves visualizing the completion of it. This is of major concern as to complete or do anything successfully one must be fully aware and present with it. CHIEN (6) is not present with physical reality as they always drift and dream away from physical reality to see things in their minds.

Balancing Description:
Only the pedantic and meticulous focus of KAN (1) can slow these trigrams enough to see how they can coexist and work cooperatively. This is true of all the axis angular relationships. KAN (1) is the required trigram to balance these complimentary energies.

Peacekeeping

Base House: 7th House -- 7 (TUI): Monk
Natal Trait: 5: Peacekeeper
Balancing Agent: 3 (CHEN): Visionary
Angle Analysis: Radial Line
I Ching Hexagram: Not Applicable

Description:
B5 (5) in the TUI (7) house produces a balancing tendency around an inward focus, meaning one who goes within to seek answers and solutions to life's dilemmas. In this case balance, unification, and the best benefit for the whole tend to be found in morale behavioral solutions or at least ones based upon strong principles. Again, because B5 encompasses all of the trigrams adding and additional TUI (7) gives the TUI (7) the most influence. In addition, because the B5 personality will take on the character traits of other trigrams, it will have a stronger tendency towards TUI (7) in this instance.

Virtuous Trait:
These individuals will be able to nicely fill the void whenever deep insight is needed in a given situation.

Divisive Trait:
The Visionary personality will have a tendency to address most issues/projects in life by filling in as a TUI (7) personality first. This may or may not be what is needed in the given situation.

Balancing Description:
CHEN (3) sits directly opposite from TUI (7) and completes the TUI-B5-CHEN axis in the Lo Shu arrangement. By providing more weight to the East side of the axis the B5 can move eastward and take its proper place. Pulling this pair to the east by adding influence from CHEN (3) will help to balance the pair.

Creativity and Zest for Life

Base House: 8th House -- 8 (KEN): Lover
Natal Trait: 6 (CHIEN): Devotee
Balancing Agent: 5: Peacekeeper
Angle Analysis: Right
I Ching Hexagram: 33, Retreat

Description:
KEN's influence causes one's focus to wander to other things. An example is when someone is trying to focus on a particular subject and they realize they are thinking about something totally unrelated. People who perform meditation experience this when they try to focus on a chakra or goal and find their attention wandering to a variety of subjects. CHIEN (6) is quite the opposite in that it is interested in mentally seeing physical reality to the smallest detail and can't afford to wander to other subjects if it wants to achieve success. As both of these trigrams are a part of the *Earthly Square* arrangement they are dedicated to carrying out the commands from heaven. Thus, the struggle here is not one of wanting to lead the situation, but rather one of each trigram wanting to perform its duty and responsibility.

CHIEN (6) in the KEN (8) house produces an inability to sustain one's mental/visual focus on a particular subject.

Virtuous Trait:
The Visionary personality type is able to see visually concepts and goals governing relationships and social interactions. However, the Visionary has trouble with its visual mental focus. Subjects regarding entertainment, intimacy, and social interaction seem to come more naturally. Thus, they are able to see the potential in relationships (i.e. people maintaining their marriage as they work through issues, business partners working out differences, friends working through disputes, etc.) where others may not.

Divisive Trait:
These individuals will have an inability to hold a mental/visual image over a sustained period and an inability to stay focused on one project or task without the awareness moving to another subject. They are easily distracted by movement in the background or area.

When the Visionary tries to "see it" in their minds, they will find their attention wandering. But what are the impacts of this?

The important talent of having this type of foresight comes with great responsibility. This talent allows Visionaries to see the danger in things or situations or how things could turn out if not addressed properly. So we see the danger in this faculty not performing correctly or being unfocused. Being able to focus on one subject or image over a long period of time gives us mastery over that subject. It prepares us the best when the time comes to work with that subject or area in our lives. Failure to have sustained focus leaves the CHEN (3) person ill prepared to handle many challenges.

Balancing Description:
B5 is able to return CHIEN's focus back to the original goal and intent by centering it in a holistic view. This will offset the wandering tendency created by KEN (8).

Intuitive Abilities

Base House: 9th House -- 9 (LI): Soldier
Natal Trait: 7 (TUI): Monk
Balancing Agent: 7 (TUI): Monk
Angle Analysis: Right
I Ching Hexagram: 49, Revolution

Description:
TUI (7) in the LI (9) house produces individuals obsessed with understanding the deeper meaning of the things of the world. They have a tireless pursuit of knowledge and wisdom concerning all subjects of interest.

TUI (7) in the LI (9) house produces the effect of one relentlessly focused on the law, counsel, the underlying mathematics of things, and understanding the proper way to go about a task or one's life. The fire of LI (9) greatly influences the inward expansiveness of TUI (7) so that much of its energy, focus, and zealousness is focused inward. TUI (7) is focused on understanding the principles governing the inner workings of things and how to act to reach those goals.

Virtuous Trait:
The Visionary individual is the master of understanding the underlying principles governing anything not yet manifested in the world. Meaning, these individuals can tell you the steps to take to achieve any goal. These steps are usually abstract and never obvious or logical in nature; thus, making some of their proclamations difficult for others to follow, believe, or understand. But this is ok, because it is not the talent of others to process in this way. This is a talent, just like the other talents produced by other trigram combinations and should be respected as such. It is not logical or respectful to expect to understand how individuals arrive at their own distinct conclusions or accomplish certain things as we are all unique. The Visionary does not depend upon logical thinking; thus, their process is not only misunderstood by most people, but often times not understood by themselves.

Visionary individuals have an ability to work toward the common good via high principles as their essential tendency is towards morality.

Divisive Trait:
This person will be over dependent on principle-based tools for success in life. These tools include oracles, law texts, religious tenants, counsel from spiritual/social/business leaders, etc. Over dependence in these areas can produce stagnation and allow others to have control over their lives or allow areas of their lives to suffer that don't fall under these abilities.

The Visionary individual can be too focused on intuitive understanding as a way to approach life's problems. This often puts them into a stalemate with themselves until they can understand the deeper meaning of life or the situation they are trying to address. Additionally, LI's fire pushes them toward intuition as the first way to approach all of life's problems and the bottom line is everything is not that serious. Often times the

Visionary has trouble looking at the situation, making the best decision, and moving on. This indecisiveness also manifests in these people undoing what they have already done (i.e. frequently taking things back to the store because they changed their mind).

The Visionary should reserve this talent for those issues or challenges that are worthy. Again, this can be difficult in an apparently "fast-paced" world where it appears that quick decisions are required for success.

Note: These individuals, due to their abilities to access information intuitively, rarely respect the works of others as they always a) believe they can do it better themselves and b) are not impressed by the intellectual aptitude of others.

Balancing Description:
The addition of a TUI (7) element will offset the fire of LI (9) and remind the original TUI (7) element of its original mission and intent. This is necessary as the LI (9) element takes TUI (7) off of its focus.

Chapter 13: SUN – The Leader

Bagua Configuration: 4

3	8	1
2	4	6
7	9	5

Summary:

The SUN (4) person, or Leader, posses a good memory and
generally, sees the oneness of all things and people in the world
and promotes unity through a vision of togetherness and the
nurturing of others. Leaders primarily view the world through
reasoning and rational thought meaning these individuals
generally call it as they see it rather than imagining what could
be. These individuals choose to experience the world by taking
control of their opportunities and leading themselves and others
to the desired goal. They also have the ability to have strong
faith in ideals and people, but again there is a rational element
that prevents this from becoming too expansive.

The Leader is passionate about forming intimate relationships
with others. This can manifest as a high interest in sexual
activity. They are highly intuitive about relationships and the
underlying principles governing them. They will have difficulty
using intuitive ability in general as the mind will tend to wander,
but they do posses well developed visual and mental imaging
ability. These individuals are very nurturing based upon a higher
moral principle; thus, they see the divine nature of all things and
people.

Communication skills are generally underdeveloped as they can
be overly talkative; thus, causing others to loose the original or
essential point. Generally, poor planners as they lack the ability

to sit still long enough to think through situations in their lives. Planning in the areas of business are the strongest for these individuals. They are overly concerned with their personal safety; therefore, risk taking only happens when a certain level of certainty has been established. They have an inability to generate a strong passion towards a subject when required.

Work Ethic

Base House: 1st House -- 1 (KAN): Conservationist
Natal Trait: 9 (LI): Soldier
Balancing Agent: 1 (KAN): Conservationist
Angle Analysis: Axis
I Ching Hexagram: 64, Before Completion

Description:
Here LI (9) is in the KAN (1) house. These elements are complements, sitting on the North (KAN) - South (LI) axis. LI's nature is external electric energy, zealousness with an unrelenting focus on building, creating, and producing in the physical environment. In this case, the cold trigram KAN (1), reduces the individual's ability to sacrifice themselves for their goals. KAN (1) has the tendency towards conservatism and self-fortification which means it is focused only on those activities that will maintain and build its own energy and capabilities for possible events to come. As these trigrams sit on the same axis the potential for conflict and the amount of work required to balance and harmonize their tendencies is great, but with that, the potential for the harnessing of great power and accomplishment is there as well.

The best way to view LI (9) is like a flame thrower of energy or fire in the direction of the trigram it interacts with, in this case LI (9) is interacting with KAN (1). KAN (1), being the compliment of LI (9), is the same intensity of energy, but focused inward. Inward means focusing on what the person or entity needs to improve or restructure in order to prepare itself for interaction with the world.

Virtuous Trait:
This trigram combination produces a tendency in the Leader to be zealous in conserving oneself and one's resources. These are also your board members of conservative organizations and political entities. The key here though is that the person must be passionate about the subject to take advantage of this talent. These individuals are not planners by nature as they need that passion about the subject they are working with to exercise this talent.

Divisive Trait:
The Leader is generally unwilling to take risks; especially at the expense of themselves or their constituents. The same holds true for their willingness to work hard as this is often times perceived as risky behavior.

Additionally, the act of intensely focusing on structure and planning and looking deeply into subjects, produces a void in the Leader's outward expression. These individuals can tend to be hermits of sorts, especially once they find a field of study or subject that interests them. When angered or excited they can move into an extremely stubborn and conservative posture. Actually, of all of the personality types, the Leaders can be the most stubborn and conservative of them all. Unlike a Conservationist who can be consistently stubborn over long periods of time because that is their inherent nature or a Devotee (6) person who chooses when to be stubborn; the Leader usually takes this posture when emotionally stimulated.

Balancing Description:
As with all trigram combinations that are on the same axis as KAN (1), what is needed to balance out the LI-KAN combination is KAN's structure and protracted consistency. The LI (9) adds additional fire behind the planning and meticulous force. Over activity of a LI (9) entity with KAN (1) should be balanced by that KAN (1) entity. The additional coolness will give one part LI (9) and two parts KAN (1) which is a happy

medium. This will allow the KAN (1) to focus without loosing a view of the whole.

Planning and Organizing Abilities

Base House: 2nd House -- 2 (KUN): Negotiator
Natal Trait: 1 (KAN): Conservationist
Balancing Agent: 3 (CHEN): Visionary
Angle Analysis: Obtuse
I Ching Hexagram: 8, Union

Description:
KAN (1) in the KUN (2) house produces one of our obtuse relationships in the BaGua; where, KAN (1) is a member of the *Heavenly Circle* and is expressing it's will with the expectation of obedience from KEN (8) while KUN (2), a member of the *Earthly Square*, is looking for guidance from LI (9). Again, a great potential for energy generation as KAN (1) and KUN (2) are three net positions away from each other, but also the challenge of coordinating two totally disparaged tendencies.

KAN (1) corresponds to the deepest and most conservative nature of an individual. This is self preservation and preparation at its most extreme in order to prepare the individual for the challenges that lay ahead.

Virtuous Trait:
The Leaders have the ability to plan around trade, marketing, and business. They also have the ability to prepare themselves for business opportunities, sales, and executing marketing strategies. They will also be protective of their assets; especially, those that they have perceived they earned through their own efforts.

Divisive Trait:
Here, there is an overall sluggishness in ability to concentrate and plan due to an excessive focus on external interaction. KAN (1) in the KUN (2) house affects one's ability to concentrate,

plan, and focus by moving their attention to the external environment.

Balancing Description:
CHEN's expansiveness breaks KAN (1) out of KUN's influence.

Social Skills

Base House: 3rd House -- 3 (CHEN): Visionary
Natal Trait: 2 (KUN): Negotiator
Balancing Agent: 5: Peacekeeper
Angle Analysis: Obtuse
I Ching Hexagram: 24, The Return

Description:
KUN (2) is the tendency to impersonally interact with the external world. It is not concerned with deep relationships outside of creating a stable environment in which its goals can be achieved. CHEN (3) also has an interest in the outside world, but only from the standpoint of offering its input to achieve a better result than what is currently present. The mix of KUN (2) in the CHEN (3) house can cause these two trigrams to get engrossed in one another and loose site of the bigger picture. Neither CHEN (3) nor KUN (2) is confrontational and both tend to take actions with the intent to produce beneficial results. From this standpoint, they rarely engage in conflict. The only conflict is when CHEN (3) wants to make a true and real impact on something and KUN (2) does not.

Virtuous Trait:
The Leaders are results oriented only to a certain extent. A Leader's goal is more often the successful interaction with others for some other purpose. CHEN's desire to interact and to experience the world and KUN's focus of maintaining harmony with the things around it produce the ability to get along with all peoples, in all situations, and make great contributions to those circles. These individuals are liked by all if that's how they want it. They will also love business and communication for its own

sake as opposed to needing outside stimulus.

Divisive Trait:
KUN (2) and CHEN (3) together will tend to get lost in their interaction and forget others and the larger picture. Here is a tendency to communicate without purpose at times; over communication.

Balancing Description:
B5 will allow KUN (2) to regain its focus and remember the larger picture and its purpose.

Creativity and Zest for Life

Base House: 4th House -- 4 (SUN): Leader
Natal Trait: 3 (CHEN): Visionary
Balancing Agent: 7 (TUI): Monk
Angle Analysis: Acute
I Ching Hexagram: 32, Duration

Description:
CHEN (3) in the SUN (4) house produces an individual who has ideas and subtle insights on how to more effectively manage things in the environment. CHEN (3) is interested in expressing and contributing its ideas and insights to the world; whereas, SUN (4) is interested in managing the world.

Virtuous Trait:
Leaders develop a number of ideas about management and leadership. They can see into the subtle nature of these disciplines to understand how they work and what are the requirements for their proper manifestation.

Divisive Trait:
Leaders give of themselves ONLY under their own terms. CHEN's expansiveness is constrained by SUN's leading nature; thus, preventing the free-flow of ideas in general. Leaders tend

to be very controlling of what they chose to experience. There will be very little impromptu behavior.

Balancing Description:
TUI (7) is required to bring the clarity to CHEN (3) so as to put SUN's influence in proper perspective.

Leadership and Resourcefulness

Base House: 5th House -- 5: Peacekeeper
Natal Trait: 4 (SUN): Leader
Balancing Agent: 9 (LI): Soldier
Angle Analysis: Radial Line
I Ching Hexagram: Not Applicable

Description:
SUN (4) in the B5 house accentuates the reasoning, rationalization, and leadership skills of SUN (4). This person's world view is based upon SUN's tendencies which revolve around properly defining the physical reality around us and organizing the resources under our control to create or achieve the goal at hand. This world view will be rooted in these leadership qualities.

Virtuous Trait:
The Leader will be able to bring harmony to their lives and the lives of others through their ability to see and understand all things involved in the particular situation. They have excellent reasoning ability.

Divisive Trait:
The Leader personality type will usually approach bringing harmony, happiness, and unity into there lives from a management and leadership standpoint. As a result, the ideas and actions they take may deter those who seek not to be managed. This approach to friendship and relationships will only bring about complete success just over 10% of the time as

142

other situations will require one of the other character traits found in the BaGua.

Balancing Description:
LI's energy, fire, and zeal will pull SUN (4) out of its cognitive outlook and help it realize that work will have to be done as well to achieve the goal. In addition, as with all of the natal trigrams rooted in B5, they must be reminded and refocused on the larger picture to achieve the goals at hand.

Peacekeeping

Base House: 6th House -- 6 (CHIEN): Devotee
Natal Trait: 5: Peacekeeper
Balancing Agent: 2 (KUN): Negotiator
Angle Analysis: Radial Line
I Ching Hexagram: Not Applicable

Description:
In the area of Peacekeeping, B5 in the CHIEN (6) house produces a balancing focus rooted in the inward visualization of the final objective. Unification as a B5 objective here is achieved through the CHIEN (6) tendency. As B5 has the ability to become the solution to life's challenges by taking on the personality of the trigram required, here the tendency will be towards CHIEN (6).

Virtuous Trait:
These individuals have the ability to focus mentally when required to bring harmony to any situation or environment that they are a part of. They can bring down the positive traits of CHIEN (6) which include seeing the final solution in their minds and staying focused on that solution through its delivery. The Leader maintains a view and purpose of the whole when performing this task and is thus effective at resolving issues needing CHIEN's talent.

Divisive Trait:
The Leaders will tend to address all of life's unification issues by working them out in their minds and trying to see the final solution. Again, this is not an issue by itself, but must be put into the proper context and tailored to the specific situation. See the details on CHIEN (6) personality under the double CHIEN (6) description in the Peacekeeper chapter.

Balancing Description:
KUN's outward focus breaks the crystallization of CHIEN's inward focus and frees B5 from CHIEN's enchantment. This allows these trigrams to work cooperatively.

Mental Acuity

Base House: 7th House -- 7 (TUI): Monk
Natal Trait: 6 (CHIEN): Devotee
Balancing Agent: 4 (SUN): Leader
Angle Analysis: Acute
I Ching Hexagram: 10, Conduct

Description:
CHIEN (6) in the TUI (7) house produces only a small conflict in tendency. Both trigrams are inward focusing, but TUI (7) has its focus on receiving while CHIEN (6) has its focus on planting. From another perspective, TUI (7) listens to heaven while CHIEN (6) talks to heaven. Thus, these individuals, when attempting to put a complete mental picture together of their goal, will have a tendency to inquire and seek clarity. There is a slight conflict here, but not one that can't be overcome. The important thing to realize here is that CHIEN (6) is being pulled backwards relative to the creative process as TUI (7) here precedes it. Additionally, it must be recognized that CHIEN (6) takes its orders from TUI (7) and must recognize this when acting. Failure to realize this may result in the cart being put before the horse. This is explained in more detail and further

understood by examining the hexagram.

Virtuous Trait:
The Leader, in terms of mental acuity, will have the ability to see the principles governing the unfolding of physical reality. Their mental processes are more aimed at law, principle, and protocol; thus, these individuals can clearly see these laws and how they unfold in the world.

Divisive Trait:
The Leader personality will attempt to see their goal, but have a slight distraction in that there will be a tendency to seek clarity, guidance, and light. This is an issue because the person at this stage should already know their goals and objectives and are thus trying to put them together in one's mind. There is no need to seek further guidance. Seeking guidance and insight is a TUI (7) function not a CHIEN (6) function.

Another perspective is the need for CHIEN (6) to recognize that TUI's influence must be acknowledged and put into the proper context before proceeding. Failure to do this may result in humiliation and delay.

Balancing Description:
SUN (4) here can offer the direction needed to CHIEN (6) to help it keep its focus inward and outward. This is accomplished by a gentle push. Harsh measures are not required.

Intuitive Abilities

Base House: 8th House -- 8 (KEN): Lover
Natal Trait: 7 (TUI): Monk
Balancing Agent: 6 (CHIEN): Devotee
Angle Analysis: Obtuse
I Ching Hexagram: 31, Influence

Description:

TUI (7) is the ability to understand the deep underlying principles governing reality. These principles are not apparent to sensory perception or a logical thought process. They must be intuited or experienced from within. In other words, these individuals have the ability to experience (or feel) manifested or non-manifested reality from within their being rather than through their senses. The closest association would be through the "mind", but this is not entirely accurate, as the symbols of that experience are displayed through one's mental visual perception. KEN (8) whose interest is connecting with others to strengthen and expand itself, has an outward looking tendency that is in conflict with TUI.

Thus, the Leader has difficulty "insperiencing" the world and thus understanding or discovering the underlying principles governing reality or the project or issue they may be focused on. KEN's tendency to move towards other things prevents this. As TUI (7) represents the first stage in creating or accomplishing anything in the world, these individuals will need great assistance in this area.

The coolness of KEN (8) prevents sustained intuitive thinking, thus, these individuals need counsel and guidance. This is a very important concept to understand about the Leader – they need wise counsel to be successful.

Virtuous Trait:
Leaders will have the tendency to gain insights on principles governing relationships and the coming together of people to work harmoniously together. Theses individuals could be contracted to start a project of this sort; however, they will need some assistance from a CHIEN (6) personality type to achieve ultimate success.

Divisive Trait:
A Leader has an inability to be still and "insperience" physical reality. These individuals cannot focus and find their minds wandering to other subjects, visions, etc. Their wisdom and knowledge generally comes through experience as opposed to

deep protracted thought.

Balancing Description:
CHIEN (6) is required to harmonize and balance the Leader's personality type. CHIEN's ability to focus deeply on any goal in their mind and hold that vision throughout any emotional influence will help TUI (7) keep its focus towards the original goal. CHIEN (6) provides that additional inward mental strength that KEN (8) tends to compromise.

Relationship Building

Base House: 9th House -- 9 (LI): Soldier
Natal Trait: 8 (KEN): Lover
Balancing Agent: 8 (KEN): Lover
Angle Analysis: Obtuse
I Ching Hexagram: 22, Grace

Description:
KEN (8) in the LI (9) house produces one who gravitates toward intimate social relationships with others. These individuals prefer the cozy closeness of a few individuals rather than partying with a large group. The cozy closeness of the few is preferred to be of high quality and intimacy.

LI (9) has the influence of accentuating the inherent tendency of any trigram it comes into contact with. As KEN (8) governs our ability to have intimate social relationships with others we can see where this trigram combination can go: abuse of sex and relationships.

Virtuous Trait:
The Leaders know how to attract the attention of others. This includes in how they dress themselves, accentuate their surroundings, and function in a social arena. Attraction doesn't mean tactfulness or social acceptance which is why many of these people end up hiding their true natures or talents or

entering careers, like entertainment, where they can express themselves more openly.

From another view, these individuals can be classified as chemists or artists from the standpoint that they can bring two or more elements together to work in harmony. They are master integrators and arbitrators through behavior. Meaning, they can show people what to do to come together and forget their differences, but they just can't explain it. If disputing parties would follow their lead and functioning they could end conflicts, but unfortunately, KEN's behavior appears out of character and is rejected as not regarding the seriousness of life. This cannot be further from the truth. KEN's behavior may not abide by the socially accepted protocols and norms, but it is the most valid and legitimate way to deal with one's social environment.

Divisive Trait:
These individuals are so into interaction with others that they approach everything in life with this behavior. Thus, the situations that call for negotiations or hard work create a challenge. Additionally, all people and situations are not meant to be intimate with and thus, the Leader can expose themselves to dangerous situations if not careful.

There is also a high probability of sexual overindulgence and abuse. LI's fiery and electric nature will ignite this individual's social behavior; which includes forming and strengthening relationships through sexual expression.

Balancing Description:
The addition of a KEN (8) element will offset the fire of LI (9) and remind the original KEN (8) element of its original mission and intent. This is necessary as the LI (9) element takes KEN (8) off of its focus.

148

Chapter 14: B5 – The Peacekeeper

BaGua Configuration: 5

4	9	2
3	5	7
8	1	6

Summary:
The B5 person, or Peacekeeper, has access to all of the talents in the BaGua. Thus, in theory, they can generate the passion and zealousness when necessary to face life's challenges without fear of personal harm. They can enter into intimate long lasting relationships with others when they choose. These individuals are highly intuitive thinkers able to understand the underlying principles governing all things in the world. Good ability to hold mental images. Their primary posture is to be unified with all things in the world as they can see the connection and interdependence of all things. They have strong reasoning skills and generally a healthy drive to experience life and contribute to the world. They also have excellent communication skills and are good planners and organizers.

That said, the Peacekeeper usually has the tendency to develop their talents based upon social importance; thus, they become over dependent on certain skills and fail to develop others. For those individuals living in modern culture those skills are generally communication and social skills. The result of developing a general social skill is usually the suffering of the ability to enter into intimate relationships that last. Another set of the B5 individual will develop strong leadership skills at the expense of one's ability to nurture others and hold clear mental images over long periods of time. It should also be noted that although the Peacekeeper has all the trigrams in the correct place (the Lo Shu) they don't become masters at all of the character traits. This is you classic "Jack of all trades, but a master of none" scenario.

Note: Please use the following double trigram descriptions as an additional resource to understanding the individual trigrams themselves (TUI, CHIEN, KAN, KEN, CHEN, SUN, LI, KUN).

Planning and Organizing Abilities

Base House: 1st House -- 1 (KAN): Conservationist
Natal Trait: 1 (KAN): Conservationist
Balancing Agent: 2 (KUN): Negotiator
Angle Analysis: Point
I Ching Hexagram: 29, The Abysmal

Description:
KAN's inherent nature is to retreat into physical places of solitude and quiet. This is beyond the mental retreat of TUI (7) as KAN (1) will go into hibernation and take everything it is connected to with it. This is a complete removal from confronting the physical environment.

These individuals are strictly focused on self preparation, rejuvenation and all of the activities commonly associated: rest, relaxation (not laziness), sleep, small/quaint social functions with well established friends only, etc. These individuals are very meticulous in taking care of themselves and not risking bodily injury. The benefit of these actions is to prepare them for the physical challenges to come, which unfortunately they don't confront due to their not being able to leave their conservative tendency. As KAN (1) and LI (9) are compliments, KAN's focus is on creating things through attraction and magnetism, but primarily strengthening itself.

Virtuous Trait:
These individuals provide that conservative element to their lives

and the lives of others. This is a true virtue in that in today's fast-paced world many activities are done without proper planning and thinking. Pure structure and planning are produced here without the influence of other elements.

Divisive Trait:

Pure structure and planning without a view or consideration of the larger picture or other elements involved can be a deficit. Too much time is spent on planning and self preparation without engaging the outside world is unbalanced. This causes major issues as these individuals can get caught up in this energy for the sake of the energy.

Balancing Description:

Double KAN (1) produces a view that is based purely on a foundational structure. Thus, the receptivity of KUN (2) will allow this purity to be guided to proper use in the larger context. KUN (2) who is interested in creating social harmony for the achievement of its goals will pull KAN (1) out of its conservative world to see the larger context of its actions.

Social Skills

Base House: 2nd House -- 2 (KUN): Negotiator
Natal Trait: 2 (KUN): Negotiator
Balancing Agent: 4 (SUN): Leader
Angle Analysis: Point
I Ching Hexagram: 2, The Receptive

Description:

KUN (2) sits between LI (9) and TUI (7) in the BaGua and has the responsibility for carrying out LI's commands. KUN (2) therefore has the ability to both physically engage world and mentally retreat within. These skills are required if KUN (2) is to complete its task(s) given by LI (9) in preparation for TUI's work. These tendencies give a clue to KUN's inherent tendency as it engages the physical world, but stays focused and receptive to principles coming from the inner regions of the mind.

KUN (2) in the KUN (2) house produces the 2nd hexagram of the I Ching, The Receptive. KUN's job is carrying out and completing the orders initiated in the TUI (7) stage (the first stage of creation). This is the last act in the creative process before rejoicing and reviewing overall implementation performance. Ultimately, KUN's master is TUI (7) as with all the trigrams in the BaGua, but KUN (2) takes direct orders from LI (9) who gives it the materials to go out into the world to fulfill its destiny.

Virtuous Trait:
These individuals are able to fit into any social setting and harmonize with others. Again, these are not deep intimate relationships, but rather superficial in nature. This is not a negative thing as superficial relationships have there place in the world just like more intimate ones do. The Peacekeeper personality type is able to easily move into this skill set provided they have not been negatively conditioned to not be familiar with this tendency.

Divisive Trait:
As with all of the doubled hexagrams the danger here is being too into one's own tendency at the expense of other tendencies. These individuals will have the challenge of not being obsessed with one's own talent and remembering the purpose of that talent relative to the whole and how to use it. These individuals can become completely docile and receptive without questioning the authoritarian figure to which they are subservient. If they are in the proper situation where the leadership has the insights, capacity, and caring to support the individual then all is well; however, if these leadership elements are lacking, problems and abuse could result.

Balancing Description:
SUN (4) provides the insightfulness to bring KUN (2) into alignment with the whole. The leadership of SUN (4) is required to reign in KUN's outward expression and focus.

Creativity and Zest for Life

Base House: 3rd House -- 3 (CHEN): Visionary
Natal Trait: 3 (CHEN): Visionary
Balancing Agent: 6 (CHIEN): Devotee
Angle Analysis: Point
I Ching Hexagram: 51, The Arousing

Description:
CHEN (3) is the complement to TUI (7) in the BaGua; where TUI (7) is a complete mental retreat for the purpose of seeking guidance. Here CHEN (3) is a complete physical or external commitment. CHEN's thought processes are strictly interested in how it can best utilize, interact with, and experience the world. These individuals have "ways" or ideas for how to create or manifest anything as their thought process is interested in utilizing the things of the world.

CHEN (3) doubled produces the 51st hexagram. CHEN (3) is interested in experiencing and contributing to the world. This tendency manifests as a rapid expansion outward into the world. From a mundane perspective this is seen as an individual who wants to explore the world, meet people, pursue interests (i.e. career, business, relationships, hobbies, etc.). CHEN (3) represents the drive for experience. Which experience and what the CHEN (3) personality type chooses to do is based on their environment, upbringing, and level of consciousness or the awareness of that individual.

Because CHEN (3) has only partial insight into the metaphysical or subtle physical world and partial insight into the physical world it cannot see what it needs to see to achieve success in its undertaking. These individuals usually have great insight into certain aspects of (1) things, processes, people, etc. and (2) the subtle structures supporting all these physical reality. From that perspective these individuals incorrectly believe they can see the whole picture and thus achieve success in any number of undertakings. Their vision is limited. Without input from CHIEN (6) and SUN (4) these individuals should not move forward on projects. This is especially true when teamed up with LI (9). Disaster can be the result.

Virtuous Trait:
These persons have the ability to see the underlying structure of physical reality; thus, the ability to know the underlying laws and principles governing the things of the world. CHEN (3) people can see beyond the veil, so to speak, and determine a person's true emotions. When this information is communicated to a SUN (4) person success can be achieved.

Because CHEN (3) has the ability to see things before they are fully manifested they are considered to be creative and generators of great ideas. It is important to note here that these ideas are really them seeing the early manifestation of physical reality.

Divisive Trait:
This person has a limited view of the world and subtle world around it. These individuals can see part of the physical world and part of the metaphysical world. From a percentage standpoint the CHEN (3) person can see about 50% of each: physical and subtle physical. As a result the phrase, "Just enough information to be dangerous." applies here. Because these individuals can see two forms of reality they tend to think they can see all of everything and thus act. This almost always leads to failure. These individuals should never act on their own ideas, but filter them through others, primarily a SUN (4) person for evaluation.

Balancing Description:
CHIEN's intense inward focus will pull back CHEN's excessive expansiveness. A double CHEN (3) will get lost in its own abilities and not be tied back to a central theme; thus, rendering its effectiveness useless.

Leadership and Resourcefulness

Base House: 4th House -- 4 (SUN): Leader
Natal Trait: 4 (SUN): Leader
Balancing Agent: 8 (KEN): Lover
Angle Analysis: Point
I Ching Hexagram: 52, The Gentle

Description:
"The first responsibility of a leader is to define reality." - Max Dupree. Sitting between CHEN (3) and LI (9) in the BaGua and being a part of the earthly circle, SUN (4) has the ability to engage the physical environment both physically and mentally. This skill is required if it is going to carry out the commands from CHEN (3) in preparation for LI's work.

SUN (4) doubled produces one with strong reasoning ability. SUN's talent is a deep penetrating insight into the function of manifested things in the world. Along with this talent is the ability to see all things in the world and understand their functions.

In order to understand SUN's talent (or any of the trigrams) we must look at the variations in our ability to maintain our focus on one thing. If we take the two extremes of wide awake and very focused versus sound asleep we see these are two different states of wakefulness. Being awake means complete awareness of all things in your environment and the ability to focus on any one or all of them. Sleeping means you have completely forfeited your ability to make conscious choices. In essence you have allowed the involuntary part of your being to have full control of your body. So those are our two extremes, but there are many variations in between. You could be awake (meaning your eyes are open and you are physically moving around), but still out in space. This can be seen in people's driving styles. People who are not present while driving tend to leave much more space between them and the car in front of them while driving on the highway. This is a subconscious precautionary measure because they know they will need an extra second to shift from whatever they are thinking of or visualizing back to the road or car in front of them. People who are completely awake and aware tend to drive closer behind the car in front of them because they are present in the driving experience and therefore know when and how to react based upon the changes around them. This is true in all situations. Those who are awake and present in a conversation, reading a book, playing sports, working, etc. are better able to respond and thus perform at that given task.

When we divide this "being present" into two divisions: (1) being aware and (2) reacting to the environment we receive the trigrams SUN (4) and LI (9). Thus, SUN (4) is that ability to be present in the situation; to see physically all things happening in the physical environment.

Virtuous Trait:
B5 (5) persons have the talent to understand, define, and ultimately manipulate all of manifested reality. These individuals are your leaders and managers. Their ability to see and understand everything around them allows them to address issues quickly and effectively. This is so because they know which people or resources to use to solve the situation. Essentially, they are very talented using the five primary senses (look, feel, hear, taste, and touch); thus, allowing them to classify and understand reality. That is why they are labeled as having good reasoning ability and being rational thinkers.

Divisive Trait:
B5 (5) persons are often labeled as dictatorial and as micromanagers in their particular fields. They can be too focused on physical reality, its management, and positioning. It is quite easy for the B5 (5) personality type to forget that their talent is not knowledge and thus limited to what is physically available. Other talents such as intuition, planning, trade, relationship building, and a strong work ethic are not necessarily natal talents that they possess. This leaves a large void when we view overall success because they are so dependent on the work of others.

It should be noted again, that in the creative process SUN (4) is the sixth overall stage; thus putting it near the end. It is not until TUI, CHIEN (6), KAN (1), KEN (8), and CHEN (3) have completed their responsibilities that SUN (4) can then have something to work with to be successful.

Balancing Description:
KEN's tendency to link and combine with other people in the environment balances double SUN's reasoning tendency. This reasoning is intensified here and the overall focus and purpose are in danger of being lost.

Peacekeeping

Base House: 5th House -- 5: Peacekeeper
Natal Trait: 5: Peacekeeper
Balancing Agent: 1: Conservation
Angle Analysis: Point
I Ching Hexagram: Not Applicable

Description:
B5 in the B5 house produces a congregative outlook/view on the world. These persons are interested in balance with all others so that everyone can play their role in the world.

The B5 individual tends to address life by taking on the character trait(s) missing in any given situation. That is why these individuals are often viewed as a bit unstable because of the constant character transformations and emotional ups and downs. Over time this takes its toll on the person and they question their place in the world. But the B5 personality needs to understand that this is their role in society. As a matter of fact, advanced cultures often use the B5 person (usually in a priesthood group) to assess the health of a community or nation. Because of their sensitivity to their environment it will become apparent through their health, visions, and dreams what needs to be addressed to bring harmony back to the community.

Virtuous Trait:

The Peacekeeper has the ability to achieve harmony, unity, and success in their lives by taking on the character traits required in that given situation. Which trigrams they have access to is largely due to the cumulative experiences in their lives and their level of consciousness. The level of consciousness is determined by the choices they have made in response to both life's challenges and specific initiations they have gone through. These consciousness levels actually span lifetimes and a separate set of criteria is required to determine where a person may be in their development. So people at a lower level my have access to KEN (8) or KUN (2) or at a slightly higher level SUN (4) and CHIEN (6). Those of higher consciousness would have access to LI (9) or KAN (1) and the finally TUI (7) or CHEN (3).

Apart from what trigrams this person may have access to is the ability to take on another character trait. This is their talent. Initiation and making the proper choices in life will simply give these individuals more of an arsenal to choose from throughout their lives. Then the individual has the power to chose and bring harmony and unity to almost any situation they encounter.

Divisive Trait:

These individuals have the weakness of not being able to see beyond this utopian view of how the world should be structured. Although, they have a balanced view of how the world should be in most societies it is not structured that way. As a result, their view is often not practical due to lack of insight in the general community. These individuals as a result become the outcasts of most communities and in many cases depressed. Another challenge is their inability to create true friendships and relationships.

Additionally, because they have the talent or tendency to take on the personality traits required in any given situation these individuals may over compensate with certain character types according to social acceptance and pressure. In western culture, the KUN (2) personality type is highly valued because of their ability to communicate verbally with all people and in most situations. This is regarded as a strength and sign of intelligence. As a result, the B5 person may find themselves cultivating this character at the expense of the others, especially, since it is the most accessible because of its closeness to the material world.

Balancing Description:
KAN (1) is the balancing answer here. When the double B5 can look at itself and prepare for the how their world, environment, organization, family, community, etc is actually structured they are better able to cope with their reality. Again the focus here is to have the proper perspective on life. If we take personal what is going on around us to the point of personal offense and depression, then we miss a valuable point of life. We are not here to directly change the world, but indirectly change it through directly changing ourselves. Look at the world around you and measure you success in life through your happiness and what manifests around you. The stronger you life force the greater the reach of you influence. Good luck.

Mental Acuity

Base House: 6th House -- 6 (CHIEN): Devotee
Natal Trait: 6 (CHIEN): Devotee
Balancing Agent: 3 (CHEN): Visionary
Angle Analysis: Point
I Ching Hexagram: 1, The Creative

Description:
CHIEN (6) sits between TUI (7) and KAN (1) in the BaGua and is a member of the *Earthly Square* arrangement. Thus it has the ability to retreat mentally into the inner regions of the mind and retreat physically to places of solitude and seclusion. These skills and tendencies are required in order for CHIEN (6) to carry out the orders given by TUI (7) in preparation for KAN (1).

CHIEN (6) in the CHIEN (6) house produces a pure inward outward focus in which one takes the word (inward or receptive action) and plants the seed (outward or intentional action). This is the ability to talk to the Creator and get a response. This is an unobstructed ability to see ones goal and hold that image in one's mind until it manifests as reality. The CHIEN (6) individual has the unique gift of being able to see the complete picture in one's mind as if it was real and in front of them.

These individuals; therefore, can see how things could change or be better. They can look at an abandoned house (a fixer upper) and see a beautiful new dwelling with the windows, fresh paint, the garden, fence, and freshly paved driveway. These individuals often times are able to take advantage of the "one person's trash is another person's treasure" scenario and make a fortune and great wealth. While at the store they can look at an outfit and visually see how it would look on them or any other person for that matter. There is no need to try it on and stand in front of the mirror for ten minutes; the image is in their head and quite clear. The CHIEN (6) function allows us to see the potential in things and how things could be improved. This ability also allows us to see the danger in things or situations or how things could turn out if not addressed properly. So we see the danger in this faculty not performing correctly.

Virtuous Trait:
Double CHIEN (6) is able to hold its focus on the goal and not be distracted by externals. This is a talent and can only be partially achieved by others with great focus and concentration. These individuals tend to have excellent memories as they see complete pictures in their minds.

Their ability to see things in their mind is so great it enables them to bring these things forth because they never loose the vision. With them it is always present.

Divisive Trait:
Double CHIEN (6) persons may have the tendency to stay in their minds and not deal with physical reality. Because pictures

and images are so clear in their mental sphere there is often neglect of the reality in front of them. Also their ability to concentrate on one thing so easily may cause them to be completely absorbed by it. This is evident in their behavior as they often times appear not to be here with us. The truth is their not. They are in a completely different world and fully committed to it.

Balancing Description:
CHEN (3) provides enough external movement to remind CHIEN (6) that its focus should be for the whole and not to get absorbed in its own nature and ability.

Intuitive Abilities

Base House: 7ᵗʰ House -- 7 (TUI): Monk
Natal Trait: 7 (TUI): Monk
Balancing Agent: 5: Peacekeeper
Angle Analysis: Point
I Ching Hexagram: 58, The Joyous Lake

Description:
TUI (7) is the compliment of CHEN (3) in the BaGua. TUI (7) represents the complete mental retreat of an individual into the vastness of one's mind for the purpose of gaining clarity and insight concerning the things of the world. TUI (7) does not look at physical manifestation to get its insight, but stays focused on the mental pictures and symbols that represent both manifested and unmanifested reality. Thus, we can say that TUI's tendency is mental - inward as opposed to CHEN (3) who is physical inward. Or in other words, TUI (7) goes from vision to physical reality; whereas, CHEN (3) goes from physical reality to mental vision (or idea).

TUI (7) in the TUI (7) house produces a doubling of the trigram which maps to the 58th hexagram, The Joyous Lake. This leads to unobstructed wisdom via a pure inward focus for guidance.

This is the ability to listen to the Creator or that inner truth within us. This energy is balanced by B5 to remind it to use its talent for the balance of all involved.

TUI (7) is the ability to understand the deep underlying principles governing reality. These principles are not apparent to the person's sensory perception or a logical thought process. They must be intuited or experienced from within. In other words, these individuals have the ability to experience (or feel) manifested or non-manifested reality from within their being rather than through their senses. The closest association would be through the "mind", but this is not entirely accurate, as the symbols of that experience are displayed through one's mental visual perception.

Virtuous Trait:
TUI-TUI people have the gift to pull back the principles or laws governing any situation. When these individuals focus on a particular subject these principles reveal themselves fairly easily.

Divisive Trait:
TUI-TUI individuals tend to approach life from a perspective of deep understanding. They tend to look at things based upon a "higher" or deeper principle and are therefore fairly slow to move forward with decisions. Even when they do make decisions they tend to reverse themselves due to a later revelation of a "deeper" insight into the situation.

Balancing Description:
B5 is the balancing energy required for the double TUI (7) as with all trigrams in the Lo Shu "base" house. All must be reminded to work for the betterment of the whole.

Relationship Building

Base House: 8th House -- 8 (KEN): Lover
Natal Trait: 8 (KEN): Lover
Balancing Agent: 7 (TUI): Monk

162

Angle Analysis: Point
I Ching Hexagram: 53, The Mountain

Description:
KEN-KEN produces one of the doubled trigrams; which, produces hexagram 52, The Mountain. KEN's talent is to bring people and things together in a tight alignment to achieve a common goal. In this coming together these people are essentially one. KEN (8) can "love" deeply and understands the actions required (what to say and do) to bring people together to work and coexist harmoniously.

It is obvious how important this skill is in both family and social arenas as well as in mate relationships. Another point of note is the image of the 53rd hexagram is the Mountain. These close relationships are ultimately to increase KEN's power. As a mountain is a collective of elements tightly formed, their overall strength is increased.

Virtuous Trait:
KEN-KEN individuals have the ability to work, socialize, and entertain. The relationships they develop are sustainable past many of the trials and tribulations that will ultimately present themselves. This talent has its obvious benefits in society.

Divisive Trait:
When trigrams are doubled their tendency is to bask in their own energy just for the sake of it. The same holds true for KEN (8). To socially and intimately interact with people without a theme or purpose can be dangerous. Plus, we shouldn't develop close relationships with all people; it's just not necessary and can be harmful depending on the situation. These are your abusive relationships where the attachment is difficult to break.

Balancing Description:
TUI's insights are able to remind KEN (8) of why these social relationships should be formed and their benefit to the overall goal. Also, TUI (7) moves inward mentally enough to change

KEN's direction.

Work Ethic

Base House: 9th House -- 9 (LI): Soldier
Natal Trait: 9 (LI): Soldier
Balancing Agent: 9 (LI): Soldier
Angle Analysis: Point
I Ching Hexagram: 30, The Clinging Fire

Description:
LI (9) is the compliment of KAN (1) in the BaGua. LI (9) represents the physical - outward tendency of an individual as opposed to KAN (1) who is mental - inward. These individuals fully commit their physical bodies and all people and things to which they are associated towards interaction with the outside environment. LI (9) in the LI (9) house produces a pure fiery, zealous, and hard-working individual. These people have the ability to be very intense, hard working individuals who operate without fear of failure or consequence. The double LI (9) element however does not give them any particular focus or insight, which, of course, can be dangerous for these individuals and those around them. In other words, here we have movement for the sake of movement or action of the sake of action.

The important note here is that LI (9) is generated as a part of passion towards a particular subject or in intense emotionalism (i.e. anger).

Virtuous Trait:
LI (9) doubled produces fearless and tireless workers. They are very deeply analytical and not afraid to bring issues to light through their action. Where as some people are calculating in their movement, double LI's act first and think later and they do it in a way that is body first and fully committed.

The important thing to realize here is this virtue comes out when the individual is zealous or passionate about a particular subject or endeavor. Ultimately, they have to choose to exercise this talent in order to take advantage of it.

Divisive Trait:
The fearlessness and tendency to move quickly can cloud the judgment and prevent proper planning. There can tend to be little thought before commitment. These individuals also have a tendency to get impatient with individuals who are not moving fast enough for their taste whether it be intellectual or physical activities. They are the one's who cut in to complete someone else's sentence to help them "get to the point."

The warning here is displayed in the name of the hexagram that is formed by doubling the two LI (9) trigrams, The Clinging Fire, which indicates that these individuals must not act without acknowledgement of the source of their power which for LI (9) is rooted in KAN (1).

Balancing Description:
With all of the LI (9) interactions between the hexagrams it may seem strange that the same trigram is required to bring harmony and balance. It is especially strange that when LI (9) is doubled an additional LI (9) element is required to harmonize the situation. The reason is that LI's original nature and tendency does not exist separate from the larger whole to which it is always associated (via B5). When we add other trigrams to a natal trigram (or personality) the original intent and tendency can be lost. It's almost like a distraction of sorts. It's like you are dancing with someone and another beautiful person walks into the room. You may tend to loose focus for a moment. That is what is taking place with all of these trigram (personality/character) combinations. When Li is combined with Li the same things happens. Li gets absorbed in its own tendency and looses its original mission. The addition of another Li element, which has the consciousness of this original mission inherent in its nature will bring back the balance. It is really all just mathematics.

Chapter 15: CHIEN – The Devotee

BaGua Configuration: 6

5	1	3
4	6	8
9	2	7

Summary:
The CHIEN (6) person, or Devotee, tends to be "spiritual" and into practices such as creative visualization, prayer, and meditation. As a general rule they play entire scenarios out in their minds when navigating through life's challenges. They have good memories and rarely forget a face. When forming friendships they look more at the moral underpinnings and principles governing the relationship. For this reason they tend to be slow in forming close friendships and relationships as well as slow to commit to others. Their preference in solving conflict is through taking control and leadership in the situation. They also have well developed intuitive abilities, but they have the tendency to shift their focus on the final outcome too quickly and thus fail to finish receiving the deeper insights.

The Devotee, is an excellent planner and organizer, but tends to take too long in the planning process; thus, movement and execution of the plan is greatly delayed at best. They are generally passionate about art, music, and the creative sciences and enjoy socializing with close friends. This can result in excessive sexual interaction although this is not the essence of why they form relationships, but rather a stage in the unfolding of these types of relationships.

Their overall ability to be zealous in completing tasks is there, but they would prefer to be in the company of others for serious projects. Leadership is a challenge as these individuals tend to be more idealistic as opposed to rational and reasonable. There is a strong tendency to explore areas of business and entrepreneurship; however there is difficulty when attempting to communicate with others as they are not very zealous in this area.

Social Skills

Base House: 1st House -- 1 (KAN): Conservationist
Natal Trait: 2 (KUN): Negotiator
Balancing Agent: 3 (CHEN): Visionary
Angle Analysis: Obtuse
I Ching Hexagram: 7, The Army

Description:
KUN (2) in the KAN (1) house produces what appears as procrastination in trading and exchanging with others due to protracted thinking and planning. This person would generally engage in commerce, but may find himself spending a long time researching and investigating commercial opportunities and focusing on one's own strengths and weaknesses relative to executing the transaction. Again, the tendency of KAN (1) is to focus on the self in such a way as to remove those weaker qualities within the person and replace with stronger qualities in preparation for events to come. KAN (1) has no interest in engaging people or the outside world. This hampers KUN's natural tendency to exchange with the surrounding environment and the person's within it.

Virtuous Trait:
These individuals are able to socialize and adjust well in conservative environments. Due to their tendency of strict adherence to structure and foundational principles they can bring conservative individuals together and interact successfully with them. An example is the ability to bring tenured religious representatives to the table to and harmoniously discuss the

common principles within their religions. That one is generally a mission impossible, but if anyone can do it the CHIEN (6) person can.

Divisive Trait:
The KUN-KAN personality will have difficulty in social arenas. It will take them some time to "warm-up" to their surroundings. This will manifest as an inability to know what to say or a tendency not to speak in general coupled with a lack of interest in engaging others. Generally, this person will avoid situations involving active exchange and interaction with others.

From another perspective these individuals will have a blind adherence to structure and foundational principles. KUN (2) being a part of the *Earthly Square* and KAN (1) being part of the *Heavenly Circle* there is a natural tendency for KUN (2) to follow KAN (1). Thus, this person will preach and follow the structures presented by KAN (1), especially, when dealing with others.

Balancing Description:
The quality of KUN (2) is obedience and the quality of KAN (1) is renewal through stillness; thus, the insightful and expanding energy of CHEN (3) will allow for healthy interaction between KUN (2) and KAN (1).

Creativity and Zest for Life

Base House: 2nd House -- 2 (KUN): Negotiator
Natal Trait: 3 (CHEN): Visionary
Balancing Agent: 5: Peacekeeper
Angle Analysis: Obtuse
I Ching Hexagram: 16, Enthusiasm

Description:
CHEN (3) in the KUN (2) house forms one of our obtuse relationships bringing together a heavenly (CHEN) and earthly

(KUN). These trigrams have different inherent natures as CHEN (3) is in a leadership position and KUN (2) is in a position of obedience. There are similarities here in that both CHEN (3) and KUN (2) have work to do in the physical world. The difference is CHEN (3) represents the start of this work and KUN (2) represents the end of it. Additionally, KUN (2) is fully vested in the physical world and has no knowledge of or interest in the metaphysical or mental realms. KUN's job is strictly the dissemination of manifested reality to its proper place. CHEN (3) however is new to the physical world and is attempting to build the inertia to leave the metaphysical mental regions. It is this drive and determination that gives double CHEN (3) the label of The Arousing in the I Ching.

Virtuous Trait:
Again, we have an obtuse relationship in CHEN (3) and KUN (2). The results here can be quite substantial and beneficial if mutual respect of each of the trigrams is given. CHEN (3) here will have deep insights into trade and commerce as well as how to cultivate superficial relationships for the achievement of various goals.

Divisive Trait:
This person will have a tendency to focus on things that are fully manifested and visible to everyone; thus, limiting their ability to generate new ideas by seeing the subtler realities of the world.

Balancing Description:
B5 is the balancing agent to bring CHEN (3) and KUN (2) into working harmony. B5 reminds CHEN (3) that it must have a balanced perspective and focus on the whole. It needs to bring into manifestation the will of TUI (7) and that means a focus on all roles in the BaGua including that of KUN (2).

Leadership and Resourcefulness

Base House: 3rd House -- 3 (CHEN): Visionary
Natal Trait: 4 (SUN): Leader
Balancing Agent: 7 (TUI): Monk
Angle Analysis: Acute
I Ching Hexagram: 42, Increase

Description:
SUN (4) in the CHEN (3) house brings together members of the *Earthly Square* and *Heavenly Circle* only one position away from one another. In this case SUN (4) is leading while being influenced by CHEN (3). This is a natural arrangement and the first fully aligned daylight consciousness arrangement in the BaGua. SUN (4), the leader of daylight, meaning conscious physical activity, must only move forward with CHEN's guidance and insight.

Virtuous Trait:
These individuals have the ability to manage their physical environment and have a particularly keen insight into the subtle laws and forces governing all things in the world. This insight allows them to expand their rational and managerial influence beyond those purely physical things. Great success is achieved when SUN (4) allows CHEN's guidance and input.

Divisive Trait:
When SUN (4) is in the CHEN (3) house it causes SUN's very intense and meticulous view of the physical world and the inspection and insight into the things around to suffer by taking its view to the metaphysical. For SUN (4) to achieve its job of managing and organizing physical reality, it cannot focus on the subtle realities of the world. SUN (4) has no time to dream, imagine, and expand beyond what it has directly in front of it. SUN (4) must remember and maintain its role and function and not get distracted by CHEN's influence beyond its stated purpose.

Balancing Description:
TUI's insight to understand the underlying principles governing any situation will help balance the relationship between SUN (4) and CHEN (3). In this case TUI (7) will be able to offer insight and guidance to SUN (4) to help in harmoniously interacting with CHEN (3) without loosing its focus.

Peacekeeping

Base House: 4th House -- 4 (SUN): Leader
Natal Trait: 5: Peacekeeper
Balancing Agent: 9 (LI): Soldier
Angle Analysis: Radial Line
I Ching Hexagram: Not Applicable

Description:
B5 in the SUN (4) house produces a tendency to unify one's life through resource management and leadership.

Virtuous Trait:
These individuals unify their lives around SUN's character traits and can unify most situations where rational thought, management, and leadership are required.

Divisive Trait:
Here the B5 person attempts to find unity through rationalization and reasoning. Although this may be good in some situations it will not work in all as SUN (4) is only one of the nine character traits used to bring about unity in one's life. Therefore overall success will only be achieved just over 10% of the time.

From another point of view, we can say that SUN (4) is the character requirement for success but the person in this case is bringing a B5 perspective. As B5 attempts to bring about unity and harmony first it is out of synch with SUN's requirement for management and leadership. If the B5 individual has been

initiated or is on a higher consciousness level it will have access
to the SUN (4) character and be able to properly address the
situation. It is however listed as a vice here as many people have
not made the choices necessary to give them access to SUN (4)
and CHIEN (6).

Balancing Description:
LI (9) is the balancing agent here. LI's energy and light allow B5
to balance SUN's dictatorial and dominating nature.

Mental Acuity

Base House: 5th House -- 5: Peacekeeper
Natal Trait: 6 (CHIEN): Devotee
Balancing Agent: 2 (KUN): Negotiator
Angle Analysis: Radial Line
I Ching Hexagram: Not Applicable

Description:
CHIEN (6) in the B5 house produces one whose world view is
centered in obedience, love, and devotion to harmony and unity.
These individuals have the tendency to solve problems and deal
with the world via internal means or mentally visualizing how
things could be better. They don't believe in confrontation with
others, but instead mobilize inwardly in their minds to clearly
define and deal with the issue at hand.

Virtuous Trait:
These individuals have the ability to see (mentally) what
harmony amongst a group or in an individual person's life would
look like. This vision would be communicated to the group and
implemented to achieve success in unity.

Divisive Trait:
These individuals will tend to view the world through the eyes of
CHIEN (6) which involves dealing with life through

visualization and mental focus. Achieving unity through CHIEN (6) is possible in the situations that require that energy. In other situations, the individuals will not achieve complete success and in many cases will fail.

Balancing Description:
KUN's outward tendency is needed to balance out CHIEN's inward focus.

Intuitive Abilities

Base House: 6th House -- 6 (CHIEN): Devotee
Natal Trait: 7 (TUI): Monk
Balancing Agent: 4 (SUN): Leader
Angle Analysis: Acute
I Ching Hexagram: 43, Breaking Through

Description:
TUI (7) in the CHIEN (6) house produces a slight focus distraction for TUI (7). TUI (7) and CHIEN (6) are both focused inward, but TUI's position in the last day or light position gives it more heat than CHIEN (6). TUI (7) is focused on gaining new insight based upon new goals and objectives and is not ready to devote itself to one course of action like CHIEN (6). CHIEN (6) follows TUI (7) in the creative process so there may be a tendency for TUI (7) to get a bit ahead of itself and plant the seeds or see the goal before all of the governing principles are identified. TUI's role is to listen (meditate) to God whereas CHIEN's is to talk (pray) to god. This trigram combination represents a common challenge for the student of meditation who can easily get caught up in directing their consciousness during the meditative process rather than simply observing what enters the sphere of awareness.

Virtuous Trait:
The TUI-CHIEN (6) individual can gain great insight into mental visions of un-manifested reality. Usually, TUI (7) is

looking at what has already occurred and attempt to fully evaluate it to see where improvements could be made. In this case, TUI (7) is able to intuit the underlying structure of the goal and see how it can manifest in its finished form. This ability to also generate the image will give TUI (7) further material to evaluate and get further direction for the upcoming cycle.

Divisive Trait:
There is a chance that TUI (7) will get ahead of itself here and attempt to see the whole picture before it has completed gathering all of the principles governing the successful implementation of the goal. These individuals may sit down to think deeply about how to solve a problem, but will find themselves jumping to a solution too quickly. This is the effect of CHIEN (6).

Balancing Description:
For balance SUN (4) gives the proper enlightenment and focus to bring TUI (7) back on its path and work cooperatively with CHIEN (6).

Relationship Building

Base House: 7th House -- 7 (TUI): Monk
Natal Trait: 8 (KEN): Lover
Balancing Agent: 6 (CHIEN): Devotee
Angle Analysis: Obtuse
I Ching Hexagram: 41, Decrease

Description:
KEN (8) in the TUI (7) house produces a conflict in KEN's intimate tendency with the people and things of the world. TUI's inward focus is in direct conflict with KEN's outward focus. TUI's additional speed, although slowing, works to pull KEN's focus away from physical reality. TUI (7) has the focus of thinking deeply on what it has seen and experienced so that future goals can be obtained.

174

Virtuous Trait:
The Devotee type has the ability to bond with others based upon the principles governing the relationship rather than for superficial reasons. These individuals also have a love for morality and spiritual law and tend to adopt these principles into their daily living.

Divisive Trait:
When the KEN-TUI personality type attempts to be social and bond with others there are delays as one tends to think deeply about the relationships in question. This additional thought process causes delays and paralyzes KEN's social nature. The conflict is partially rooted in the net position difference (NPD) of three places between these trigrams. These two energies are almost directly at odds with one another.

Balancing Description:
CHIEN's inward focus and ability to hold its goals and objectives mentally will help KEN (8) keep its focus on its original goal and purpose. CHIEN's understanding and clarity on the results it wishes to achieve will reduce the inquisitive influence TUI (7) brings to the equation.

Work Ethic

Base House: 8th House -- 8 (KEN): Lover
Natal Trait: 9 (LI): Soldier
Balancing Agent: 8 (KEN): Lover
Angle Analysis: Obtuse
I Ching Hexagram: 56, The Wanderer

Description:
LI (9) in the KEN (8) house produces one whose passion is in intimacy and quaint "socialness" with others. These individuals are very sensual and like intimate contact with others. This

however does not necessarily translate into sexual passion. Sexual passion falls under the more fiery trigrams like SUN (4), LI (9), and KUN (2). For KEN (8) it is enough to have the close, touchy, quality interaction without necessarily the need to take things all the way. That said, these individuals are very sexual and tend to go there quite often, but the mistake is to think that is their main focus. Sexual intercourse for them is simply one of many expressions of this social intimate interaction.

In children this often manifests as the boy or girl who is always hugging and kissing the rest of the class. They just want to be close to others, especially, when they are excited.

Virtuous Trait:
The talent here is that these persons can resolve conflicts well when they or someone they care about is involved. For example, when family disagreements arise the Devotee personality is usually the best to bring harmony and resolution. They move towards creating and harmonizing relationships when a conflict arises.

From another view, these individuals can be classified as chemists or artists from the standpoint that they can bring two or more elements together to work in harmony when they care enough about the outcome. They are master integrators and arbitrators through behavior. Meaning, they can show people what to do to come together and forget their differences, but they just can't explain it. If disputing parties would follow their lead and functioning they could end conflicts, but unfortunately, KEN's behavior appears out of character and is rejected as not regarding the seriousness of life. This cannot be further from the truth. KEN's behavior may not abide by the socially accepted protocols and norms, but it is the most valid and legitimate way to deal with one's environment.

Divisive Trait:
When passionate about a person or subject the Devotee likes to get very close to them/it. They move to intimacy as a way to deal with the person. Again, trying to approach someone in this

way is dangerous especially if that is not the approach required. The result can be this person getting hurt and feeling betrayed by others. The Devotee mindset is they let this person into their life and were abused as a result. The fault here is they created a social intimate relationship when they should have been approaching the person from a different perspective (i.e. business, negotiation, sales, etc.).

This is true of loved ones as well. The Devotee person may feel love toward a son, daughter, spouse, or close relative, but must remember they can't approach all situations involving those people the same way. Sometimes it is necessary to bring another trigram personality in to ultimately create harmony.

Balancing Description:
KEN (8) is the element needed to return KEN's original focus back to the overall goal and purpose of its original intent. This is true for all trigram interactions with LI (9) where the natal trigram is the balancing agent when LI (9) interacts with it.

Planning and Organizing Abilities

Base House: 9th House -- 9 (LI): Soldier
Natal Trait: 1 (KAN): Conservationist
Balancing Agent: 1 (KAN): Conservationist
Angle Analysis: Axis
I Ching Hexagram: 63, After Completion

Description:
KAN (1) in the LI (9) house produces an enhanced ability to think deeply when one attempts to do so. These elements are complements, sitting on the same axis. LI's nature is external energy, zealousness, and unrelenting focus. LI's fire and focus serve to enhance the inherent tendency of any trigram it interacts with. In this case the cold trigram KAN (1), influenced by LI (9), enhances the individual's ability to plan, strategize, self-fortify, and think deeply about subjects.

177

KAN (1), being the compliment of LI (9), is the same intensity of energy, but focused inward. Inward means focusing on what the person or entity needs to improve or restructure in order to prepare itself for interaction with the world.

KAN (1) in the LI (9) house produces one who is very much into seclusion and internalization. These individuals are not the outgoing social types although they are very loyal to their core constituency. This person takes a long time to make decisions; tending to meditate deeply on subjects of interest or life matters.

Virtuous Trait:
The KAN-LI trigram combination produces your most talented master planners and strategic thinkers of any trigram combination. These individuals can also think deeply and intensely on a number of subjects which allows them to see into the inner structure and workings of the subject of their focus. Often times these will be your Ph. Ds of a particular field of study.

Divisive Trait:
The act of intensely focusing on structure and planning and looking deeply into subjects has its advantages, but can also cause stagnation when it is time to act or make a decision.

Balancing Description:
KAN (1) is what is needed to balance out the KAN-LI combination. LI (9) adds additional fire behind the planning and meticulous force. Over activity of a LI (9) entity with KAN (1) should be balanced by that KAN (1) entity. The additional coolness will give one part LI (9) and two parts KAN (1) which is a happy medium. This will allow the KAN (1) focus without loosing a view of the whole.

Chapter 16: TUI – The Monk

BaGua Configuration: 7

6	2	4
5	7	9
1	3	8

Summary:
The TUI (7) person, or Monk, is a person who views the world based upon principle. In other words, there is a right and a wrong way to do most things and in certain areas they can be quite fanatical. This principled view of the world in many cases makes them slow/resistant to change. They really have to see and understand that a new way of doing things is "true" and correct in the larger scheme of things. They may have an affinity for the arts and creative sciences, but not a lot of natural talent here. These individuals have trouble forming friendships as they tend to play out scenarios of what to say and how to function in their minds which inhibits their ability to be natural and truthful. These individuals have good memories. There is good mental acuity here and a talent for skillfully managing their mental space, thoughts, and visions.

The TUI (7) person, or Monk, has a natural ability to communicate with others for the sake of accomplishing a task or goal. This may manifest as well developed writing, presentation, and verbal communication abilities. These are your natural marketing persons. This, however, does not necessarily mean these individuals are willing to open up to others. They are excellent planners and organizers of people and social events. These persons are very passionate about spirituality and morality. The passion around morality and doing the right thing can be so strong that it can cause them to frequently second guess themselves; thus, stifling their ability to make decisions.

They tend to seek unity and balance through giving, sharing, and having faith in others. This often times leads to disaster as people just don't consistently deliver as they should. They tend to lead through strong communication, but are very controlling of what they say to others. They can also be verbally abusive at times. These individuals are not daring or expansive in their functioning; thus, lacking a drive to go out and experience life.

Creativity and Zest for Life

Base House: 1st House -- 1 (KAN): Conservationist
Natal Trait: 3 (CHEN): Faith
Balancing Agent: 4 (SUN): Leader
Angle Analysis: Right
I Ching Hexagram: 40, Deliverance

Description:
CHEN (3) has the ability to see parts of the physical world around them and parts of the subtle world, but doesn't have the ability to see all of either. CHEN (3) also has a drive to experience the world and offer its talents to achieve something. KAN (1) is focused on only those things which build its internal strength and power. This is accomplished through rest and conservative activities that don't stress the body. Both CHEN (3) and KAN (1) are members of the *Heavenly Circle* and are in the position to command others; thus, we have a conflict here.

Here one is slow to expand outward into the world. Ideas and concepts tend to come slowly. However, once the CHEN (3) personality breaks through KAN's conservative nature one's ideas and expansiveness are focused and intense. The ideas "generated" are deep and meaningful and if properly implemented have a lasting affect in the world.

CHEN (3) in the KAN (1) house produces a slowing in one's ability to perceive the subtle physical forces in the material world. The slow movement of KAN (1) burdens CHEN's expansiveness and forces perception inward.

Virtuous Trait:

Once these individuals grow accustomed to KAN's conservative nature they have deep insights (ideas actually) into what structures can be put into place as foundations and new ways to implement them.

Divisive Trait:

The CHEN-KAN personality is slow to generate ideas. Dysfunctional behavior occurs when attempting to go out into the world. These individuals want to expand outward, but once they take that step they revert back to a conservative posture.

From another perspective, the CHEN-KAN combination causes one to be overly expanding in the need and role of structure beyond the physical supports available.

Balancing Description:

The balancing requirement would be SUN (4). Translated, the focus and rationality of SUN (4) will enable CHEN (3) to properly manage itself in this environment. SUN's focus and ability to define physical are the balancing requirements here.

Leadership and Resourcefulness

Base House: 2nd House -- 2 (KUN): Negotiator
Natal Trait: 4 (SUN): Leader
Balancing Agent: 6 (CHIEN): Devotee
Angle Analysis: Right
I Ching Hexagram: 20, Contemplation

Description:

SUN (4) in the KUN (2) house produces one who is normally focused on defining the physical reality with a tendency to interact with that environment. SUN (4) generally is not interested in interacting with the physical environment, but rather putting into place those resources that can effectively deal with it. SUN (4) is like KUN (2) in that it takes its orders from another trigram. This is due to the fact that they are both members of the *Earthly Square* and are in place for servitude of the higher *Heavenly Circle* trigrams. Thus, again from this standpoint they are both in a position of servitude and obedience and their directions simply harmonize. SUN (4) is in servitude to CHEN (3) whose job it is to identify the first signs of creative expression in the physical world and KUN (2) is obedient to LI (9) whose job it is to produce all physical manifestation.

Virtuous Trait:
Here one has the insight to see clearly what relationships are all about. As KUN (2) is here to form superficial relationships, SUN's ability to see and define physical reality will allow them to see what these relationships are trying to accomplish. This is key, as KUN's effectiveness in forming superficial relationships provides the needed insight to allow SUN (4) to see clearly into most types of relationships.

Divisive Trait:
As SUN (4) and KUN (2) are both members of the *Earthly Square* they take their orders from one of the heavenly trigrams: KUN (2) from LI (9) and SUN (4) from CHEN (3). Here one is called to interact and form social relationships in the world, but has the tendency to define, manage, and control them instead. This causes for stagnation in the forming of relationships as one comes across as too controlling.

Balancing Description:
CHIEN's inward focus balances out the outward focus of both KUN (2) and CHIEN (6).

Peacekeeping

Base House: 3rd House -- 3 (CHEN): Visionary
Natal Trait: 5: Peacekeeper
Balancing Agent: 8 (KEN): Lover
Angle Analysis: Radial Line
I Ching Hexagram: Not Applicable

Description:
B5 is interested in the balance and unity amongst those things/people that it interacts with in order to achieve its goals in life. To achieve this it tends to take on the personality or fill the void of those people/energies/character traits that are missing to help achieve its goals. The B5 personality type is therefore largely subject to the conditions it has experienced over time and those factors influencing its life. When B5 mixes with CHEN (3) it takes on some of CHEN's tendency which is to experience the world through offering insight to address various issues and circumstances. B5 adopts some of this tendency and looses some of its balanced perspective. It looses its consciousness of the other tendencies in the world and focuses more from a dreamy, idealistic mental state.

Virtuous Trait:
These individuals have the ability to harmonize and unify a situation by becoming the CHEN (3) personality type. The B5 person's focus, already towards achievement, now has the trait of seeing the underlying principles governing all things in the world. This gives them additional perspective when viewing and evaluating the things around them.

Divisive Trait:
This individual will have a tendency to bring about balance in their lives through the generation of ideas first. This can be a problem as all problems/issues do not require a new idea. Again, the B5 person has the ability to take on many personality types to achieve its goal, but the tendency here will be a heavy leniency

183

towards the CHEN (3) personality type.

Balancing Description:
KEN (8) is required to help CHEN (3) focus more towards what is directly in front of it rather than trying to achieve the world as CHEN (3) can get very expansive and idealistic.

Mental Acuity

Base House: 4th House -- 4 (SUN): Leader
Natal Trait: 6 (CHIEN): Devotee
Balancing Agent: 1 (KAN): Conservationist
Angle Analysis: Axis
I Ching Hexagram: 44, Coming to Meet

Description:
CHIEN (6) in the SUN (4) house generates one of the four axis and one of the eight complimentary arrangements. Although these trigrams are complementary their coordination and interaction will take a great deal of understanding and deliberateness. CHIEN's movement is inward while SUN's movement is outward. They both serve different masters and complete two complimentary phases of the creative process. CHIEN (6) is taking its queue from TUI (7) and SUN (4) from CHEN (3). This is the source of potential conflicts as each is a member of the *Earthly Square* and committed to obedience.

Virtuous Trait:
These individuals will have the ability to see mentally what is presented physically by SUN (4). They will be able to see what is required to be an effective leader and manager of manifested reality. Because they can see more physical reality, they have greater potential to add mental images to its visualization process.

Divisive Trait:
As CHIEN (6) and SUN (4) are on the same axis they are

compliments. For the Monk this character conflict produces some of the greatest challenges in their lives. In a situation that calls for management and control these individuals will retreat inward to address the issues through mental processing. It is almost equivalent to closing one's eyes when attempting to complete a project. Failure is of course the result. Because CHIEN (6) is so focused on mental processing one of its character traits is receptivity and deference to that which is physical. This is implied in the fact that it is a member of the *Earthly Square* and by default takes its orders from heaven, in this case TUI (7). In a SUN (4) situation, deference is not the way to function. This is where we must take control of our lives.

As one attempts to see mentally the goals to be achieved there will be a strong tendency to manage and define these images. In addition, CHIEN (6) will be pulled to focus on manifested things and suffer from an inability to concentrate and hold images mentally.

Balancing Description:
KAN's deliberateness and structure are required to balance out these energies. Without this intervention, SUN's dominating nature will be unraveled by extreme emotionalism and an inability to focus on physical reality.

Intuitive Abilities

Base House: 5th House -- 5: Peacekeeper
Natal Trait: 7 (TUI): Monk
Balancing Agent: 3 (CHEN): Visionary
Angle Analysis: Radial Line
I Ching Hexagram: Not Applicable

Description:
TUI (7) in the B5 house produces an effect of a worldly viewpoint through the eyes of TUI (7) which involves assessment of the past to intuitively address the future. TUI (7)

is also focused on identifying those laws and principles which will address as many needs as possible with one solution. TUI (7) is centered on doing things as efficiently as possible and with the least amount of waist. Thus, TUI (7) here will address all of the world's issues from this vantage point. It will use its talents to unify and bring harmony to its life and its general environment (i.e. work, family, etc.).

Virtuous Trait:
These individuals are able to see the underlying principles required to bring forth harmony and unity in their lives and the lives of others. Through there mental processes they are able to reveal what the group must do to achieve unity and success. These individuals are also able to live by these tenants and be the example to others.

Divisive Trait:
The Monk will tend to bring unity and harmony in their lives through revealing and understanding the underlying principle governing the situation. The issue here is not in the sincere attempt to resolve conflict in this way, but in viewing it from this perspective first without an honest unbiased assessment of the situation. These individuals will normally not only view the situation from a TUI (7) perspective, but often address it from that perspective as well. Because TUI (7) is only one of the nine possible traits to bring harmony to a situation overall success will only be achieved just over 10% of the time. We will also find a tendency for the Monk to "actively promote" (I won't say force) their principles upon others.

Balancing Description:
CHEN (3) is the necessary balancing agent to pull TUI (7) out of its inward focus to also look outward. The CHEN (3) addition adds the outward expansiveness and focus on physical reality to balance TUI's inward focus, which in this case is greater than normal due to B5's inherent TUI (7) energy.

Relationship Building

Base House: 6th House -- 6 (CHIEN): Prayer
Natal Trait: 8 (KEN): Relationships
Balancing Agent: 5: Peacekeeper
Angle Analysis: Right
I Ching Hexagram: 26, The Taming Power of the Great

Description:
KEN (8) in the CHIEN (6) house produces a conflict in focus as KEN (8) is attempting to move slowly outward into the environment while CHIEN (6) is pulled well away from the external environment and focused inward. The balancing requirement is B5 with a view and consideration of the whole. CHIEN (6) is inward and down and KEN (8) is outward and down. Both are members of the *Earthly Square* so there is no leader here.

Virtuous Trait:
KEN (8) here is able to mentally see how relationships can be formed and what needs to be done to sustain them. These visions can be turned into actuality without much effort at all. These individuals have an affinity for Tantric exercises and tend to have out of body experiences during sex.

Divisive Trait:
KEN (8) usually the intimate relationship type becomes more introverted when interacting with CHIEN (6). As a result, KEN's ability to connect with all people in all environments is compromised by its hesitancy on engaging others.

Balancing Description:
B5 is needed to refocus KEN's tendency towards the whole.

Work Ethic

Base House: 7ᵗʰ House -- 7 (TUI): Monk
Natal Trait: 9 (LI): Soldier
Balancing Agent: 7 (TUI): Monk
Angle Analysis: Right
I Ching Hexagram: 38, Opposition

Description:
LI (9) in the TUI (7) house produces the effect of one relentlessly focused on the law, counsel, and understanding the proper way to go about a task or one's life. The fire of LI (9) is greatly influenced by the inward expansiveness of TUI (7) so much of this energy and zealousness is focused inward. TUI (7) is focused on understanding the principles governing the inner workings of things and how to act to reach those goals.

Here we have TUI (7) as the center of this person's outlook on life and all of the intuitive and moral talents that go with it and additionally, we have LI (9) in the TUI (7) house which further intensifies TUI's nature and talents here. In essence we have a triple TUI (7) influence at work here; thus, the virtuous and decisive traits are intensified exponentially. From that standpoint, we cannot escape including the Monk's natal TUI (7) personality as a part of the LI-TUI influence here. What that means is it won't only be passion and zealousness that drives the characteristics of this trigram combination but also the natal tendency of TUI (7) as well.

Virtuous Trait:
The LI-TUI individual is the master of understanding the underlying principles governing anything not yet manifested in the world. Meaning, these individuals can tell you the steps to take to achieve any goal. These steps are usually abstract and never obvious or logical in nature; thus, making some of their proclamations difficult for others to follow, believe, or understand. But this is ok, because it is not other people's talent

188

to process in this way. This is a talent, just like the other talents produced by trigram combinations and should be respected as such. It is not logical or respectful to expect to understand how people arrive at their conclusions or accomplish certain things as we are not the same. This is not logical thinking; thus, their process is not only misunderstood by most people, but often times not understood by themselves.

LI-TUI individuals have an ability to work toward the common good through high principles as their essential tendency is towards morality.

Divisive Trait:
The LI-TUI individual can be overly focused on intuitive understanding as a way to approach life's problems. This often puts them into a stalemate with themselves until they can understand the deeper meaning of life or the situation they are trying to address. Additionally, LI's fire pushes them toward intuition as the first way to approach all of life's problems and the bottom line is everything is not that serious. Often times we need to look at the situation, make the best decision, and move on. This indecisiveness also manifests in these people undoing what they have already done (i.e. frequently taking things back to the store because they changed their mind).

The LI-TUI person should reserve this talent for those issues or challenges that are worthy of their intuitive ability. Again, this can be difficult in an apparently "fast-paced" world where it appears that quick decisions are required for success.

Balancing Description:
TUI (7) is the balancing trigram here. As LI (9) has excited TUI (7) to the point where it is into its own talent for its talent's sake, an additional TUI (7) element will remind TUI (7) of how it is supposed to relate to other trigrams and the overall goal.

Planning and Organizing Abilities

Base House: 8th House -- 8 (KEN): Lover
Natal Trait: 1 (KAN): Conservationist
Balancing Agent: 9 (LI): Soldier
Angle Analysis: Acute
I Ching Hexagram: 39, Obstruction

Description:

KAN (1) in the KEN (8) house produces one who thinks deeply and takes time to properly structure their relationships. The structuring and planning ability of KAN (1) is greatly influenced by KEN's intimate social nature. Thus, these individuals are slow to get into relationships wanting to be sure everything is structured the right way. Because both of these trigrams are slow in nature the movement here is almost paralyzed. Once these individuals do get into relationships they demand the proper structure (i.e. no dating without marriage, etc.).

This also translates into one's ability to plan in general. KAN's ability to focus on those things to improve itself will be slightly affected by KEN's tendency to bond with others. KEN (8) looks outside of itself for strength; thus, the goals of KEN (8) and KAN (1) are the same, but the methods and stages are different.

Virtuous Trait:

KAN-KEN produces one who thinks deeply about the meaning of relationships and their structures. These individuals, although slow to move, ensure all of the proper structure and foundations are in place before committing to long term relationship. This being the case, they tend to be in relationships for the duration. This also holds true for the types of relationships they pursue. Although, the Monk is into long-term relationships they also have the ability to structure alternative relationships that may involve more than one partner. Generally, if an individual fits the bill they include them within their relationship structure. Again, these behaviors as described by the trigram combinations

190

are not limited to one type of manifested reality, but rather indicate a behavior pattern that can be seen in all related situations.

Divisive Trait:
KAN-KEN indicates one whose ability to plan and organize lacks the internal focus needed to be effective. The stillness required is violated by KEN's movement (although slow in itself). Organization is still possible, but the depth and protracted focus cannot be sustained.

Balancing Description:
LI's light and external focus help KAN (1) regain its internal focus. The light and fire of LI (9) may seem to be a bit extreme especially because KAN (1) and KEN (8) are so close together in the creative process. It should be noted that KEN (8) is very close to the earthly realm, meaning it has deep attachments to material items and desires as opposed to the will to follow principles. To break the bond KEN (8) has on KAN (1) does require LI's fire. KAN (1) is not of the earth, it is part of the *Heavenly Circle*. The fire and light of LI (9) breaks KAN (1) from KEN's enchantment.

Social Skills

Base House: 9th House -- 9 (LI): Soldier
Natal Trait: 2 (KUN): Negotiator
Balancing Agent: 2 (KUN): Negotiator
Angle Analysis: Acute
I Ching Hexagram: 36, Darkening of the Light

Description:
KUN (2) in the LI (9) house produces one intensely focused on interacting with and exchanging with the surrounding environment. This manifests in trade, commerce, social interaction, and business. These individuals have the ability to enter any environment and (a) fit in and (b) bring social

harmony. They have a chameleon-like ability to blend in, but can also direct and change the mood of the interaction through witty words and actions. KUN's goal is to achieve this social harmony not for harmony's sake but for the achievement of specific objective. It should be noted that these individuals rarely have anything deep or substantial to offer in many cases, unless the conversation is around one of their core principles. This is your typical salesmen.

Virtuous Trait:
The Monk is your master of interaction with people and the environment. They can in essence make friends with all people and in any situation. They are trusted and liked by all and have success in arenas where social interaction is a requirement. These people are your master sales persons, and in some cases, your magicians. They also tend to be excellent communicators: oral and written. Sales and marketing are possible career paths.

Divisive Trait:
The Monk interacts well with others, but tends to lean to heavily on this talent. As a result, the substance required to complete tasks, which often times is the purpose of the social interaction, is lacking. In addition, this talent must be used sparingly and with regard to the overall situation. Addressing serious problems using this talent will lead to greater problems down the road as the core issue is not addressed, but only the social mood of those involved.

Balancing Description:
The addition of a KUN (2) element to bring KUN's original intent and focus back to earth is required here. This will offset LI's exciting nature.

Chapter 17: KEN – The Lover

BaGua Configuration: 8

7	3	5
6	8	1
2	4	9

Summary:
The KEN (8) person, or Lover, primarily looks at the world through creating and cultivating close friendships and relationships. They can really see concepts, pictures, and images in their mind and can recall anything when challenged. These individuals have a tendency to let moral principles run their lives rather than using these principles to strengthen their character. This manifests as not being able to get past certain things that happen in the world that violate their moral tenants. They do have a deep understanding of the principles governing leadership. The KEN (8) person also has a good work ethic and will spend a lot of time seeing the end goal which helps them succeed in the end.

The KEN (8) person, or Lover, tends to be expansive in wanting to experience the world. This manifests as an extreme nature toward food, stimulants like drugs and alcohol, sex, travel, trying new things, etc. These individuals don't set the same boundaries for themselves as others would. In theory these individuals have good communication skills; although, their ability to communicate is obstructed by their longing to be close to others. Generally, they are good planners and organizers, but can get too deep into the theory of the plan itself; thus, causing some stagnation in this area.

There is difficulty here when these individuals try to focus and concentrate on a mental picture as the mind wanders on to other things. In times of disharmony they try to restore balance through communication. Leadership skills are lacking here.

Leadership and Resourcefulness

Base House: 1st House -- 1 (KAN): Conservationist
Natal Trait: 4 (SUN): Leader
Balancing Agent: 5: Peacekeeper
Angle Analysis: Obtuse
I Ching Hexagram: 59, Dispersion

Description:
SUN's talent is the ability to see, define, and mobilize the physical reality around it while KAN (1) has the ability to identify and carry out those conservative and self preserving activities that will strengthen it over time. Here we have a difference in direction and focus between these two trigrams. SUN (4) is a member of the *Earthly Square* arrangement while KAN (1) is a member of the *Heavenly Circle*. SUN (4) receives orders while KAN (1) sets direction and gives them. The angular analysis produces an obtuse angle with a net position difference of three places; thus, indicating these trigrams to be far apart in placement and function. This produces the potential for conflict but also the potential for harnessing of great energy and accomplishment.

SUN (4) in KAN (1) produces an ability to see into foundational tenants governing any point of analysis. Meaning not only can SUN (4) see and understand the physical reality around it, but it can also see and understand the structural components supporting physical reality. SUN (4) generally is not interested in interacting with the physical environment, but rather putting into place those resources that can effectively manage and define it. When mixed with KAN (1) it is focused on putting these resources together in such a way as to build foundational structures rather than superficial ones.

Virtuous Trait:
These individuals have great insight into the structural components of physical reality. In other words, they can easily see those supporting elements that provide the foundation for things in the world. An example is understanding and appreciating the framing, rough plumbing, and concrete foundations of a building rather than just the exterior siding or brick facing. These individuals would have greater insight and appreciation for these hidden details as opposed to those details more easily processed by the eye and five senses.

Ability to stay focused on one object and vet it thoroughly through reasoning and rationalization. Once they are able to lock in on an objective they can stay focused on it intently. It never leaves their state of consciousness. These are your financial analysts who track business performance through the use of metrics, ratios, and indicators. As soon as a company's financials violate these measures, it is immediately put into an "underperforming" category.

Divisive Trait:
Here we have a manifestation of an unusual and intense stubbornness. This manifests as an intense focus on rationalizing the object of focus to the point of losing the view of the whole. These individuals can easily get caught up in details beyond their relativity to the goal. The issue is once they enter this realm, it is very difficult to bring them out. These are you dictators in the world stuck on a particular belief/concept at the expense of the nation and its people. Their downfall usually comes by force.

Balancing Description:
B5 will provide a view from a balanced life perspective and will greatly aid these individuals. Another help here is a general detachment from any particular tendency.

Peacekeeping

Base House: 2nd House -- 2 (KUN): Negotiator
Natal Trait: 5: Peacekeeper
Balancing Agent: 7 (TUI): Monk
Angle Analysis: Radial Line
I Ching Hexagram: Not Applicable

Description:

B5 in the KUN (2) house produces one whose tendency is
focused on balance through the external trading of resources
communication, and the building of superficial relationships.
While B5 attempts to balance the primary eight energies of the
universe KUN (2) pulls its influence into the arena of external
interaction and resource reallocation. From this perspective B5
views its way to unify with the world through KUN's natal
tendency.

Virtuous Trait:

When there is a situation to solve regarding a KUN (2) tendency
or skill (communication and relationship building) these
individuals are able to rise to the occasion. They mostly bring
forth this energy to balance and maintain a larger environment or
a particular time in their life. The key here is that KUN (2) is not
the natal skill of these individuals, but they can call it forth to
restore harmony in the world.

Divisive Trait:

Here the person's general view and centeredness revolves around
KUN (2). This issue here of course is that only one ninth of
life's scenarios call for KUN's tendency to solve.

Balancing Description:

TUI's knowledge, wisdom, and insight enable B5 to understand
how to integrate the additional KUN (2) tendencies into the
whole.

Mental Acuity

Base House: 3rd House -- 3 (CHEN): Visionary
Natal Trait: 6 (CHIEN): Devotee
Balancing Agent: 9 (LI): Soldier
Angle Analysis: Obtuse
I Ching Hexagram: 25, Innocence

Description:
CHIEN (6) is the ability to create and see visually one's goal. These individuals go within to address their problems and achieve their goals in life. CHEN (3) is the tendency to experience its creative powers in the world through experience and bringing forth ideas. CHIEN (6) in a CHEN (3) environment causes CHEN (3) to have a more outward focus, thus loosing its mental vision; as a result, CHIEN's devotion waivers from its goal. CHEN's vision is partly physical and partly subtle physical; whereas, CHIEN's vision is purely subtle physical. CHIEN's level of awareness can only be achieved with intense focus just like its compliment SUN (4). Neither of these trigrams can achieve success with distraction. From this standpoint CHEN (3) is the definition of distraction whose functioning appears to be that of a curious child. That is why LI's fire is required to restore balance and harmony to this situation.

Virtuous Trait:
The Lover has the ability to generate a number of ideas to further a goal or purpose. However, their ability to hold on to a particular idea for the purpose of furthering it is limited. In addition, they don't have the ability to see all the details associated with the idea they have presented. The CHIEN-CHEN person has the ability to see the details of ideas generated and hold that idea in their mental sphere long enough to transfer it to others. This is important as many people have the ability to generate an idea of some sort, but often times cannot hold onto the details long enough to make use of it. This is the equivalent

of having an insightful dream, but forgetting it upon waking.

Divisive Trait:
These individuals will find it very hard to maintain their inward focus and concentration. The outward expansiveness of CHEN (3) will pull these persons from a mental focus to outward physical exploration. These persons find it very hard to concentrate and would rather go out and do things or even dream of new ideas.

Balancing Description:
LI's fire is required to return's CHIEN's focus inward with the amount of intensity required to escape the physical constraints of the world through mental focus. LI (9) will offset the dreaminess of CHEN (3).

Intuitive Abilities

Base House: 4th House -- 4 (SUN): Leader
Natal Trait: 7 (TUI): Monk
Balancing Agent: 2 (KUN): Negotiator
Angle Analysis: Obtuse
I Ching Hexagram: 28, Preponderance of the Great

Description:
TUI (7) in the SUN (4) house will cause one focused on evaluation of past performance and understanding the laws governing future success to gravitate toward control of the physical resources in the surrounding environment. TUI (7) here is concerned with the underlying principles governing a project or situation while SUN (4) is focused on seeing, managing, tracking, and placing these resources. A conflict is here in that TUI's focus is inward and SUN's focus is outward.

Virtuous Trait:
The TUI-SUN personality is able to gain insights into the things

of the world for the purpose of better managing and defining them. These individuals are in essence able to provide leadership with the best techniques, tools, and strategies for doing their job.

Divisive Trait:
These individuals in their attempt to find the laws governing a particular situation will instead find themselves determining the best use of these laws during the intuitive process. They will grab onto and grasp the first insights that come to them and try to make sense of them instantly. This interrupts the process of thinking deeply. Genuine TUI (7) tendency involves understanding and discovering life's principles, not applying them.

During the meditation process these individuals will also attach themselves to particular thoughts and images that enter their sphere of awareness. Thus, they switch from a receptive and inquisitive state to a controlling state.

Balancing Description:
KUN's outward focus with the multitudes will help harmonize TUI (7) and SUN's interaction.

Relationship Building

Base House: 5th House -- 5: Peacekeeper
Natal Trait: 8 (KEN): Lover
Balancing Agent: 4 (SUN): Leader
Angle Analysis: Radial Line
I Ching Hexagram: Not Applicable

Description:
KEN (8) in the B5 house produces an effect of a worldly perspective based upon interacting harmoniously and intimately with others. This person's perspectives and view points will be centered in everyone having close relationships. These are your

199

flower children types who believe that we should all just be friends.

Virtuous Trait:
These individuals are able to bring harmony to their lives and certain situations through the use of intimate and close relationships between all the parties involved. In this scenario, KEN's socialness is used as a unifying agent. Where the Negotiator is able to bring everyone to the table and work together for the sake of the goal, the Lover is able to get everyone to truly care for one another and stay together regardless of the circumstances. This is a rare and valuable talent that is the ultimate goal of "conflict resolution".

Divisive Trait:
The Lover will always attempt to bring about unity and harmony through the forming of intimate relationships with others. KEN (8) being one of the nine available character traits will give it a low percentage of success, relative to the multitude of life's challenges, in its attempts to harmonize its life and the general environment.

Balancing Description:
SUN's reasoning and direction are required to direct KEN (8) where it needs to go in these situations.

Work Ethic

Base House: 6ᵗʰ House -- 6 (CHIEN): Devotee
Natal Trait: 9 (LI): Soldier
Balancing Agent: 6 (CHIEN): Devotee
Angle Analysis: Obtuse
I Ching Hexagram: 14, Possession in Great Measure

Description:
LI (9) in the CHIEN (6) house produces a strong tendency to go within in situations where passion and/or stress are involved.

The fire of LI (9) ignites one's mental visual ability. Entire scenarios and pictures can be seen in the mind's eye with ease and clarity. The prerequisite is this person must have a genuine interest in the person or subject in order to manifest these qualities.

Virtuous Trait:
The Lover is a master seer of un-manifested reality when they chose to do that. These individuals can hold in their minds a complete picture with sounds, colors, and intricate details as if the thing was right in front of them (i.e. the photographic memory). The only trigram combination that can perform this talent better is CHIEN (6) in the LI (9) house (the Negotiator). The key here though, again as with all LI (9) in the natal house positions, is that these persons must have the genuine interest and passion for the subject to do this. Thus, this talent tends to manifest when these individuals are involved in a conflict of sorts. It allows them to see the end of the conflict in their minds and everyone working harmoniously.

This talent goes beyond just being able to see a picture in one's mind. It also involves seeing and adding in parts of that picture that could not normally be seen even if the image was manifest in front of them. The adding in of additional pieces connects the dots of what is being communicated and gives these individuals a complete understanding of the subject. When these individuals are allowed to process their reality in this way they are labeled as geniuses in their field of study or expertise. This is because they have worked out all of the inconsistencies in their minds and now have ownership of the subject. This can be seen in some children who are consistently "spacey" and often "not present" in class or a conversation. That's correct; they are not here, they are in their minds looking at a complete picture and experiencing a complete reality in even more detail than those who are "paying attention." This is the best way to own information or a lesson; to see all aspects of it in your mind. Now it is a part of you and will not be forgotten.

There is one key difference here from the Negotiator and that is the Lover manifests these talents when they are intently focused on something. You can see this in these children when they are coloring or doing artwork. There projects seem to be so much more colorful and complete compared to the other children. They have really become 'one' with their work.

This is the key to learning and gives us great insight into how our brains process information and thus how our educators should teach. The idea is not to continuously feed our children information, but to give them enough to create a picture in their minds. A picture is worth a thousand words. Once this picture has been created the teacher can move on with the next part of the lesson and the process repeated accordingly. As all students will not be LI-CHIEN people classes should be divided based upon how each child processes information rather than random groupings.

Divisive Trait:
The LI-CHIEN person tends to internalize and create these mental pictures in many of their daily activities. This primarily manifests for subjects they are passionate about or have a great concern with. And yes this does manifest as "a spacing out" of that person. Obviously, these individuals tend not to be present in situations where they need to be, like driving a car, working with dangerous machinery, or on guard as a security worker. There are just many activities in life where you need to be present and focused on what is physically in front of you in order to have success. Nothing else needs to be said here.

From another perspective, these individuals when confronted with serious challenges have the tendency to retreat inward and visualize resolution to the conflict or challenge. This has its place, but often times manifests and is viewed as escapism by other parties involved.

Balancing Description:
What is required for balance is an additional CHIEN (6) element to bring LI (9) full circle and restore its path. These individuals will be too extreme with their inward focus and must be brought

back to earth so to speak. The additional CHIEN (6) trigram will not eliminate LI-CHIEN's talent, but simply put into a right perspective relative to the whole picture.

Planning and Organizing Abilities

Base House: 7th House -- 7 (TUI): Monk
Natal Trait: 1 (KAN): Conservationist
Balancing Agent: 8 (KEN): Lover
Angle Analysis: Right
I Ching Hexagram: 60, Limitation

Description:
KAN (1) in the TUI (7) house produces a conflict in KAN's focus on building the internal foundations that will be needed to deal with the upcoming work in the spring and summer. TUI's energy will cause KAN (1) to look inward and search for answers and truth rather than taking what it already knows in preparing for the future. KAN (1) is the first stage of self preparation, where TUI (7) is focused on understanding what needs to take place in the future. Both these trigrams belong to the *Heavenly Circle* and are responsible for initiating commands to be followed by others. From that standpoint there is a conflict as well.

Virtuous Trait:
The KAN-TUI individual is willing to make plans based upon sound morale, spiritual, and principled tenants. These individuals are often your morale or religious persons who are interested in building a "kingdom of god" on earth. From a more general sense these persons are able to plan more effectively than others because they have a deep insight into the underlying principles governing the project in question.

Divisive Trait:
These individuals are your conservative religious types. They refuse to move or make progress without alignment to their spiritual philosophies. Again, this is not a bad thing in itself, but

the context of everything we do must be kept in the forefront. An extreme example, just to drive the point home, is not going to a funeral because the religion of the deceased was different than your own or not pursuing any material goals in life because money is bad/corrupt and so forth. The point of going to a funeral is to support those living who may need the support and on another level to honor the deceased if one chooses that as the method to honor them. Money is not at the root of corruption, but rather peoples own weaknesses that are exposed with issues surrounding money. Living in the modern world we need money and material resources to survive, so these "morale" attachments just can't be applied with the same zealousness in all situations.

Balancing Description:
KEN (8) provides just enough movement to pull KAN (1) back onto its normal path. This will allow the TUI (7) and KAN (1) trigrams to work cooperatively without affecting each others core nature.

Social Skills

Base House: 8th House -- 8 (KEN): Lover
Natal Trait: 2 (KUN): Negotiator
Balancing Agent: 1 (KAN): Conservationist
Angle Analysis: Axis
I Ching Hexagram: 15, Modesty

Description:
KUN (2) in the KEN (8) house consists of the southwest-northeastern axis in the BaGua. These trigrams are closest to the earth plane and physical manifestation and therefore have the greatest "direct" impact to material manifestation than any other there other trigrams. This is seen in the Net Position Difference analysis done in the chapter "Natal House Configurations". These energies are complements and dynamically opposed. KUN (2) wishes to interact with the world through trade, commerce, and communication while KEN (8) wishes to have intimate relations. KUN (2) in the KEN (8) house produces one

who wishes to trade only in close circles. With KEN (8), the expansiveness due to KUN's inherited heat from LI (9), is cooled by KEN's coldness as inherited by KAN (1). So although a tendency to trade and interact with the world is there, the coolness of KEN (8) prevents very much movement.

Virtuous Trait:
The KUN-KEN personality has the potential to cultivate the most powerful relationships possible. KUN's talent of creating social harmony and KEN's talent of creating close relationships with those of like mind and similar goals can make for a powerful combination. Additionally, as both these trigrams are part of the *Earthly Square* they take their commands from others, so both are receptive to direction. Here is where the greatest of social harmonies can be achieved.

Divisive Trait:
The KUN-KEN trigram combination produces one of the four axes in the BaGua. As a result the potential for both conflict and success is great. In addition, KUN (2) and KEN (8) are the closest to the earthly realm, both being members of the *Earthly Square* arrangement and aligned to matter. As a result, these individuals will have a tendency toward materialism and their lower animalistic natures in general. This is why KAN (1), Conservatism, is the balancing agent who is saying always be ready to put on the brakes.

Balancing Description:
KAN (1) is the balancing agent for the KUN-KEN personality type. Both KUN (2) and KEN (8) have an external focus (KEN (8) is apparently external, but not really) so the internal focus of KAN (1) will help balance these elements. If these individuals take time to look at themselves it will break them from the enchantment of connecting and bonding with others.

Creativity and Zest for Life

Base House: 9th House -- 9 (LI): Soldier
Natal Trait: 3 (CHEN): Visionary
Balancing Agent: 3 (CHEN): Visionary
Angle Analysis: Right
I Ching Hexagram: 55, Abundance

Description:
CHEN (3) in the LI (9) house produces one with the ability to see both the subtle and overt physical realities of the world. As LI's influence on other trigrams is to intensify their natural tendencies, CHEN's ability to see un-manifested reality is greatly enhanced. In addition, the ideas that CHEN (3) generates will come much faster (not necessarily deeper). So in essence this personality type will be able to generate a multitude of ideas that could be used to achieve one's goal.

Virtuous Trait:
The CHEN-LI person can see and identify things in the formative stages. For this, they are often labeled as great inventors. This is because other charts cannot see the same reality and thus think this idea came from no where. But that could be farther from the truth as these ideas and visions are simply what were initiated in the TUI (7) and CHIEN (6) stages of creation. CHEN (3) people are the first ones to be able to see its subtle manifestation on the physical plane. Their ideas are more readily accepted than that of the CHIEN (6) person because by the time the CHEN (3) person sees it there are traces of physical manifestation. When the CHIEN (6) person is visualizing the complete picture it may lack any physical construct or support mechanism. Not only that, but because the CHEN-LI person is rooted in both the physical and metaphysical realms they can better communicate this reality to others, especially to the SUN (4) person who needs it the most.

These persons can also see a bit deeper into physical and mental things than the average person. This manifests as someone being able to read the aura of another person. This goes beyond the five primary senses and gives them extra ability or intensity.

Divisive Trait:

The CHEN-LI person is one who stretches physical reality beyond its physical supports. These individuals want to implement ideas that most individuals cannot comprehend and thus cannot support. As a result, when they try to implement these ideas they often fail; especially, when the correct individuals are not there to carry them out.

Balancing Description:

The balancing factor here is an additional CHEN (3) trigram to help balance and anchor it considering the influence of LI (9). As CHEN's expansiveness can go way beyond its bounds; which includes the manifestation of ideas and goals beyond reach, an additional CHEN (3) element is required to bring its energy back into focus.

Chapter 18: LI – The Soldier

BaGua Configuration: 9

8	4	6
7	9	2
3	5	1

Summary:
The LI (9) person, or Soldier, is generally your "go-getter" type and is up for most challenges when required. These individuals have a strong ability to plan and organize things in their mind. Their demeanor is one of being ready for action. They have a good ability to enter into close relationships with others, but have a tendency to be a bit controlling and overbearing.

The LI (9) person, or Soldier, has strong leadership and reasoning capabilities. They are very expansive when it comes to socializing, forming relationships, entertainment, and sex. Good communication skills with a tendency to preach.

They lack the ability to see the deeper underlying meaning of the world around them although they have moments when they are overly expansive when thinking intuitively. Their memories are generally poor as they are hampered when attempting to hold mental images in their mind. These persons attempt to bring balance to situations in their lives by retreating within themselves and being generally conservative. They are also slow to address the unbalanced aspects of their lives.

Unifying & Balancing Abilities

Base House: 1st House -- 1 (KAN): Conservationist
Natal Trait: 5: Peacekeeper
Balancing Agent: 6 (CHIEN): Devotee
Angle Analysis: Radial Line
I Ching Hexagram: Not Applicable

Description:
B5 in KAN (1) produces unification around fundamental and foundational precepts. The B5 individual tends to address life by taking on the character trait(s) missing in any given situation. That is why these individuals are often viewed as a bit unstable because of the constant character transformations. Over time this takes its toll on the person and they question their place in the world. But the B5 personality needs to understand that this is their role in society. As a matter of fact advanced cultures often use the B5 person (usually in a priesthood group) to assess the health of a community or nation. Because of their sensitivity to their environment it will become apparent through their health, visions, and dreams what needs to be addressed to bring harmony back to the community.

When combined with KAN (1) this person is a bit slower to fill these voids and tends to do so in a conservative manner.

Virtuous Trait:
Although slow to bring forth the required unifying talent in a given situation once this talent comes forth (could be any of the eight) it comes through strong and pure. This is because of the methodical nature in which these individuals go through to bring forth these talents.

In addition, these individuals have a real ability to view and feel for the world, their environment, and family's needs. They tend to find their peace and centeredness in making sure the world is properly structured in all areas (politics, environment, social, etc.).

Divisive Trait:
These individuals will be slow to bring forth the necessary talents in their lives to unify their lives and environments. Under normal circumstances the B5 person naturally generates the missing talent required to achieve the goal. This process is much slower when B5 mixes with a KAN (1) consciousness. Their first tendency will be to withdrawal from the challenges presented by life or deal with them in a conservative nature.

From another perspective these individuals are overly centered in the world, environment, and family unity.

Balancing Description:
CHIEN's intense focus on the goal through its mental vision will bring the B5 consciousness back outward to the original goal or intent. KAN (1) tends to focus on the self; whereas, CHIEN (6) tends to focus on the goal.

The power of prayer and meditation will greatly aid these individuals. Their caring for the world in and of itself is not sufficient to bring about the world changes they so passionately want.

Mental Acuity

Base House: 2nd House -- 2 (KUN): Negotiator
Natal Trait: 6 (CHIEN): Devotee
Balancing Agent: 8 (KEN): Lover
Angle Analysis: Right
I Ching Hexagram: 12, Stagnation

Description:
CHIEN (6) in the KUN (2) house produces one who is attempting to focus inward but pulled outward. CHIEN's focus is internal while KUN's focus is external, but both trigrams are active in completing their assigned tasks. CHIEN (6) receives its orders from TUI (7) while KUN (2) receives its orders from LI (9). From that standpoint both personalities are in an obedient

210

position; thus, only their directions of movement must be balanced. This is where KEN's effect of working intimately with others brings CHIEN (6) and KUN (2) into harmony.

CHIEN (6) and KUN (2) are both members of the *Earthly Square* and form a right angle relationships based upon their positioning in the BaGua. Their nature is to follow and take orders from a heavenly influence. From this aspect there is a similarity. The difference is in their focus areas: KUN (2) external and worldly and CHIEN (6) internal and reserved. So the position (one of obedience) and "energetics" are the same, but their direction is different (outward v. inward).

Virtuous Trait:
This person will be able to influence the outcome of relationships through thought. They can see how relationships need to be formed, the people involved, and the final outcome all in their minds eye. This gives them a significant advantage in this area as they can almost read the future so to speak.

Divisive Trait:
Here one is called to deal with the outside world and form superficial relationships, but CHIEN (6) refuses to deal with the outside world; thus, we have conflict. This person will have a tendency to space out and live inside their head when attempting to deal with others and conduct business.

Balancing Description:
KEN (8) is the balancing agent. Also part of the *Earthly Square* KEN (8) will pull CHIEN (6) to the outside world just enough to balance out its relationship with KUN (2).

Intuitive Abilities

Base House: 3rd House -- 3 (CHEN): Visionary
Natal Trait: 7 (TUI): Monk
Balancing Agent: 1 (KAN): Conservationist

Angle Analysis: Axis
I Ching Hexagram: 17, Following

Description:
Here we have one of our eight axis relationships formed with the coming together of TUI (7) and CHEN (3). As with any of the axis' there is great potential for both success and failure as the centripetal force created is at its peak. To further state the case CHEN (3) and TUI (7) are members of the *Heavenly Circle* and are closest to the originating elements of creation.

In this case the TUI (7) is outwardly influenced by CHEN (3) and this is incorrect. TUI (7) is responsible for setting the pace for all things in creation and should be thus giving the orders and insights to the other trigrams.

Virtuous Trait:
These individuals will have a deep penetrating insight into both the physical and subtle physical world. This insight will increase the potency of TUI's intuitive abilities and allow them to deeply understand the laws governing un-manifested reality.

Divisive Trait:
These individuals should not make decisions too hastily. The insight TUI (7) is attempting to achieve will be influenced by CHEN's current incomplete view of the physical and subtle physical reality around it. From this perspective TUI (7) must remember its purpose and not get distracted by the physical world. TUI (7) must also be able to go internal without effort, but this too will be adversely influenced by CHEN (3).

Balancing Description:
KAN's conservative nature is required to balance CHEN's expansive tendency.

Relationship Building

Base House: 4th House -- 4 (SUN): Leader
Natal Trait: 8 (KEN): Lover
Balancing Agent: 3 (CHEN): Visionary
Angle Analysis: Right
I Ching Hexagram: 18, Decay

Description:
KEN (8) and SUN (4) are both a part of the *Earthly Square* configuration and are in obedience to other trigrams. These individuals take orders, or complete their assigned work, from KAN (1) and CHEN (3) respectively. There job is again direct interaction with the things of the world. Thus, the tendency towards the physical environment is the commonality between KEN (8) and SUN (4), but the difference is in the purpose of that interaction. KEN's goal is to create close intimate alliances to ultimately strengthen itself, while SUN's goal is to identify how these resources can come together to produce a given outcome/product.

Virtuous Trait:
The KEN-SUN personality will have the ability to see the qualities of relationships and understand what each of the persons involved is all about. This will allow them to chose wisely who they interact with and advise others in the same way.

Divisive Trait:
The KEN-SUN person will have the tendency to over rationalize when attempting to form close relationships with others. SUN's inspective nature will prevent the natural flow of KEN (8) when it comes to forming intimate relationships with others. As KEN (8) attempts to form these partnerships it will find itself defining and managing those relationships which ultimately stagnates the flow of people coming together.

This is actually a common issue in relationships where one

partner attempts to manage the other one for their own personal comfort rather than for the success of the relationship itself. KEN's ability to form these close unions is based on its ability not to judge and not to rationalize the traits of the people it is dealing with, but to determine how everyone can fit under the same mountain top.

Balancing Description:
CHEN's ability to project physical reality based only upon its embryonic form and potential allows KEN (8) and SUN (4) to see deeply enough into one another's relationship and role to work harmoniously.

Work Ethic

Base House: 5th House -- 5: Peacekeeper
Natal Trait: 9 (LI): Soldier
Balancing Agent: 5: Peacekeeper
Angle Analysis: Radial Line
I Ching Hexagram: Not Applicable

Description:
LI (9) in the B5 house produces an individual focused on oneness, uniting, and balance in their lives. The Soldier manifests a moral sense that wants all things to be successful rather than any one person or thing getting more than their share of the spoils. These personalities show themselves as someone who is conservative, but active, in nature who doesn't want to create too many ruffles by making chaotic movements.

Virtuous Trait:
Soldiers are morally centered and balanced in their approach and outlook to life. These are your master unifiers in the world who function out of a state of fairness and balance. These individuals have the ability to take on any one of the nine personality types in order to keep balance and harmony in a group or situation.

214

Note: There is a conflict here as the B5 in the KAN (1) house will hamper this unification ability for the soldier type. So yes, the talent is there, but great effort will be required to bring it forth.

Note: The only limitations here is the person's level of awareness which will determine which trigrams (talents) they have access to and how they view the situation (i.e. the situation itself needs to change versus the individuals need to change to fit the situation). These are important factors as our environmental influences have shaped our belief systems regarding our power as human beings; therefore, we tend to use only one or two talents available to us to solve all of our problems. Additionally, our conditioning prevents many of us from looking introspectively at ourselves as the possible problem which means we loose the opportunity to make the changes necessary.

Divisive Trait:
Soldier's tend to be zealous by nature and not concerned with maintaining balance in their personal lives or with their personal health when focused on a goal. This is an extreme posture to take when attempting to achieve anything in the world as we must take care of ourselves as we pursue life.

Balancing Description:
B5 is needed to bring LI's fire full circle and back on focus. B5 provides the universal view LI (9) needs.

Planning and Organizing Ability

Base House: 6th House -- 6 (CHIEN): Devotee
Natal Trait: 1 (KAN): Conservationist
Balancing Agent: 7 (TUI): Monk
Angle Analysis: Acute
I Ching Hexagram: 5, Waiting (Nourishment)

Description:
KAN (1) in the CHIEN (6) house produces a slightly limiting affect on KAN (1). KAN (1) is focused on self strengthening in preparation for the coming season where CHIEN (6) is focused on the planting of the creative seed, which goes beyond the initiating entity. Both tendencies however are focused inward, have slow movements, and cold temperaments; thus, they are closely related.

Virtuous Trait:
These individuals are able to plan very well based upon a communicated vision. As all planning starts with a vision or map of the goal this is a very valuable talent.

Divisive Trait:
KAN's focus is on one's own person and activities that conserve and build one's energy. CHIEN's focus is on the goal to be obtained via a mental image. Here when one sits down to plan, strategize, and map out one's activity there will be a tendency to focus on the vision and goal rather than the planning task itself. As KAN's focus is inward on the self, CHIEN's focus is inward and outward on the task to be achieved. This is the source of the conflict.

Balancing Description:
Only the cooling temperament of TUI (7) is required to establish balance.

Social Skills

Base House: 7th House -- 7 (TUI): Monk
Natal Trait: 2 (KUN): Negotiator
Balancing Agent: 9 (LI): Soldier
Angle Analysis: Acute
I Ching Hexagram: 19, Approach

Description:

KUN (2) in the TUI (7) house produces a slight directional conflict. KUN's nature is obedience to serve and distribute the fruits of LI's labor. Thus, its focus is on interacting via trade, communication, and commerce with others. It is not attempting to befriend or break bread with others, but exchange with them fairly. TUI (7) is focused on the physical landscape following KUN's work. Its focus is inward to gain insight on improving and creating processes to produce a more favorable outcome for the following cycle. Naturally, TUI (7) would be very focused on KUN (2), but in this case KUN (2) is stifled from looking outward due to TUI's inward tendency.

Virtuous Trait:

The KUN-TUI person will function in a moral and upright manner with others. As these individuals are often in business and sales they can be trusted with your investments. These are also the type of individuals who tend not to gossip, talk with forked tongue, and play hurtful pranks on others. For them there is a moral conflict in behaving this way.

Divisive Trait:

The KUN-TUI person will tend to allow deep spiritual and moral principles to govern the relationship between persons where not applicable. There is a time and place for all things and we should not try to force our belief system upon other people. In addition, we should have the freedom to mingle and interact with others without limiting the interaction with deep moral complexity. We are not saying to violate your morale principles in your interaction with others, but they should be put into context. Further more, the KUN (2) interaction is not an intimate close interaction with others, but rather an arms length interaction without the emotional attachments. This is further reason not to add too much complexity here.

Balancing Description:

Note: All balancing trigrams are the number of the chart

whenever an element is in the TUI (7) house, with the exception of B5. The energy of LI (9) is needed to break the crystallization of KUN (2) and TUI (7) because their tendencies would be to stay in awe of one another.

Creativity and Zest for Life

Base House: 8th House -- 8 (KEN): Lover
Natal Trait: 3 (CHEN): Visionary
Balancing Agent: 2 (KUN): Negotiator
Angle Analysis: Acute
I Ching Hexagram: 62, Preponderance of the Small

Description:
The CHEN-KEN personality type is one who is social, likes to work with others, likes to contribute to projects and people, and who has a number of ideas concerning how individuals can come together. CHEN (3) and KEN (8) are closely related in that their focus is both outside of themselves. The only difference here is the intensity and range of their expansiveness. From this standpoint there is not a major conflict. As CHEN (3) is the natal here, its expansiveness will be slightly compromised and forced more into bonding types of arenas. These individuals are the playwrights, script writers, authors, etc. in the entertainment field.

CHEN (3) in the KEN (8) house produces one who can see deeply into relationships and focuses on how individuals can be together. Due to KEN's selectiveness any social groups or memberships are on a smaller scale as opposed to larger gatherings.

Virtuous Trait:
These individuals can make great contributions to social programs in society. They are often on the idea side of the entertainment industry and are the ones suggesting ideas of what people can do socially to improve their relationships. They also

218

have the ability to see the deeper meaning of art and how it communicates to the psyche of people. The can generate ideas of how art and entertainment can accomplish this end.

Divisive Trait:
The CHEN-KEN personality may have a tendency to expand too much into social arenas. This expansiveness may show as excessive partying, entertainment seeking, etc. which will distract from more serious concerns or objectives at hand.

Balancing Description:
KUN's outward focus and dispassion for a deep connection with others will help balance the relationship between CHEN (3) and KEN (8).

Leadership and Resourcefulness

Base House: 9th House -- 9 (LI): Soldier
Natal Trait: 4 (SUN): Leader
Balancing Agent: 4 (SUN): Leader
Angle Analysis: Acute
I Ching Hexagram: 37, The Family

Description:
SUN (4) in the LI (9) house produces an intense focus on reasoning and rationalization as one attempts to define the reality around them. As LI's influence on other trigrams is to intensify their natural tendencies these person's ability to see how physical reality fits together to create the complete picture is greatly increased. This sight not only includes the pieces required for assembly, but the supporting resources and elements that are required to complete it. SUN's talent is a deep penetrating insight into the function of manifested things in the world. Along with this talent is the ability to see all things in the world and understand their functions.

Virtuous Trait:

The SUN-LI person has the talent to understand, define, and ultimately manipulate all of manifested reality. These individuals are your master leaders and managers. Their ability to see and understand everything around them allows them to address issues quickly and effectively. This is so because they know which people or resources to use to solve the situation. Essentially, they are masters of the five primary senses (look, feel, hear, taste, and touch); thus, allowing them to classify and understand reality. That is why they are labeled good rational thinkers.

Divisive Trait:
SUN-LI persons are often labeled as dictatorial and as micromanagers in their particular fields. They can be too focused on physical reality, its management, and positioning. It is quite easy for the SUN-LI personality type to forget that their talent is not knowledge and thus limited to what is physically available. Other talents such as intuition, planning, trade, and relationship building are not necessarily natal talents that they possess. This leaves a large void when we view overall success because they are so dependent on the work of others.

It should be noted again, that in the creative process SUN (4) is the sixth overall stage; thus putting it near the end. It is not until TUI (7), CHIEN (6), KAN (1), KEN (8), and CHEN (3) have completed their responsibilities that SUN (4) can then have something to work with to be successful.

Balancing Description:
An additional SUN (4) element will refocus LI's influence back on the purpose of SUN's natal tendency in the larger picture of reality.

Appendices

Yearly Cycle Chart

Year	Female BaGua	Female Trigram	Male BaGua	Male Trigram
1900	5	N/A	1	KAN
1901	6	CHIEN	9	LI
1902	7	TUI	8	KEN
1903	8	KEN	7	TUI
1904	9	LI	6	CHIEN
1905	1	KAN	5	N/A
1906	2	KUN	4	SUN
1907	3	CHEN	3	CHEN
1908	4	SUN	2	KUN
1909	5	N/A	1	KAN
1910	6	CHIEN	9	LI
1911	7	TUI	8	KEN
1912	8	KEN	7	TUI
1913	9	LI	6	CHIEN
1914	1	KAN	5	N/A
1915	2	KUN	4	SUN
1916	3	CHEN	3	CHEN
1917	4	SUN	2	KUN
1918	5	N/A	1	KAN
1919	6	CHIEN	9	LI
1920	7	TUI	8	KEN
1921	8	KEN	7	TUI
1922	9	LI	6	CHIEN
1923	1	KAN	5	N/A
1924	2	KUN	4	SUN
1925	3	CHEN	3	CHEN
1926	4	SUN	2	KUN
1927	5	N/A	1	KAN
1928	6	CHIEN	9	LI
1929	7	TUI	8	KEN

Year	Female BaGua	Female Trigram	Male BaGua	Male Trigram
1930	8	KEN	7	TUI
1931	9	LI	6	CHIEN
1932	1	KAN	5	N/A
1933	2	KUN	4	SUN
1934	3	CHEN	3	CHEN
1935	4	SUN	2	KUN
1936	5	N/A	1	KAN
1937	6	CHIEN	9	LI
1938	7	TUI	8	KEN
1939	8	KEN	7	TUI
1940	9	LI	6	CHIEN
1941	1	KAN	5	N/A
1942	2	KUN	4	SUN
1943	3	CHEN	3	CHEN
1944	4	SUN	2	KUN
1945	5	N/A	1	KAN
1946	6	CHIEN	9	LI
1947	7	TUI	8	KEN
1948	8	KEN	7	TUI
1949	9	LI	6	CHIEN
1950	1	KAN	5	N/A
1951	2	KUN	4	SUN
1952	3	CHEN	3	CHEN
1953	4	SUN	2	KUN
1954	5	N/A	1	KAN
1955	6	CHIEN	9	LI
1956	7	TUI	8	KEN
1957	8	KEN	7	TUI
1958	9	LI	6	CHIEN
1959	1	KAN	5	N/A
1960	2	KUN	4	SUN
1961	3	CHEN	3	CHEN
1962	4	SUN	2	KUN
1963	5	N/A	1	KAN
1964	6	CHIEN	9	LI

Year	Female BaGua	Female Trigram	Male BaGua	Male Trigram
1965	7	TUI	8	KEN
1966	8	KEN	7	TUI
1967	9	LI	6	CHIEN
1968	1	KAN	5	N/A
1969	2	KUN	4	SUN
1970	3	CHEN	3	CHEN
1971	4	SUN	2	KUN
1972	5	N/A	1	KAN
1973	6	CHIEN	9	LI
1974	7	TUI	8	KEN
1975	8	KEN	7	TUI
1976	9	LI	6	CHIEN
1977	1	KAN	5	N/A
1978	2	KUN	4	SUN
1979	3	CHEN	3	CHEN
1980	4	SUN	2	KUN
1981	5	N/A	1	KAN
1982	6	CHIEN	9	LI
1983	7	TUI	8	KEN
1984	8	KEN	7	TUI
1985	9	LI	6	CHIEN
1986	1	KAN	5	N/A
1987	2	KUN	4	SUN
1988	3	CHEN	3	CHEN
1989	4	SUN	2	KUN
1990	5	N/A	1	KAN
1991	6	CHIEN	9	LI
1992	7	TUI	8	KEN
1993	8	KEN	7	TUI
1994	9	LI	6	CHIEN
1995	1	KAN	5	N/A
1996	2	KUN	4	SUN
1997	3	CHEN	3	CHEN
1998	4	SUN	2	KUN
1999	5	N/A	1	KAN

Year	Female BaGua	Female Trigram	Male BaGua	Male Trigram
2000	6	CHIEN	9	LI
2001	7	TUI	8	KEN
2002	8	KEN	7	TUI
2003	9	LI	6	CHIEN
2004	1	KAN	5	N/A
2005	2	KUN	4	SUN
2006	3	CHEN	3	CHEN
2007	4	SUN	2	KUN
2008	5	N/A	1	KAN
2009	6	CHIEN	9	LI
2010	7	TUI	8	KEN
2011	8	KEN	7	TUI
2012	9	LI	6	CHIEN
2013	1	KAN	5	N/A
2014	2	KUN	4	SUN
2015	3	CHEN	3	CHEN
2016	4	SUN	2	KUN
2017	5	N/A	1	KAN
2018	6	CHIEN	9	LI
2019	7	TUI	8	KEN
2020	8	KEN	7	TUI
2021	9	LI	6	CHIEN
2022	1	KAN	5	N/A
2023	2	KUN	4	SUN
2024	3	CHEN	3	CHEN
2025	4	SUN	2	KUN
2026	5	N/A	1	KAN
2027	6	CHIEN	9	LI
2028	7	TUI	8	KEN
2029	8	KEN	7	TUI
2030	9	LI	6	CHIEN
2031	1	KAN	5	N/A
2032	2	KUN	4	SUN
2033	3	CHEN	3	CHEN
2034	4	SUN	2	KUN

Year	Female BaGua	Female Trigram	Male BaGua	Male Trigram
2035	5	N/A	1	KAN
2036	6	CHIEN	9	LI
2037	7	TUI	8	KEN
2038	8	KEN	7	TUI
2039	9	LI	6	CHIEN
2040	1	KAN	5	N/A
2041	2	KUN	4	SUN
2042	3	CHEN	3	CHEN
2043	4	SUN	2	KUN
2044	5	N/A	1	KAN
2045	6	CHIEN	9	LI
2046	7	TUI	8	KEN
2047	8	KEN	7	TUI
2048	9	LI	6	CHIEN
2049	1	KAN	5	N/A
2050	2	KUN	4	SUN
2051	3	CHEN	3	CHEN
2052	4	SUN	2	KUN
2053	5	N/A	1	KAN
2054	6	CHIEN	9	LI
2055	7	TUI	8	KEN
2056	8	KEN	7	TUI
2057	9	LI	6	CHIEN
2058	1	KAN	5	N/A
2059	2	KUN	4	SUN
2060	3	CHEN	3	CHEN
2061	4	SUN	2	KUN
2062	5	N/A	1	KAN
2063	6	CHIEN	9	LI
2064	7	TUI	8	KEN
2065	8	KEN	7	TUI
2066	9	LI	6	CHIEN
2067	1	KAN	5	N/A
2068	2	KUN	4	SUN
2069	3	CHEN	3	CHEN

Year	Female BaGua	Female Trigram	Male BaGua	Male Trigram
2070	4	SUN	2	KUN
2071	5	N/A	1	KAN
2072	6	CHIEN	9	LI
2073	7	TUI	8	KEN
2074	8	KEN	7	TUI
2075	9	LI	6	CHIEN
2076	1	KAN	5	N/A
2077	2	KUN	4	SUN
2078	3	CHEN	3	CHEN
2079	4	SUN	2	KUN
2080	5	N/A	1	KAN
2081	6	CHIEN	9	LI
2082	7	TUI	8	KEN
2083	8	KEN	7	TUI
2084	9	LI	6	CHIEN
2085	1	KAN	5	N/A
2086	2	KUN	4	SUN
2087	3	CHEN	3	CHEN
2088	4	SUN	2	KUN
2089	5	N/A	1	KAN
2090	6	CHIEN	9	LI
2091	7	TUI	8	KEN
2092	8	KEN	7	TUI
2093	9	LI	6	CHIEN
2094	1	KAN	5	N/A
2095	2	KUN	4	SUN
2096	3	CHEN	3	CHEN
2097	4	SUN	2	KUN

Monthly Cycle Chart

NOTE: Start with the 'Month Name' column as the starting point for determining the correct month. Then review the 'Adjusted Monthly Number' and 'Year' columns. Remember the year begins on February 5th (not January 1st), thus month '1' is February and month '12' is January. This is denoted in the 'Adjusted Month Number'.

Year	Yearly Male	Yearly Female	Adjusted Monthly Number	Month Name	Male Monthly Number	Female Monthly Number
1910	9	6	1	Feb	6	9
1910	9	6	2	Mar	5	1
1910	9	6	3	Apr	4	2
1910	9	6	4	May	3	3
1910	9	6	5	Jun	2	4
1910	9	6	6	Jul	1	5
1910	9	6	7	Aug	9	6
1910	9	6	8	Sep	8	7
1910	9	6	9	Oct	7	8
1910	9	6	10	Nov	6	9
1910	9	6	11	Dec	5	1
1910	9	6	12	Jan	4	2
1911	8	7	1	Feb	3	3
1911	8	7	2	Mar	2	4
1911	8	7	3	Apr	1	5
1911	8	7	4	May	9	6
1911	8	7	5	Jun	8	7
1911	8	7	6	Jul	7	8
1911	8	7	7	Aug	6	9
1911	8	7	8	Sep	5	1
1911	8	7	9	Oct	4	2
1911	8	7	10	Nov	3	3
1911	8	7	11	Dec	2	4
1911	8	7	12	Jan	1	5
1912	7	8	1	Feb	9	6
1912	7	8	2	Mar	8	7
1912	7	8	3	Apr	7	8
1912	7	8	4	May	6	9
1912	7	8	5	Jun	5	1
1912	7	8	6	Jul	4	2
1912	7	8	7	Aug	3	3
1912	7	8	8	Sep	2	4
1912	7	8	9	Oct	1	5

Year	Yearly Male	Yearly Female	Adjusted Monthly Number	Month Name	Male Monthly Number	Female Monthly Number
1912	7	8	10	Nov	9	6
1912	7	8	11	Dec	8	7
1912	7	8	12	Jan	7	8
1913	6	9	1	Feb	6	9
1913	6	9	2	Mar	5	1
1913	6	9	3	Apr	4	2
1913	6	9	4	May	3	3
1913	6	9	5	Jun	2	4
1913	6	9	6	Jul	1	5
1913	6	9	7	Aug	9	6
1913	6	9	8	Sep	8	7
1913	6	9	9	Oct	7	8
1913	6	9	10	Nov	6	9
1913	6	9	11	Dec	5	1
1913	6	9	12	Jan	4	2
1914	5	1	1	Feb	3	3
1914	5	1	2	Mar	2	4
1914	5	1	3	Apr	1	5
1914	5	1	4	May	9	6
1914	5	1	5	Jun	8	7
1914	5	1	6	Jul	7	8
1914	5	1	7	Aug	6	9
1914	5	1	8	Sep	5	1
1914	5	1	9	Oct	4	2
1914	5	1	10	Nov	3	3
1914	5	1	11	Dec	2	4
1914	5	1	12	Jan	1	5
1915	4	2	1	Feb	9	6
1915	4	2	2	Mar	8	7
1915	4	2	3	Apr	7	8
1915	4	2	4	May	6	9
1915	4	2	5	Jun	5	1
1915	4	2	6	Jul	4	2
1915	4	2	7	Aug	3	3
1915	4	2	8	Sep	2	4
1915	4	2	9	Oct	1	5
1915	4	2	10	Nov	9	6
1915	4	2	11	Dec	8	7
1915	4	2	12	Jan	7	8
1916	3	3	1	Feb	6	9
1916	3	3	2	Mar	5	1
1916	3	3	3	Apr	4	2
1916	3	3	4	May	3	3
1916	3	3	5	Jun	2	4
1916	3	3	6	Jul	1	5

Year	Yearly Male	Yearly Female	Adjusted Monthly Number	Month Name	Male Monthly Number	Female Monthly Number
1916	3	3	7	Aug	9	6
1916	3	3	8	Sep	8	7
1916	3	3	9	Oct	7	8
1916	3	3	10	Nov	6	9
1916	3	3	11	Dec	5	1
1916	3	3	12	Jan	4	2
1917	2	4	1	Feb	3	3
1917	2	4	2	Mar	2	4
1917	2	4	3	Apr	1	5
1917	2	4	4	May	9	6
1917	2	4	5	Jun	8	7
1917	2	4	6	Jul	7	8
1917	2	4	7	Aug	6	9
1917	2	4	8	Sep	5	1
1917	2	4	9	Oct	4	2
1917	2	4	10	Nov	3	3
1917	2	4	11	Dec	2	4
1917	2	4	12	Jan	1	5
1918	1	5	1	Feb	9	6
1918	1	5	2	Mar	8	7
1918	1	5	3	Apr	7	8
1918	1	5	4	May	6	9
1918	1	5	5	Jun	5	1
1918	1	5	6	Jul	4	2
1918	1	5	7	Aug	3	3
1918	1	5	8	Sep	2	4
1918	1	5	9	Oct	1	5
1918	1	5	10	Nov	9	6
1918	1	5	11	Dec	8	7
1918	1	5	12	Jan	7	8
1919	9	6	1	Feb	6	9
1919	9	6	2	Mar	5	1
1919	9	6	3	Apr	4	2
1919	9	6	4	May	3	3
1919	9	6	5	Jun	2	4
1919	9	6	6	Jul	1	5
1919	9	6	7	Aug	9	6
1919	9	6	8	Sep	8	7
1919	9	6	9	Oct	7	8
1919	9	6	10	Nov	6	9
1919	9	6	11	Dec	5	1
1919	9	6	12	Jan	4	2
1920	8	7	1	Feb	3	3
1920	8	7	2	Mar	2	4
1920	8	7	3	Apr	1	5

Year	Yearly Male	Yearly Female	Adjusted Monthly Number	Month Name	Male Monthly Number	Female Monthly Number
1920	8	7	4	May	9	6
1920	8	7	5	Jun	8	7
1920	8	7	6	Jul	7	8
1920	8	7	7	Aug	6	9
1920	8	7	8	Sep	5	1
1920	8	7	9	Oct	4	2
1920	8	7	10	Nov	3	3
1920	8	7	11	Dec	2	4
1920	8	7	12	Jan	1	5
1921	7	8	1	Feb	9	6
1921	7	8	2	Mar	8	7
1921	7	8	3	Apr	7	8
1921	7	8	4	May	6	9
1921	7	8	5	Jun	5	1
1921	7	8	6	Jul	4	2
1921	7	8	7	Aug	3	3
1921	7	8	8	Sep	2	4
1921	7	8	9	Oct	1	5
1921	7	8	10	Nov	9	6
1921	7	8	11	Dec	8	7
1921	7	8	12	Jan	7	8
1922	6	9	1	Feb	6	9
1922	6	9	2	Mar	5	1
1922	6	9	3	Apr	4	2
1922	6	9	4	May	3	3
1922	6	9	5	Jun	2	4
1922	6	9	6	Jul	1	5
1922	6	9	7	Aug	9	6
1922	6	9	8	Sep	8	7
1922	6	9	9	Oct	7	8
1922	6	9	10	Nov	6	9
1922	6	9	11	Dec	5	1
1922	6	9	12	Jan	4	2
1923	5	1	1	Feb	3	3
1923	5	1	2	Mar	2	4
1923	5	1	3	Apr	1	5
1923	5	1	4	May	9	6
1923	5	1	5	Jun	8	7
1923	5	1	6	Jul	7	8
1923	5	1	7	Aug	6	9
1923	5	1	8	Sep	5	1
1923	5	1	9	Oct	4	2
1923	5	1	10	Nov	3	3
1923	5	1	11	Dec	2	4
1923	5	1	12	Jan	1	5

Year	Yearly Male	Yearly Female	Adjusted Monthly Number	Month Name	Male Monthly Number	Female Monthly Number
1924	4	2	1	Feb	9	6
1924	4	2	2	Mar	8	7
1924	4	2	3	Apr	7	8
1924	4	2	4	May	6	9
1924	4	2	5	Jun	5	1
1924	4	2	6	Jul	4	2
1924	4	2	7	Aug	3	3
1924	4	2	8	Sep	2	4
1924	4	2	9	Oct	1	5
1924	4	2	10	Nov	9	6
1924	4	2	11	Dec	8	7
1924	4	2	12	Jan	7	8
1925	3	3	1	Feb	6	9
1925	3	3	2	Mar	5	1
1925	3	3	3	Apr	4	2
1925	3	3	4	May	3	3
1925	3	3	5	Jun	2	4
1925	3	3	6	Jul	1	5
1925	3	3	7	Aug	9	6
1925	3	3	8	Sep	8	7
1925	3	3	9	Oct	7	8
1925	3	3	10	Nov	6	9
1925	3	3	11	Dec	5	1
1925	3	3	12	Jan	4	2
1926	2	4	1	Feb	3	3
1926	2	4	2	Mar	2	4
1926	2	4	3	Apr	1	5
1926	2	4	4	May	9	6
1926	2	4	5	Jun	8	7
1926	2	4	6	Jul	7	8
1926	2	4	7	Aug	6	9
1926	2	4	8	Sep	5	1
1926	2	4	9	Oct	4	2
1926	2	4	10	Nov	3	3
1926	2	4	11	Dec	2	4
1926	2	4	12	Jan	1	5
1927	1	5	1	Feb	9	6
1927	1	5	2	Mar	8	7
1927	1	5	3	Apr	7	8
1927	1	5	4	May	6	9
1927	1	5	5	Jun	5	1
1927	1	5	6	Jul	4	2
1927	1	5	7	Aug	3	3
1927	1	5	8	Sep	2	4
1927	1	5	9	Oct	1	5

Year	Yearly Male	Yearly Female	Adjusted Monthly Number	Month Name	Male Monthly Number	Female Monthly Number
1927	1	5	10	Nov	9	6
1927	1	5	11	Dec	8	7
1927	1	5	12	Jan	7	8
1928	9	6	1	Feb	6	9
1928	9	6	2	Mar	5	1
1928	9	6	3	Apr	4	2
1928	9	6	4	May	3	3
1928	9	6	5	Jun	2	4
1928	9	6	6	Jul	1	5
1928	9	6	7	Aug	9	6
1928	9	6	8	Sep	8	7
1928	9	6	9	Oct	7	8
1928	9	6	10	Nov	6	9
1928	9	6	11	Dec	5	1
1928	9	6	12	Jan	4	2
1929	8	7	1	Feb	3	3
1929	8	7	2	Mar	2	4
1929	8	7	3	Apr	1	5
1929	8	7	4	May	9	6
1929	8	7	5	Jun	8	7
1929	8	7	6	Jul	7	8
1929	8	7	7	Aug	6	9
1929	8	7	8	Sep	5	1
1929	8	7	9	Oct	4	2
1929	8	7	10	Nov	3	3
1929	8	7	11	Dec	2	4
1929	8	7	12	Jan	1	5
1930	7	8	1	Feb	9	6
1930	7	8	2	Mar	8	7
1930	7	8	3	Apr	7	8
1930	7	8	4	May	6	9
1930	7	8	5	Jun	5	1
1930	7	8	6	Jul	4	2
1930	7	8	7	Aug	3	3
1930	7	8	8	Sep	2	4
1930	7	8	9	Oct	1	5
1930	7	8	10	Nov	9	6
1930	7	8	11	Dec	8	7
1930	7	8	12	Jan	7	8
1931	6	9	1	Feb	6	9
1931	6	9	2	Mar	5	1
1931	6	9	3	Apr	4	2
1931	6	9	4	May	3	3
1931	6	9	5	Jun	2	4
1931	6	9	6	Jul	1	5

Year	Yearly Male	Yearly Female	Adjusted Monthly Number	Month Name	Male Monthly Number	Female Monthly Number
1931	6	9	7	Aug	9	6
1931	6	9	8	Sep	8	7
1931	6	9	9	Oct	7	8
1931	6	9	10	Nov	6	9
1931	6	9	11	Dec	5	1
1931	6	9	12	Jan	4	2
1932	5	1	1	Feb	3	3
1932	5	1	2	Mar	2	4
1932	5	1	3	Apr	1	5
1932	5	1	4	May	9	6
1932	5	1	5	Jun	8	7
1932	5	1	6	Jul	7	8
1932	5	1	7	Aug	6	9
1932	5	1	8	Sep	5	1
1932	5	1	9	Oct	4	2
1932	5	1	10	Nov	3	3
1932	5	1	11	Dec	2	4
1932	5	1	12	Jan	1	5
1933	4	2	1	Feb	9	6
1933	4	2	2	Mar	8	7
1933	4	2	3	Apr	7	8
1933	4	2	4	May	6	9
1933	4	2	5	Jun	5	1
1933	4	2	6	Jul	4	2
1933	4	2	7	Aug	3	3
1933	4	2	8	Sep	2	4
1933	4	2	9	Oct	1	5
1933	4	2	10	Nov	9	6
1933	4	2	11	Dec	8	7
1933	4	2	12	Jan	7	8
1934	3	3	1	Feb	6	9
1934	3	3	2	Mar	5	1
1934	3	3	3	Apr	4	2
1934	3	3	4	May	3	3
1934	3	3	5	Jun	2	4
1934	3	3	6	Jul	1	5
1934	3	3	7	Aug	9	6
1934	3	3	8	Sep	8	7
1934	3	3	9	Oct	7	8
1934	3	3	10	Nov	6	9
1934	3	3	11	Dec	5	1
1934	3	3	12	Jan	4	2
1935	2	4	1	Feb	3	3
1935	2	4	2	Mar	2	4
1935	2	4	3	Apr	1	5

Year	Yearly Male	Yearly Female	Adjusted Monthly Number	Month Name	Male Monthly Number	Female Monthly Number
1935	2	4	4	May	9	6
1935	2	4	5	Jun	8	7
1935	2	4	6	Jul	7	8
1935	2	4	7	Aug	6	9
1935	2	4	8	Sep	5	1
1935	2	4	9	Oct	4	2
1935	2	4	10	Nov	3	3
1935	2	4	11	Dec	2	4
1935	2	4	12	Jan	1	5
1936	1	5	1	Feb	9	6
1936	1	5	2	Mar	8	7
1936	1	5	3	Apr	7	8
1936	1	5	4	May	6	9
1936	1	5	5	Jun	5	1
1936	1	5	6	Jul	4	2
1936	1	5	7	Aug	3	3
1936	1	5	8	Sep	2	4
1936	1	5	9	Oct	1	5
1936	1	5	10	Nov	9	6
1936	1	5	11	Dec	8	7
1936	1	5	12	Jan	7	8
1937	9	6	1	Feb	6	9
1937	9	6	2	Mar	5	1
1937	9	6	3	Apr	4	2
1937	9	6	4	May	3	3
1937	9	6	5	Jun	2	4
1937	9	6	6	Jul	1	5
1937	9	6	7	Aug	9	6
1937	9	6	8	Sep	8	7
1937	9	6	9	Oct	7	8
1937	9	6	10	Nov	6	9
1937	9	6	11	Dec	5	1
1937	9	6	12	Jan	4	2
1938	8	7	1	Feb	3	3
1938	8	7	2	Mar	2	4
1938	8	7	3	Apr	1	5
1938	8	7	4	May	9	6
1938	8	7	5	Jun	8	7
1938	8	7	6	Jul	7	8
1938	8	7	7	Aug	6	9
1938	8	7	8	Sep	5	1
1938	8	7	9	Oct	4	2
1938	8	7	10	Nov	3	3
1938	8	7	11	Dec	2	4
1938	8	7	12	Jan	1	5

Year	Yearly Male	Yearly Female	Adjusted Monthly Number	Month Name	Male Monthly Number	Female Monthly Number
1939	7	8	1	Feb	9	6
1939	7	8	2	Mar	8	7
1939	7	8	3	Apr	7	8
1939	7	8	4	May	6	9
1939	7	8	5	Jun	5	1
1939	7	8	6	Jul	4	2
1939	7	8	7	Aug	3	3
1939	7	8	8	Sep	2	4
1939	7	8	9	Oct	1	5
1939	7	8	10	Nov	9	6
1939	7	8	11	Dec	8	7
1939	7	8	12	Jan	7	8
1940	6	9	1	Feb	6	9
1940	6	9	2	Mar	5	1
1940	6	9	3	Apr	4	2
1940	6	9	4	May	3	3
1940	6	9	5	Jun	2	4
1940	6	9	6	Jul	1	5
1940	6	9	7	Aug	9	6
1940	6	9	8	Sep	8	7
1940	6	9	9	Oct	7	8
1940	6	9	10	Nov	6	9
1940	6	9	11	Dec	5	1
1940	6	9	12	Jan	4	2
1941	5	1	1	Feb	3	3
1941	5	1	2	Mar	2	4
1941	5	1	3	Apr	1	5
1941	5	1	4	May	9	6
1941	5	1	5	Jun	8	7
1941	5	1	6	Jul	7	8
1941	5	1	7	Aug	6	9
1941	5	1	8	Sep	5	1
1941	5	1	9	Oct	4	2
1941	5	1	10	Nov	3	3
1941	5	1	11	Dec	2	4
1941	5	1	12	Jan	1	5
1942	4	2	1	Feb	9	6
1942	4	2	2	Mar	8	7
1942	4	2	3	Apr	7	8
1942	4	2	4	May	6	9
1942	4	2	5	Jun	5	1
1942	4	2	6	Jul	4	2
1942	4	2	7	Aug	3	3
1942	4	2	8	Sep	2	4
1942	4	2	9	Oct	1	5

Year	Yearly Male	Yearly Female	Adjusted Monthly Number	Month Name	Male Monthly Number	Female Monthly Number
1942	4	2	10	Nov	9	6
1942	4	2	11	Dec	8	7
1942	4	2	12	Jan	7	8
1943	3	3	1	Feb	6	9
1943	3	3	2	Mar	5	1
1943	3	3	3	Apr	4	2
1943	3	3	4	May	3	3
1943	3	3	5	Jun	2	4
1943	3	3	6	Jul	1	5
1943	3	3	7	Aug	9	6
1943	3	3	8	Sep	8	7
1943	3	3	9	Oct	7	8
1943	3	3	10	Nov	6	9
1943	3	3	11	Dec	5	1
1943	3	3	12	Jan	4	2
1944	2	4	1	Feb	3	3
1944	2	4	2	Mar	2	4
1944	2	4	3	Apr	1	5
1944	2	4	4	May	9	6
1944	2	4	5	Jun	8	7
1944	2	4	6	Jul	7	8
1944	2	4	7	Aug	6	9
1944	2	4	8	Sep	5	1
1944	2	4	9	Oct	4	2
1944	2	4	10	Nov	3	3
1944	2	4	11	Dec	2	4
1944	2	4	12	Jan	1	5
1945	1	5	1	Feb	9	6
1945	1	5	2	Mar	8	7
1945	1	5	3	Apr	7	8
1945	1	5	4	May	6	9
1945	1	5	5	Jun	5	1
1945	1	5	6	Jul	4	2
1945	1	5	7	Aug	3	3
1945	1	5	8	Sep	2	4
1945	1	5	9	Oct	1	5
1945	1	5	10	Nov	9	6
1945	1	5	11	Dec	8	7
1945	1	5	12	Jan	7	8
1946	9	6	1	Feb	6	9
1946	9	6	2	Mar	5	1
1946	9	6	3	Apr	4	2
1946	9	6	4	May	3	3
1946	9	6	5	Jun	2	4
1946	9	6	6	Jul	1	5

Year	Yearly Male	Yearly Female	Adjusted Monthly Number	Month Name	Male Monthly Number	Female Monthly Number
1946	9	6	7	Aug	9	6
1946	9	6	8	Sep	8	7
1946	9	6	9	Oct	7	8
1946	9	6	10	Nov	6	9
1946	9	6	11	Dec	5	1
1946	9	6	12	Jan	4	2
1947	8	7	1	Feb	3	3
1947	8	7	2	Mar	2	4
1947	8	7	3	Apr	1	5
1947	8	7	4	May	9	6
1947	8	7	5	Jun	8	7
1947	8	7	6	Jul	7	8
1947	8	7	7	Aug	6	9
1947	8	7	8	Sep	5	1
1947	8	7	9	Oct	4	2
1947	8	7	10	Nov	3	3
1947	8	7	11	Dec	2	4
1947	8	7	12	Jan	1	5
1948	7	8	1	Feb	9	6
1948	7	8	2	Mar	8	7
1948	7	8	3	Apr	7	8
1948	7	8	4	May	6	9
1948	7	8	5	Jun	5	1
1948	7	8	6	Jul	4	2
1948	7	8	7	Aug	3	3
1948	7	8	8	Sep	2	4
1948	7	8	9	Oct	1	5
1948	7	8	10	Nov	9	6
1948	7	8	11	Dec	8	7
1948	7	8	12	Jan	7	8
1949	6	9	1	Feb	6	9
1949	6	9	2	Mar	5	1
1949	6	9	3	Apr	4	2
1949	6	9	4	May	3	3
1949	6	9	5	Jun	2	4
1949	6	9	6	Jul	1	5
1949	6	9	7	Aug	9	6
1949	6	9	8	Sep	8	7
1949	6	9	9	Oct	7	8
1949	6	9	10	Nov	6	9
1949	6	9	11	Dec	5	1
1949	6	9	12	Jan	4	2
1950	5	1	1	Feb	3	3
1950	5	1	2	Mar	2	4
1950	5	1	3	Apr	1	5

Year	Yearly Male	Yearly Female	Adjusted Monthly Number	Month Name	Male Monthly Number	Female Monthly Number
1950	5	1	4	May	9	6
1950	5	1	5	Jun	8	7
1950	5	1	6	Jul	7	8
1950	5	1	7	Aug	6	9
1950	5	1	8	Sep	5	1
1950	5	1	9	Oct	4	2
1950	5	1	10	Nov	3	3
1950	5	1	11	Dec	2	4
1950	5	1	12	Jan	1	5
1951	4	2	1	Feb	9	6
1951	4	2	2	Mar	8	7
1951	4	2	3	Apr	7	8
1951	4	2	4	May	6	9
1951	4	2	5	Jun	5	1
1951	4	2	6	Jul	4	2
1951	4	2	7	Aug	3	3
1951	4	2	8	Sep	2	4
1951	4	2	9	Oct	1	5
1951	4	2	10	Nov	9	6
1951	4	2	11	Dec	8	7
1951	4	2	12	Jan	7	8
1952	3	3	1	Feb	6	9
1952	3	3	2	Mar	5	1
1952	3	3	3	Apr	4	2
1952	3	3	4	May	3	3
1952	3	3	5	Jun	2	4
1952	3	3	6	Jul	1	5
1952	3	3	7	Aug	9	6
1952	3	3	8	Sep	8	7
1952	3	3	9	Oct	7	8
1952	3	3	10	Nov	6	9
1952	3	3	11	Dec	5	1
1952	3	3	12	Jan	4	2
1953	2	4	1	Feb	3	3
1953	2	4	2	Mar	2	4
1953	2	4	3	Apr	1	5
1953	2	4	4	May	9	6
1953	2	4	5	Jun	8	7
1953	2	4	6	Jul	7	8
1953	2	4	7	Aug	6	9
1953	2	4	8	Sep	5	1
1953	2	4	9	Oct	4	2
1953	2	4	10	Nov	3	3
1953	2	4	11	Dec	2	4
1953	2	4	12	Jan	1	5

Year	Yearly Male	Yearly Female	Adjusted Monthly Number	Month Name	Male Monthly Number	Female Monthly Number
1954	1	5	1	Feb	9	6
1954	1	5	2	Mar	8	7
1954	1	5	3	Apr	7	8
1954	1	5	4	May	6	9
1954	1	5	5	Jun	5	1
1954	1	5	6	Jul	4	2
1954	1	5	7	Aug	3	3
1954	1	5	8	Sep	2	4
1954	1	5	9	Oct	1	5
1954	1	5	10	Nov	9	6
1954	1	5	11	Dec	8	7
1954	1	5	12	Jan	7	8
1955	9	6	1	Feb	6	9
1955	9	6	2	Mar	5	1
1955	9	6	3	Apr	4	2
1955	9	6	4	May	3	3
1955	9	6	5	Jun	2	4
1955	9	6	6	Jul	1	5
1955	9	6	7	Aug	9	6
1955	9	6	8	Sep	8	7
1955	9	6	9	Oct	7	8
1955	9	6	10	Nov	6	9
1955	9	6	11	Dec	5	1
1955	9	6	12	Jan	4	2
1956	8	7	1	Feb	3	3
1956	8	7	2	Mar	2	4
1956	8	7	3	Apr	1	5
1956	8	7	4	May	9	6
1956	8	7	5	Jun	8	7
1956	8	7	6	Jul	7	8
1956	8	7	7	Aug	6	9
1956	8	7	8	Sep	5	1
1956	8	7	9	Oct	4	2
1956	8	7	10	Nov	3	3
1956	8	7	11	Dec	2	4
1956	8	7	12	Jan	1	5
1957	7	8	1	Feb	9	6
1957	7	8	2	Mar	8	7
1957	7	8	3	Apr	7	8
1957	7	8	4	May	6	9
1957	7	8	5	Jun	5	1
1957	7	8	6	Jul	4	2
1957	7	8	7	Aug	3	3
1957	7	8	8	Sep	2	4
1957	7	8	9	Oct	1	5

Year	Yearly Male	Yearly Female	Adjusted Monthly Number	Month Name	Male Monthly Number	Female Monthly Number
1957	7	8	10	Nov	9	6
1957	7	8	11	Dec	8	7
1957	7	8	12	Jan	7	8
1958	6	9	1	Feb	6	9
1958	6	9	2	Mar	5	1
1958	6	9	3	Apr	4	2
1958	6	9	4	May	3	3
1958	6	9	5	Jun	2	4
1958	6	9	6	Jul	1	5
1958	6	9	7	Aug	9	6
1958	6	9	8	Sep	8	7
1958	6	9	9	Oct	7	8
1958	6	9	10	Nov	6	9
1958	6	9	11	Dec	5	1
1958	6	9	12	Jan	4	2
1959	5	1	1	Feb	3	3
1959	5	1	2	Mar	2	4
1959	5	1	3	Apr	1	5
1959	5	1	4	May	9	6
1959	5	1	5	Jun	8	7
1959	5	1	6	Jul	7	8
1959	5	1	7	Aug	6	9
1959	5	1	8	Sep	5	1
1959	5	1	9	Oct	4	2
1959	5	1	10	Nov	3	3
1959	5	1	11	Dec	2	4
1959	5	1	12	Jan	1	5
1960	4	2	1	Feb	9	6
1960	4	2	2	Mar	8	7
1960	4	2	3	Apr	7	8
1960	4	2	4	May	6	9
1960	4	2	5	Jun	5	1
1960	4	2	6	Jul	4	2
1960	4	2	7	Aug	3	3
1960	4	2	8	Sep	2	4
1960	4	2	9	Oct	1	5
1960	4	2	10	Nov	9	6
1960	4	2	11	Dec	8	7
1960	4	2	12	Jan	7	8
1961	3	3	1	Feb	6	9
1961	3	3	2	Mar	5	1
1961	3	3	3	Apr	4	2
1961	3	3	4	May	3	3
1961	3	3	5	Jun	2	4
1961	3	3	6	Jul	1	5

Year	Yearly Male	Yearly Female	Adjusted Monthly Number	Month Name	Male Monthly Number	Female Monthly Number
1961	3	3	7	Aug	9	6
1961	3	3	8	Sep	8	7
1961	3	3	9	Oct	7	8
1961	3	3	10	Nov	6	9
1961	3	3	11	Dec	5	1
1961	3	3	12	Jan	4	2
1962	2	4	1	Feb	3	3
1962	2	4	2	Mar	2	4
1962	2	4	3	Apr	1	5
1962	2	4	4	May	9	6
1962	2	4	5	Jun	8	7
1962	2	4	6	Jul	7	8
1962	2	4	7	Aug	6	9
1962	2	4	8	Sep	5	1
1962	2	4	9	Oct	4	2
1962	2	4	10	Nov	3	3
1962	2	4	11	Dec	2	4
1962	2	4	12	Jan	1	5
1963	1	5	1	Feb	9	6
1963	1	5	2	Mar	8	7
1963	1	5	3	Apr	7	8
1963	1	5	4	May	6	9
1963	1	5	5	Jun	5	1
1963	1	5	6	Jul	4	2
1963	1	5	7	Aug	3	3
1963	1	5	8	Sep	2	4
1963	1	5	9	Oct	1	5
1963	1	5	10	Nov	9	6
1963	1	5	11	Dec	8	7
1963	1	5	12	Jan	7	8
1964	9	6	1	Feb	6	9
1964	9	6	2	Mar	5	1
1964	9	6	3	Apr	4	2
1964	9	6	4	May	3	3
1964	9	6	5	Jun	2	4
1964	9	6	6	Jul	1	5
1964	9	6	7	Aug	9	6
1964	9	6	8	Sep	8	7
1964	9	6	9	Oct	7	8
1964	9	6	10	Nov	6	9
1964	9	6	11	Dec	5	1
1964	9	6	12	Jan	4	2
1965	8	7	1	Feb	3	3
1965	8	7	2	Mar	2	4
1965	8	7	3	Apr	1	5

Year	Yearly Male	Yearly Female	Adjusted Monthly Number	Month Name	Male Monthly Number	Female Monthly Number
1965	8	7	4	May	9	6
1965	8	7	5	Jun	8	7
1965	8	7	6	Jul	7	8
1965	8	7	7	Aug	6	9
1965	8	7	8	Sep	5	1
1965	8	7	9	Oct	4	2
1965	8	7	10	Nov	3	3
1965	8	7	11	Dec	2	4
1965	8	7	12	Jan	1	5
1966	7	8	1	Feb	9	6
1966	7	8	2	Mar	8	7
1966	7	8	3	Apr	7	8
1966	7	8	4	May	6	9
1966	7	8	5	Jun	5	1
1966	7	8	6	Jul	4	2
1966	7	8	7	Aug	3	3
1966	7	8	8	Sep	2	4
1966	7	8	9	Oct	1	5
1966	7	8	10	Nov	9	6
1966	7	8	11	Dec	8	7
1966	7	8	12	Jan	7	8
1967	6	9	1	Feb	6	9
1967	6	9	2	Mar	5	1
1967	6	9	3	Apr	4	2
1967	6	9	4	May	3	3
1967	6	9	5	Jun	2	4
1967	6	9	6	Jul	1	5
1967	6	9	7	Aug	9	6
1967	6	9	8	Sep	8	7
1967	6	9	9	Oct	7	8
1967	6	9	10	Nov	6	9
1967	6	9	11	Dec	5	1
1967	6	9	12	Jan	4	2
1968	5	1	1	Feb	3	3
1968	5	1	2	Mar	2	4
1968	5	1	3	Apr	1	5
1968	5	1	4	May	9	6
1968	5	1	5	Jun	8	7
1968	5	1	6	Jul	7	8
1968	5	1	7	Aug	6	9
1968	5	1	8	Sep	5	1
1968	5	1	9	Oct	4	2
1968	5	1	10	Nov	3	3
1968	5	1	11	Dec	2	4
1968	5	1	12	Jan	1	5

Year	Yearly Male	Yearly Female	Adjusted Monthly Number	Month Name	Male Monthly Number	Female Monthly Number
1969	4	2	1	Feb	9	6
1969	4	2	2	Mar	8	7
1969	4	2	3	Apr	7	8
1969	4	2	4	May	6	9
1969	4	2	5	Jun	5	1
1969	4	2	6	Jul	4	2
1969	4	2	7	Aug	3	3
1969	4	2	8	Sep	2	4
1969	4	2	9	Oct	1	5
1969	4	2	10	Nov	9	6
1969	4	2	11	Dec	8	7
1969	4	2	12	Jan	7	8
1970	3	3	1	Feb	6	9
1970	3	3	2	Mar	5	1
1970	3	3	3	Apr	4	2
1970	3	3	4	May	3	3
1970	3	3	5	Jun	2	4
1970	3	3	6	Jul	1	5
1970	3	3	7	Aug	9	6
1970	3	3	8	Sep	8	7
1970	3	3	9	Oct	7	8
1970	3	3	10	Nov	6	9
1970	3	3	11	Dec	5	1
1970	3	3	12	Jan	4	2
1971	2	4	1	Feb	3	3
1971	2	4	2	Mar	2	4
1971	2	4	3	Apr	1	5
1971	2	4	4	May	9	6
1971	2	4	5	Jun	8	7
1971	2	4	6	Jul	7	8
1971	2	4	7	Aug	6	9
1971	2	4	8	Sep	5	1
1971	2	4	9	Oct	4	2
1971	2	4	10	Nov	3	3
1971	2	4	11	Dec	2	4
1971	2	4	12	Jan	1	5
1972	1	5	1	Feb	9	6
1972	1	5	2	Mar	8	7
1972	1	5	3	Apr	7	8
1972	1	5	4	May	6	9
1972	1	5	5	Jun	5	1
1972	1	5	6	Jul	4	2
1972	1	5	7	Aug	3	3
1972	1	5	8	Sep	2	4
1972	1	5	9	Oct	1	5

Year	Yearly Male	Yearly Female	Adjusted Monthly Number	Month Name	Male Monthly Number	Female Monthly Number
1972	1	5	10	Nov	9	6
1972	1	5	11	Dec	8	7
1972	1	5	12	Jan	7	8
1973	9	6	1	Feb	6	9
1973	9	6	2	Mar	5	1
1973	9	6	3	Apr	4	2
1973	9	6	4	May	3	3
1973	9	6	5	Jun	2	4
1973	9	6	6	Jul	1	5
1973	9	6	7	Aug	9	6
1973	9	6	8	Sep	8	7
1973	9	6	9	Oct	7	8
1973	9	6	10	Nov	6	9
1973	9	6	11	Dec	5	1
1973	9	6	12	Jan	4	2
1974	8	7	1	Feb	3	3
1974	8	7	2	Mar	2	4
1974	8	7	3	Apr	1	5
1974	8	7	4	May	9	6
1974	8	7	5	Jun	8	7
1974	8	7	6	Jul	7	8
1974	8	7	7	Aug	6	9
1974	8	7	8	Sep	5	1
1974	8	7	9	Oct	4	2
1974	8	7	10	Nov	3	3
1974	8	7	11	Dec	2	4
1974	8	7	12	Jan	1	5
1975	7	8	1	Feb	9	6
1975	7	8	2	Mar	8	7
1975	7	8	3	Apr	7	8
1975	7	8	4	May	6	9
1975	7	8	5	Jun	5	1
1975	7	8	6	Jul	4	2
1975	7	8	7	Aug	3	3
1975	7	8	8	Sep	2	4
1975	7	8	9	Oct	1	5
1975	7	8	10	Nov	9	6
1975	7	8	11	Dec	8	7
1975	7	8	12	Jan	7	8
1976	6	9	1	Feb	6	9
1976	6	9	2	Mar	5	1
1976	6	9	3	Apr	4	2
1976	6	9	4	May	3	3
1976	6	9	5	Jun	2	4
1976	6	9	6	Jul	1	5

Year	Yearly Male	Yearly Female	Adjusted Monthly Number	Month Name	Male Monthly Number	Female Monthly Number
1976	6	9	7	Aug	9	6
1976	6	9	8	Sep	8	7
1976	6	9	9	Oct	7	8
1976	6	9	10	Nov	6	9
1976	6	9	11	Dec	5	1
1976	6	9	12	Jan	4	2
1977	5	1	1	Feb	3	3
1977	5	1	2	Mar	2	4
1977	5	1	3	Apr	1	5
1977	5	1	4	May	9	6
1977	5	1	5	Jun	8	7
1977	5	1	6	Jul	7	8
1977	5	1	7	Aug	6	9
1977	5	1	8	Sep	5	1
1977	5	1	9	Oct	4	2
1977	5	1	10	Nov	3	3
1977	5	1	11	Dec	2	4
1977	5	1	12	Jan	1	5
1978	4	2	1	Feb	9	6
1978	4	2	2	Mar	8	7
1978	4	2	3	Apr	7	8
1978	4	2	4	May	6	9
1978	4	2	5	Jun	5	1
1978	4	2	6	Jul	4	2
1978	4	2	7	Aug	3	3
1978	4	2	8	Sep	2	4
1978	4	2	9	Oct	1	5
1978	4	2	10	Nov	9	6
1978	4	2	11	Dec	8	7
1978	4	2	12	Jan	7	8
1979	3	3	1	Feb	6	9
1979	3	3	2	Mar	5	1
1979	3	3	3	Apr	4	2
1979	3	3	4	May	3	3
1979	3	3	5	Jun	2	4
1979	3	3	6	Jul	1	5
1979	3	3	7	Aug	9	6
1979	3	3	8	Sep	8	7
1979	3	3	9	Oct	7	8
1979	3	3	10	Nov	6	9
1979	3	3	11	Dec	5	1
1979	3	3	12	Jan	4	2
1980	2	4	1	Feb	3	3
1980	2	4	2	Mar	2	4
1980	2	4	3	Apr	1	5

Year	Yearly Male	Yearly Female	Adjusted Monthly Number	Month Name	Male Monthly Number	Female Monthly Number
1980	2	4	4	May	9	6
1980	2	4	5	Jun	8	7
1980	2	4	6	Jul	7	8
1980	2	4	7	Aug	6	9
1980	2	4	8	Sep	5	1
1980	2	4	9	Oct	4	2
1980	2	4	10	Nov	3	3
1980	2	4	11	Dec	2	4
1980	2	4	12	Jan	1	5
1981	1	5	1	Feb	9	6
1981	1	5	2	Mar	8	7
1981	1	5	3	Apr	7	8
1981	1	5	4	May	6	9
1981	1	5	5	Jun	5	1
1981	1	5	6	Jul	4	2
1981	1	5	7	Aug	3	3
1981	1	5	8	Sep	2	4
1981	1	5	9	Oct	1	5
1981	1	5	10	Nov	9	6
1981	1	5	11	Dec	8	7
1981	1	5	12	Jan	7	8
1982	9	6	1	Feb	6	9
1982	9	6	2	Mar	5	1
1982	9	6	3	Apr	4	2
1982	9	6	4	May	3	3
1982	9	6	5	Jun	2	4
1982	9	6	6	Jul	1	5
1982	9	6	7	Aug	9	6
1982	9	6	8	Sep	8	7
1982	9	6	9	Oct	7	8
1982	9	6	10	Nov	6	9
1982	9	6	11	Dec	5	1
1982	9	6	12	Jan	4	2
1983	8	7	1	Feb	3	3
1983	8	7	2	Mar	2	4
1983	8	7	3	Apr	1	5
1983	8	7	4	May	9	6
1983	8	7	5	Jun	8	7
1983	8	7	6	Jul	7	8
1983	8	7	7	Aug	6	9
1983	8	7	8	Sep	5	1
1983	8	7	9	Oct	4	2
1983	8	7	10	Nov	3	3
1983	8	7	11	Dec	2	4
1983	8	7	12	Jan	1	5

Year	Yearly Male	Yearly Female	Adjusted Monthly Number	Month Name	Male Monthly Number	Female Monthly Number
1984	7	8	1	Feb	9	6
1984	7	8	2	Mar	8	7
1984	7	8	3	Apr	7	8
1984	7	8	4	May	6	9
1984	7	8	5	Jun	5	1
1984	7	8	6	Jul	4	2
1984	7	8	7	Aug	3	3
1984	7	8	8	Sep	2	4
1984	7	8	9	Oct	1	5
1984	7	8	10	Nov	9	6
1984	7	8	11	Dec	8	7
1984	7	8	12	Jan	7	8
1985	6	9	1	Feb	6	9
1985	6	9	2	Mar	5	1
1985	6	9	3	Apr	4	2
1985	6	9	4	May	3	3
1985	6	9	5	Jun	2	4
1985	6	9	6	Jul	1	5
1985	6	9	7	Aug	9	6
1985	6	9	8	Sep	8	7
1985	6	9	9	Oct	7	8
1985	6	9	10	Nov	6	9
1985	6	9	11	Dec	5	1
1985	6	9	12	Jan	4	2
1986	5	1	1	Feb	3	3
1986	5	1	2	Mar	2	4
1986	5	1	3	Apr	1	5
1986	5	1	4	May	9	6
1986	5	1	5	Jun	8	7
1986	5	1	6	Jul	7	8
1986	5	1	7	Aug	6	9
1986	5	1	8	Sep	5	1
1986	5	1	9	Oct	4	2
1986	5	1	10	Nov	3	3
1986	5	1	11	Dec	2	4
1986	5	1	12	Jan	1	5
1987	4	2	1	Feb	9	6
1987	4	2	2	Mar	8	7
1987	4	2	3	Apr	7	8
1987	4	2	4	May	6	9
1987	4	2	5	Jun	5	1
1987	4	2	6	Jul	4	2
1987	4	2	7	Aug	3	3
1987	4	2	8	Sep	2	4
1987	4	2	9	Oct	1	5

Year	Yearly Male	Yearly Female	Adjusted Monthly Number	Month Name	Male Monthly Number	Female Monthly Number
1987	4	2	10	Nov	9	6
1987	4	2	11	Dec	8	7
1987	4	2	12	Jan	7	8
1988	3	3	1	Feb	6	9
1988	3	3	2	Mar	5	1
1988	3	3	3	Apr	4	2
1988	3	3	4	May	3	3
1988	3	3	5	Jun	2	4
1988	3	3	6	Jul	1	5
1988	3	3	7	Aug	9	6
1988	3	3	8	Sep	8	7
1988	3	3	9	Oct	7	8
1988	3	3	10	Nov	6	9
1988	3	3	11	Dec	5	1
1988	3	3	12	Jan	4	2
1989	2	4	1	Feb	3	3
1989	2	4	2	Mar	2	4
1989	2	4	3	Apr	1	5
1989	2	4	4	May	9	6
1989	2	4	5	Jun	8	7
1989	2	4	6	Jul	7	8
1989	2	4	7	Aug	6	9
1989	2	4	8	Sep	5	1
1989	2	4	9	Oct	4	2
1989	2	4	10	Nov	3	3
1989	2	4	11	Dec	2	4
1989	2	4	12	Jan	1	5
1990	1	5	1	Feb	9	6
1990	1	5	2	Mar	8	7
1990	1	5	3	Apr	7	8
1990	1	5	4	May	6	9
1990	1	5	5	Jun	5	1
1990	1	5	6	Jul	4	2
1990	1	5	7	Aug	3	3
1990	1	5	8	Sep	2	4
1990	1	5	9	Oct	1	5
1990	1	5	10	Nov	9	6
1990	1	5	11	Dec	8	7
1990	1	5	12	Jan	7	8
1991	9	6	1	Feb	6	9
1991	9	6	2	Mar	5	1
1991	9	6	3	Apr	4	2
1991	9	6	4	May	3	3
1991	9	6	5	Jun	2	4
1991	9	6	6	Jul	1	5

Year	Yearly Male	Yearly Female	Adjusted Monthly Number	Month Name	Male Monthly Number	Female Monthly Number
1991	9	6	7	Aug	9	6
1991	9	6	8	Sep	8	7
1991	9	6	9	Oct	7	8
1991	9	6	10	Nov	6	9
1991	9	6	11	Dec	5	1
1991	9	6	12	Jan	4	2
1992	8	7	1	Feb	3	3
1992	8	7	2	Mar	2	4
1992	8	7	3	Apr	1	5
1992	8	7	4	May	9	6
1992	8	7	5	Jun	8	7
1992	8	7	6	Jul	7	8
1992	8	7	7	Aug	6	9
1992	8	7	8	Sep	5	1
1992	8	7	9	Oct	4	2
1992	8	7	10	Nov	3	3
1992	8	7	11	Dec	2	4
1992	8	7	12	Jan	1	5
1993	7	8	1	Feb	9	6
1993	7	8	2	Mar	8	7
1993	7	8	3	Apr	7	8
1993	7	8	4	May	6	9
1993	7	8	5	Jun	5	1
1993	7	8	6	Jul	4	2
1993	7	8	7	Aug	3	3
1993	7	8	8	Sep	2	4
1993	7	8	9	Oct	1	5
1993	7	8	10	Nov	9	6
1993	7	8	11	Dec	8	7
1993	7	8	12	Jan	7	8
1994	6	9	1	Feb	6	9
1994	6	9	2	Mar	5	1
1994	6	9	3	Apr	4	2
1994	6	9	4	May	3	3
1994	6	9	5	Jun	2	4
1994	6	9	6	Jul	1	5
1994	6	9	7	Aug	9	6
1994	6	9	8	Sep	8	7
1994	6	9	9	Oct	7	8
1994	6	9	10	Nov	6	9
1994	6	9	11	Dec	5	1
1994	6	9	12	Jan	4	2
1995	5	1	1	Feb	3	3
1995	5	1	2	Mar	2	4
1995	5	1	3	Apr	1	5

Year	Yearly Male	Yearly Female	Adjusted Monthly Number	Month Name	Male Monthly Number	Female Monthly Number
1995	5	1	4	May	9	6
1995	5	1	5	Jun	8	7
1995	5	1	6	Jul	7	8
1995	5	1	7	Aug	6	9
1995	5	1	8	Sep	5	1
1995	5	1	9	Oct	4	2
1995	5	1	10	Nov	3	3
1995	5	1	11	Dec	2	4
1995	5	1	12	Jan	1	5
1996	4	2	1	Feb	9	6
1996	4	2	2	Mar	8	7
1996	4	2	3	Apr	7	8
1996	4	2	4	May	6	9
1996	4	2	5	Jun	5	1
1996	4	2	6	Jul	4	2
1996	4	2	7	Aug	3	3
1996	4	2	8	Sep	2	4
1996	4	2	9	Oct	1	5
1996	4	2	10	Nov	9	6
1996	4	2	11	Dec	8	7
1996	4	2	12	Jan	7	8
1997	3	3	1	Feb	6	9
1997	3	3	2	Mar	5	1
1997	3	3	3	Apr	4	2
1997	3	3	4	May	3	3
1997	3	3	5	Jun	2	4
1997	3	3	6	Jul	1	5
1997	3	3	7	Aug	9	6
1997	3	3	8	Sep	8	7
1997	3	3	9	Oct	7	8
1997	3	3	10	Nov	6	9
1997	3	3	11	Dec	5	1
1997	3	3	12	Jan	4	2
1998	2	4	1	Feb	3	3
1998	2	4	2	Mar	2	4
1998	2	4	3	Apr	1	5
1998	2	4	4	May	9	6
1998	2	4	5	Jun	8	7
1998	2	4	6	Jul	7	8
1998	2	4	7	Aug	6	9
1998	2	4	8	Sep	5	1
1998	2	4	9	Oct	4	2
1998	2	4	10	Nov	3	3
1998	2	4	11	Dec	2	4
1998	2	4	12	Jan	1	5

Year	Yearly Male	Yearly Female	Adjusted Monthly Number	Month Name	Male Monthly Number	Female Monthly Number
1999	1	5	1	Feb	9	6
1999	1	5	2	Mar	8	7
1999	1	5	3	Apr	7	8
1999	1	5	4	May	6	9
1999	1	5	5	Jun	5	1
1999	1	5	6	Jul	4	2
1999	1	5	7	Aug	3	3
1999	1	5	8	Sep	2	4
1999	1	5	9	Oct	1	5
1999	1	5	10	Nov	9	6
1999	1	5	11	Dec	8	7
1999	1	5	12	Jan	7	8
2000	9	6	1	Feb	6	9
2000	9	6	2	Mar	5	1
2000	9	6	3	Apr	4	2
2000	9	6	4	May	3	3
2000	9	6	5	Jun	2	4
2000	9	6	6	Jul	1	5
2000	9	6	7	Aug	9	6
2000	9	6	8	Sep	8	7
2000	9	6	9	Oct	7	8
2000	9	6	10	Nov	6	9
2000	9	6	11	Dec	5	1
2000	9	6	12	Jan	4	2
2001	8	7	1	Feb	3	3
2001	8	7	2	Mar	2	4
2001	8	7	3	Apr	1	5
2001	8	7	4	May	9	6
2001	8	7	5	Jun	8	7
2001	8	7	6	Jul	7	8
2001	8	7	7	Aug	6	9
2001	8	7	8	Sep	5	1
2001	8	7	9	Oct	4	2
2001	8	7	10	Nov	3	3
2001	8	7	11	Dec	2	4
2001	8	7	12	Jan	1	5
2002	7	8	1	Feb	9	6
2002	7	8	2	Mar	8	7
2002	7	8	3	Apr	7	8
2002	7	8	4	May	6	9
2002	7	8	5	Jun	5	1
2002	7	8	6	Jul	4	2
2002	7	8	7	Aug	3	3
2002	7	8	8	Sep	2	4
2002	7	8	9	Oct	1	5

Year	Yearly Male	Yearly Female	Adjusted Monthly Number	Month Name	Male Monthly Number	Female Monthly Number
2002	7	8	10	Nov	9	6
2002	7	8	11	Dec	8	7
2002	7	8	12	Jan	7	8
2003	6	9	1	Feb	6	9
2003	6	9	2	Mar	5	1
2003	6	9	3	Apr	4	2
2003	6	9	4	May	3	3
2003	6	9	5	Jun	2	4
2003	6	9	6	Jul	1	5
2003	6	9	7	Aug	9	6
2003	6	9	8	Sep	8	7
2003	6	9	9	Oct	7	8
2003	6	9	10	Nov	6	9
2003	6	9	11	Dec	5	1
2003	6	9	12	Jan	4	2
2004	5	1	1	Feb	3	3
2004	5	1	2	Mar	2	4
2004	5	1	3	Apr	1	5
2004	5	1	4	May	9	6
2004	5	1	5	Jun	8	7
2004	5	1	6	Jul	7	8
2004	5	1	7	Aug	6	9
2004	5	1	8	Sep	5	1
2004	5	1	9	Oct	4	2
2004	5	1	10	Nov	3	3
2004	5	1	11	Dec	2	4
2004	5	1	12	Jan	1	5
2005	4	2	1	Feb	9	6
2005	4	2	2	Mar	8	7
2005	4	2	3	Apr	7	8
2005	4	2	4	May	6	9
2005	4	2	5	Jun	5	1
2005	4	2	6	Jul	4	2
2005	4	2	7	Aug	3	3
2005	4	2	8	Sep	2	4
2005	4	2	9	Oct	1	5
2005	4	2	10	Nov	9	6
2005	4	2	11	Dec	8	7
2005	4	2	12	Jan	7	8
2006	3	3	1	Feb	6	9
2006	3	3	2	Mar	5	1
2006	3	3	3	Apr	4	2
2006	3	3	4	May	3	3
2006	3	3	5	Jun	2	4
2006	3	3	6	Jul	1	5

Year	Yearly Male	Yearly Female	Adjusted Monthly Number	Month Name	Male Monthly Number	Female Monthly Number
2006	3	3	7	Aug	9	6
2006	3	3	8	Sep	8	7
2006	3	3	9	Oct	7	8
2006	3	3	10	Nov	6	9
2006	3	3	11	Dec	5	1
2006	3	3	12	Jan	4	2
2007	2	4	1	Feb	3	3
2007	2	4	2	Mar	2	4
2007	2	4	3	Apr	1	5
2007	2	4	4	May	9	6
2007	2	4	5	Jun	8	7
2007	2	4	6	Jul	7	8
2007	2	4	7	Aug	6	9
2007	2	4	8	Sep	5	1
2007	2	4	9	Oct	4	2
2007	2	4	10	Nov	3	3
2007	2	4	11	Dec	2	4
2007	2	4	12	Jan	1	5
2008	1	5	1	Feb	9	6
2008	1	5	2	Mar	8	7
2008	1	5	3	Apr	7	8
2008	1	5	4	May	6	9
2008	1	5	5	Jun	5	1
2008	1	5	6	Jul	4	2
2008	1	5	7	Aug	3	3
2008	1	5	8	Sep	2	4
2008	1	5	9	Oct	1	5
2008	1	5	10	Nov	9	6
2008	1	5	11	Dec	8	7
2008	1	5	12	Jan	7	8
2009	9	6	1	Feb	6	9
2009	9	6	2	Mar	5	1
2009	9	6	3	Apr	4	2
2009	9	6	4	May	3	3
2009	9	6	5	Jun	2	4
2009	9	6	6	Jul	1	5
2009	9	6	7	Aug	9	6
2009	9	6	8	Sep	8	7
2009	9	6	9	Oct	7	8
2009	9	6	10	Nov	6	9
2009	9	6	11	Dec	5	1
2009	9	6	12	Jan	4	2
2010	8	7	1	Feb	3	3
2010	8	7	2	Mar	2	4
2010	8	7	3	Apr	1	5

Year	Yearly Male	Yearly Female	Adjusted Monthly Number	Month Name	Male Monthly Number	Female Monthly Number
2010	8	7	4	May	9	6
2010	8	7	5	Jun	8	7
2010	8	7	6	Jul	7	8
2010	8	7	7	Aug	6	9
2010	8	7	8	Sep	5	1
2010	8	7	9	Oct	4	2
2010	8	7	10	Nov	3	3
2010	8	7	11	Dec	2	4
2010	8	7	12	Jan	1	5
2011	7	8	1	Feb	9	6
2011	7	8	2	Mar	8	7
2011	7	8	3	Apr	7	8
2011	7	8	4	May	6	9
2011	7	8	5	Jun	5	1
2011	7	8	6	Jul	4	2
2011	7	8	7	Aug	3	3
2011	7	8	8	Sep	2	4
2011	7	8	9	Oct	1	5
2011	7	8	10	Nov	9	6
2011	7	8	11	Dec	8	7
2011	7	8	12	Jan	7	8
2012	6	9	1	Feb	6	9
2012	6	9	2	Mar	5	1
2012	6	9	3	Apr	4	2
2012	6	9	4	May	3	3
2012	6	9	5	Jun	2	4
2012	6	9	6	Jul	1	5
2012	6	9	7	Aug	9	6
2012	6	9	8	Sep	8	7
2012	6	9	9	Oct	7	8
2012	6	9	10	Nov	6	9
2012	6	9	11	Dec	5	1
2012	6	9	12	Jan	4	2
2013	5	1	1	Feb	3	3
2013	5	1	2	Mar	2	4
2013	5	1	3	Apr	1	5
2013	5	1	4	May	9	6
2013	5	1	5	Jun	8	7
2013	5	1	6	Jul	7	8
2013	5	1	7	Aug	6	9
2013	5	1	8	Sep	5	1
2013	5	1	9	Oct	4	2
2013	5	1	10	Nov	3	3
2013	5	1	11	Dec	2	4
2013	5	1	12	Jan	1	5

Year	Yearly Male	Yearly Female	Adjusted Monthly Number	Month Name	Male Monthly Number	Female Monthly Number
2014	4	2	1	Feb	9	6
2014	4	2	2	Mar	8	7
2014	4	2	3	Apr	7	8
2014	4	2	4	May	6	9
2014	4	2	5	Jun	5	1
2014	4	2	6	Jul	4	2
2014	4	2	7	Aug	3	3
2014	4	2	8	Sep	2	4
2014	4	2	9	Oct	1	5
2014	4	2	10	Nov	9	6
2014	4	2	11	Dec	8	7
2014	4	2	12	Jan	7	8
2015	3	3	1	Feb	6	9
2015	3	3	2	Mar	5	1
2015	3	3	3	Apr	4	2
2015	3	3	4	May	3	3
2015	3	3	5	Jun	2	4
2015	3	3	6	Jul	1	5
2015	3	3	7	Aug	9	6
2015	3	3	8	Sep	8	7
2015	3	3	9	Oct	7	8
2015	3	3	10	Nov	6	9
2015	3	3	11	Dec	5	1
2015	3	3	12	Jan	4	2
2016	2	4	1	Feb	3	3
2016	2	4	2	Mar	2	4
2016	2	4	3	Apr	1	5
2016	2	4	4	May	9	6
2016	2	4	5	Jun	8	7
2016	2	4	6	Jul	7	8
2016	2	4	7	Aug	6	9
2016	2	4	8	Sep	5	1
2016	2	4	9	Oct	4	2
2016	2	4	10	Nov	3	3
2016	2	4	11	Dec	2	4
2016	2	4	12	Jan	1	5
2017	1	5	1	Feb	9	6
2017	1	5	2	Mar	8	7
2017	1	5	3	Apr	7	8
2017	1	5	4	May	6	9
2017	1	5	5	Jun	5	1
2017	1	5	6	Jul	4	2
2017	1	5	7	Aug	3	3
2017	1	5	8	Sep	2	4
2017	1	5	9	Oct	1	5

Year	Yearly Male	Yearly Female	Adjusted Monthly Number	Month Name	Male Monthly Number	Female Monthly Number
2017	1	5	10	Nov	9	6
2017	1	5	11	Dec	8	7
2017	1	5	12	Jan	7	8
2018	9	6	1	Feb	6	9
2018	9	6	2	Mar	5	1
2018	9	6	3	Apr	4	2
2018	9	6	4	May	3	3
2018	9	6	5	Jun	2	4
2018	9	6	6	Jul	1	5
2018	9	6	7	Aug	9	6
2018	9	6	8	Sep	8	7
2018	9	6	9	Oct	7	8
2018	9	6	10	Nov	6	9
2018	9	6	11	Dec	5	1
2018	9	6	12	Jan	4	2
2019	8	7	1	Feb	3	3
2019	8	7	2	Mar	2	4
2019	8	7	3	Apr	1	5
2019	8	7	4	May	9	6
2019	8	7	5	Jun	8	7
2019	8	7	6	Jul	7	8
2019	8	7	7	Aug	6	9
2019	8	7	8	Sep	5	1
2019	8	7	9	Oct	4	2
2019	8	7	10	Nov	3	3
2019	8	7	11	Dec	2	4
2019	8	7	12	Jan	1	5
2020	7	8	1	Feb	9	6
2020	7	8	2	Mar	8	7
2020	7	8	3	Apr	7	8
2020	7	8	4	May	6	9
2020	7	8	5	Jun	5	1
2020	7	8	6	Jul	4	2
2020	7	8	7	Aug	3	3
2020	7	8	8	Sep	2	4
2020	7	8	9	Oct	1	5
2020	7	8	10	Nov	9	6
2020	7	8	11	Dec	8	7
2020	7	8	12	Jan	7	8
2021	6	9	1	Feb	6	9
2021	6	9	2	Mar	5	1
2021	6	9	3	Apr	4	2
2021	6	9	4	May	3	3
2021	6	9	5	Jun	2	4
2021	6	9	6	Jul	1	5

Year	Yearly Male	Yearly Female	Adjusted Monthly Number	Month Name	Male Monthly Number	Female Monthly Number
2021	6	9	7	Aug	9	6
2021	6	9	8	Sep	8	7
2021	6	9	9	Oct	7	8
2021	6	9	10	Nov	6	9
2021	6	9	11	Dec	5	1
2021	6	9	12	Jan	4	2
2022	5	1	1	Feb	3	3
2022	5	1	2	Mar	2	4
2022	5	1	3	Apr	1	5
2022	5	1	4	May	9	6
2022	5	1	5	Jun	8	7
2022	5	1	6	Jul	7	8
2022	5	1	7	Aug	6	9
2022	5	1	8	Sep	5	1
2022	5	1	9	Oct	4	2
2022	5	1	10	Nov	3	3
2022	5	1	11	Dec	2	4
2022	5	1	12	Jan	1	5
2023	4	2	1	Feb	9	6
2023	4	2	2	Mar	8	7
2023	4	2	3	Apr	7	8
2023	4	2	4	May	6	9
2023	4	2	5	Jun	5	1
2023	4	2	6	Jul	4	2
2023	4	2	7	Aug	3	3
2023	4	2	8	Sep	2	4
2023	4	2	9	Oct	1	5
2023	4	2	10	Nov	9	6
2023	4	2	11	Dec	8	7
2023	4	2	12	Jan	7	8
2024	3	3	1	Feb	6	9
2024	3	3	2	Mar	5	1
2024	3	3	3	Apr	4	2
2024	3	3	4	May	3	3
2024	3	3	5	Jun	2	4
2024	3	3	6	Jul	1	5
2024	3	3	7	Aug	9	6
2024	3	3	8	Sep	8	7
2024	3	3	9	Oct	7	8
2024	3	3	10	Nov	6	9
2024	3	3	11	Dec	5	1
2024	3	3	12	Jan	4	2
2025	2	4	1	Feb	3	3
2025	2	4	2	Mar	2	4
2025	2	4	3	Apr	1	5

Year	Yearly Male	Yearly Female	Adjusted Monthly Number	Month Name	Male Monthly Number	Female Monthly Number
2025	2	4	4	May	9	6
2025	2	4	5	Jun	8	7
2025	2	4	6	Jul	7	8
2025	2	4	7	Aug	6	9
2025	2	4	8	Sep	5	1
2025	2	4	9	Oct	4	2
2025	2	4	10	Nov	3	3
2025	2	4	11	Dec	2	4
2025	2	4	12	Jan	1	5
2026	1	5	1	Feb	9	6
2026	1	5	2	Mar	8	7
2026	1	5	3	Apr	7	8
2026	1	5	4	May	6	9
2026	1	5	5	Jun	5	1
2026	1	5	6	Jul	4	2
2026	1	5	7	Aug	3	3
2026	1	5	8	Sep	2	4
2026	1	5	9	Oct	1	5
2026	1	5	10	Nov	9	6
2026	1	5	11	Dec	8	7
2026	1	5	12	Jan	7	8
2027	9	6	1	Feb	6	9
2027	9	6	2	Mar	5	1
2027	9	6	3	Apr	4	2
2027	9	6	4	May	3	3
2027	9	6	5	Jun	2	4
2027	9	6	6	Jul	1	5
2027	9	6	7	Aug	9	6
2027	9	6	8	Sep	8	7
2027	9	6	9	Oct	7	8
2027	9	6	10	Nov	6	9
2027	9	6	11	Dec	5	1
2027	9	6	12	Jan	4	2
2028	8	7	1	Feb	3	3
2028	8	7	2	Mar	2	4
2028	8	7	3	Apr	1	5
2028	8	7	4	May	9	6
2028	8	7	5	Jun	8	7
2028	8	7	6	Jul	7	8
2028	8	7	7	Aug	6	9
2028	8	7	8	Sep	5	1
2028	8	7	9	Oct	4	2
2028	8	7	10	Nov	3	3
2028	8	7	11	Dec	2	4
2028	8	7	12	Jan	1	5

Year	Yearly Male	Yearly Female	Adjusted Monthly Number	Month Name	Male Monthly Number	Female Monthly Number
2029	7	8	1	Feb	9	6
2029	7	8	2	Mar	8	7
2029	7	8	3	Apr	7	8
2029	7	8	4	May	6	9
2029	7	8	5	Jun	5	1
2029	7	8	6	Jul	4	2
2029	7	8	7	Aug	3	3
2029	7	8	8	Sep	2	4
2029	7	8	9	Oct	1	5
2029	7	8	10	Nov	9	6
2029	7	8	11	Dec	8	7
2029	7	8	12	Jan	7	8
2030	6	9	1	Feb	6	9
2030	6	9	2	Mar	5	1
2030	6	9	3	Apr	4	2
2030	6	9	4	May	3	3
2030	6	9	5	Jun	2	4
2030	6	9	6	Jul	1	5
2030	6	9	7	Aug	9	6
2030	6	9	8	Sep	8	7
2030	6	9	9	Oct	7	8
2030	6	9	10	Nov	6	9
2030	6	9	11	Dec	5	1
2030	6	9	12	Jan	4	2
2031	5	1	1	Feb	3	3
2031	5	1	2	Mar	2	4
2031	5	1	3	Apr	1	5
2031	5	1	4	May	9	6
2031	5	1	5	Jun	8	7
2031	5	1	6	Jul	7	8
2031	5	1	7	Aug	6	9
2031	5	1	8	Sep	5	1
2031	5	1	9	Oct	4	2
2031	5	1	10	Nov	3	3
2031	5	1	11	Dec	2	4
2031	5	1	12	Jan	1	5
2032	4	2	1	Feb	9	6
2032	4	2	2	Mar	8	7
2032	4	2	3	Apr	7	8
2032	4	2	4	May	6	9
2032	4	2	5	Jun	5	1
2032	4	2	6	Jul	4	2
2032	4	2	7	Aug	3	3
2032	4	2	8	Sep	2	4
2032	4	2	9	Oct	1	5

Year	Yearly Male	Yearly Female	Adjusted Monthly Number	Month Name	Male Monthly Number	Female Monthly Number
2032	4	2	10	Nov	9	6
2032	4	2	11	Dec	8	7
2032	4	2	12	Jan	7	8
2033	3	3	1	Feb	6	9
2033	3	3	2	Mar	5	1
2033	3	3	3	Apr	4	2
2033	3	3	4	May	3	3
2033	3	3	5	Jun	2	4
2033	3	3	6	Jul	1	5
2033	3	3	7	Aug	9	6
2033	3	3	8	Sep	8	7
2033	3	3	9	Oct	7	8
2033	3	3	10	Nov	6	9
2033	3	3	11	Dec	5	1
2033	3	3	12	Jan	4	2
2034	2	4	1	Feb	3	3
2034	2	4	2	Mar	2	4
2034	2	4	3	Apr	1	5
2034	2	4	4	May	9	6
2034	2	4	5	Jun	8	7
2034	2	4	6	Jul	7	8
2034	2	4	7	Aug	6	9
2034	2	4	8	Sep	5	1
2034	2	4	9	Oct	4	2
2034	2	4	10	Nov	3	3
2034	2	4	11	Dec	2	4
2034	2	4	12	Jan	1	5
2035	1	5	1	Feb	9	6
2035	1	5	2	Mar	8	7
2035	1	5	3	Apr	7	8
2035	1	5	4	May	6	9
2035	1	5	5	Jun	5	1
2035	1	5	6	Jul	4	2
2035	1	5	7	Aug	3	3
2035	1	5	8	Sep	2	4
2035	1	5	9	Oct	1	5
2035	1	5	10	Nov	9	6
2035	1	5	11	Dec	8	7
2035	1	5	12	Jan	7	8
2036	9	6	1	Feb	6	9
2036	9	6	2	Mar	5	1
2036	9	6	3	Apr	4	2
2036	9	6	4	May	3	3
2036	9	6	5	Jun	2	4
2036	9	6	6	Jul	1	5

Year	Yearly Male	Yearly Female	Adjusted Monthly Number	Month Name	Male Monthly Number	Female Monthly Number
2036	9	6	7	Aug	9	6
2036	9	6	8	Sep	8	7
2036	9	6	9	Oct	7	8
2036	9	6	10	Nov	6	9
2036	9	6	11	Dec	5	1
2036	9	6	12	Jan	4	2
2037	8	7	1	Feb	3	3
2037	8	7	2	Mar	2	4
2037	8	7	3	Apr	1	5
2037	8	7	4	May	9	6
2037	8	7	5	Jun	8	7
2037	8	7	6	Jul	7	8
2037	8	7	7	Aug	6	9
2037	8	7	8	Sep	5	1
2037	8	7	9	Oct	4	2
2037	8	7	10	Nov	3	3
2037	8	7	11	Dec	2	4
2037	8	7	12	Jan	1	5
2038	7	8	1	Feb	9	6
2038	7	8	2	Mar	8	7
2038	7	8	3	Apr	7	8
2038	7	8	4	May	6	9
2038	7	8	5	Jun	5	1
2038	7	8	6	Jul	4	2
2038	7	8	7	Aug	3	3
2038	7	8	8	Sep	2	4
2038	7	8	9	Oct	1	5
2038	7	8	10	Nov	9	6
2038	7	8	11	Dec	8	7
2038	7	8	12	Jan	7	8
2039	6	9	1	Feb	6	9
2039	6	9	2	Mar	5	1
2039	6	9	3	Apr	4	2
2039	6	9	4	May	3	3
2039	6	9	5	Jun	2	4
2039	6	9	6	Jul	1	5
2039	6	9	7	Aug	9	6
2039	6	9	8	Sep	8	7
2039	6	9	9	Oct	7	8
2039	6	9	10	Nov	6	9
2039	6	9	11	Dec	5	1
2039	6	9	12	Jan	4	2
2040	5	1	1	Feb	3	3
2040	5	1	2	Mar	2	4
2040	5	1	3	Apr	1	5

Year	Yearly Male	Yearly Female	Adjusted Monthly Number	Month Name	Male Monthly Number	Female Monthly Number
2040	5	1	4	May	9	6
2040	5	1	5	Jun	8	7
2040	5	1	6	Jul	7	8
2040	5	1	7	Aug	6	9
2040	5	1	8	Sep	5	1
2040	5	1	9	Oct	4	2
2040	5	1	10	Nov	3	3
2040	5	1	11	Dec	2	4
2040	5	1	12	Jan	1	5
2041	4	2	1	Feb	9	6
2041	4	2	2	Mar	8	7
2041	4	2	3	Apr	7	8
2041	4	2	4	May	6	9
2041	4	2	5	Jun	5	1
2041	4	2	6	Jul	4	2
2041	4	2	7	Aug	3	3
2041	4	2	8	Sep	2	4
2041	4	2	9	Oct	1	5
2041	4	2	10	Nov	9	6
2041	4	2	11	Dec	8	7
2041	4	2	12	Jan	7	8
2042	3	3	1	Feb	6	9
2042	3	3	2	Mar	5	1
2042	3	3	3	Apr	4	2
2042	3	3	4	May	3	3
2042	3	3	5	Jun	2	4
2042	3	3	6	Jul	1	5
2042	3	3	7	Aug	9	6
2042	3	3	8	Sep	8	7
2042	3	3	9	Oct	7	8
2042	3	3	10	Nov	6	9
2042	3	3	11	Dec	5	1
2042	3	3	12	Jan	4	2
2043	2	4	1	Feb	3	3
2043	2	4	2	Mar	2	4
2043	2	4	3	Apr	1	5
2043	2	4	4	May	9	6
2043	2	4	5	Jun	8	7
2043	2	4	6	Jul	7	8
2043	2	4	7	Aug	6	9
2043	2	4	8	Sep	5	1
2043	2	4	9	Oct	4	2
2043	2	4	10	Nov	3	3
2043	2	4	11	Dec	2	4
2043	2	4	12	Jan	1	5

Year	Yearly Male	Yearly Female	Adjusted Monthly Number	Month Name	Male Monthly Number	Female Monthly Number
2044	1	5	1	Feb	9	6
2044	1	5	2	Mar	8	7
2044	1	5	3	Apr	7	8
2044	1	5	4	May	6	9
2044	1	5	5	Jun	5	1
2044	1	5	6	Jul	4	2
2044	1	5	7	Aug	3	3
2044	1	5	8	Sep	2	4
2044	1	5	9	Oct	1	5
2044	1	5	10	Nov	9	6
2044	1	5	11	Dec	8	7
2044	1	5	12	Jan	7	8
2045	9	6	1	Feb	6	9
2045	9	6	2	Mar	5	1
2045	9	6	3	Apr	4	2
2045	9	6	4	May	3	3
2045	9	6	5	Jun	2	4
2045	9	6	6	Jul	1	5
2045	9	6	7	Aug	9	6
2045	9	6	8	Sep	8	7
2045	9	6	9	Oct	7	8
2045	9	6	10	Nov	6	9
2045	9	6	11	Dec	5	1
2045	9	6	12	Jan	4	2
2046	8	7	1	Feb	3	3
2046	8	7	2	Mar	2	4
2046	8	7	3	Apr	1	5
2046	8	7	4	May	9	6
2046	8	7	5	Jun	8	7
2046	8	7	6	Jul	7	8
2046	8	7	7	Aug	6	9
2046	8	7	8	Sep	5	1
2046	8	7	9	Oct	4	2
2046	8	7	10	Nov	3	3
2046	8	7	11	Dec	2	4
2046	8	7	12	Jan	1	5
2047	7	8	1	Feb	9	6
2047	7	8	2	Mar	8	7
2047	7	8	3	Apr	7	8
2047	7	8	4	May	6	9
2047	7	8	5	Jun	5	1
2047	7	8	6	Jul	4	2
2047	7	8	7	Aug	3	3
2047	7	8	8	Sep	2	4
2047	7	8	9	Oct	1	5

Year	Yearly Male	Yearly Female	Adjusted Monthly Number	Month Name	Male Monthly Number	Female Monthly Number
2047	7	8	10	Nov	9	6
2047	7	8	11	Dec	8	7
2047	7	8	12	Jan	7	8
2048	6	9	1	Feb	6	9
2048	6	9	2	Mar	5	1
2048	6	9	3	Apr	4	2
2048	6	9	4	May	3	3
2048	6	9	5	Jun	2	4
2048	6	9	6	Jul	1	5
2048	6	9	7	Aug	9	6
2048	6	9	8	Sep	8	7
2048	6	9	9	Oct	7	8
2048	6	9	10	Nov	6	9
2048	6	9	11	Dec	5	1
2048	6	9	12	Jan	4	2
2049	5	1	1	Feb	3	3
2049	5	1	2	Mar	2	4
2049	5	1	3	Apr	1	5
2049	5	1	4	May	9	6
2049	5	1	5	Jun	8	7
2049	5	1	6	Jul	7	8
2049	5	1	7	Aug	6	9
2049	5	1	8	Sep	5	1
2049	5	1	9	Oct	4	2
2049	5	1	10	Nov	3	3
2049	5	1	11	Dec	2	4
2049	5	1	12	Jan	1	5
2050	4	2	1	Feb	9	6
2050	4	2	2	Mar	8	7
2050	4	2	3	Apr	7	8
2050	4	2	4	May	6	9
2050	4	2	5	Jun	5	1
2050	4	2	6	Jul	4	2
2050	4	2	7	Aug	3	3
2050	4	2	8	Sep	2	4
2050	4	2	9	Oct	1	5
2050	4	2	10	Nov	9	6
2050	4	2	11	Dec	8	7
2050	4	2	12	Jan	7	8
2051	3	3	1	Feb	6	9
2051	3	3	2	Mar	5	1
2051	3	3	3	Apr	4	2
2051	3	3	4	May	3	3
2051	3	3	5	Jun	2	4
2051	3	3	6	Jul	1	5

Year	Yearly Male	Yearly Female	Adjusted Monthly Number	Month Name	Male Monthly Number	Female Monthly Number
2051	3	3	7	Aug	9	6
2051	3	3	8	Sep	8	7
2051	3	3	9	Oct	7	8
2051	3	3	10	Nov	6	9
2051	3	3	11	Dec	5	1
2051	3	3	12	Jan	4	2
2052	2	4	1	Feb	3	3
2052	2	4	2	Mar	2	4
2052	2	4	3	Apr	1	5
2052	2	4	4	May	9	6
2052	2	4	5	Jun	8	7
2052	2	4	6	Jul	7	8
2052	2	4	7	Aug	6	9
2052	2	4	8	Sep	5	1
2052	2	4	9	Oct	4	2
2052	2	4	10	Nov	3	3
2052	2	4	11	Dec	2	4
2052	2	4	12	Jan	1	5
2053	1	5	1	Feb	9	6
2053	1	5	2	Mar	8	7
2053	1	5	3	Apr	7	8
2053	1	5	4	May	6	9
2053	1	5	5	Jun	5	1
2053	1	5	6	Jul	4	2
2053	1	5	7	Aug	3	3
2053	1	5	8	Sep	2	4
2053	1	5	9	Oct	1	5
2053	1	5	10	Nov	9	6
2053	1	5	11	Dec	8	7
2053	1	5	12	Jan	7	8
2054	9	6	1	Feb	6	9
2054	9	6	2	Mar	5	1
2054	9	6	3	Apr	4	2
2054	9	6	4	May	3	3
2054	9	6	5	Jun	2	4
2054	9	6	6	Jul	1	5
2054	9	6	7	Aug	9	6
2054	9	6	8	Sep	8	7
2054	9	6	9	Oct	7	8
2054	9	6	10	Nov	6	9
2054	9	6	11	Dec	5	1
2054	9	6	12	Jan	4	2
2055	8	7	1	Feb	3	3
2055	8	7	2	Mar	2	4
2055	8	7	3	Apr	1	5

Year	Yearly Male	Yearly Female	Adjusted Monthly Number	Month Name	Male Monthly Number	Female Monthly Number
2055	8	7	4	May	9	6
2055	8	7	5	Jun	8	7
2055	8	7	6	Jul	7	8
2055	8	7	7	Aug	6	9
2055	8	7	8	Sep	5	1
2055	8	7	9	Oct	4	2
2055	8	7	10	Nov	3	3
2055	8	7	11	Dec	2	4
2055	8	7	12	Jan	1	5
2056	7	8	1	Feb	9	6
2056	7	8	2	Mar	8	7
2056	7	8	3	Apr	7	8
2056	7	8	4	May	6	9
2056	7	8	5	Jun	5	1
2056	7	8	6	Jul	4	2
2056	7	8	7	Aug	3	3
2056	7	8	8	Sep	2	4
2056	7	8	9	Oct	1	5
2056	7	8	10	Nov	9	6
2056	7	8	11	Dec	8	7
2056	7	8	12	Jan	7	8
2057	6	9	1	Feb	6	9
2057	6	9	2	Mar	5	1
2057	6	9	3	Apr	4	2
2057	6	9	4	May	3	3
2057	6	9	5	Jun	2	4
2057	6	9	6	Jul	1	5
2057	6	9	7	Aug	9	6
2057	6	9	8	Sep	8	7
2057	6	9	9	Oct	7	8
2057	6	9	10	Nov	6	9
2057	6	9	11	Dec	5	1
2057	6	9	12	Jan	4	2
2058	5	1	1	Feb	3	3
2058	5	1	2	Mar	2	4
2058	5	1	3	Apr	1	5
2058	5	1	4	May	9	6
2058	5	1	5	Jun	8	7
2058	5	1	6	Jul	7	8
2058	5	1	7	Aug	6	9
2058	5	1	8	Sep	5	1
2058	5	1	9	Oct	4	2
2058	5	1	10	Nov	3	3
2058	5	1	11	Dec	2	4
2058	5	1	12	Jan	1	5

Year	Yearly Male	Yearly Female	Adjusted Monthly Number	Month Name	Male Monthly Number	Female Monthly Number
2059	4	2	1	Feb	9	6
2059	4	2	2	Mar	8	7
2059	4	2	3	Apr	7	8
2059	4	2	4	May	6	9
2059	4	2	5	Jun	5	1
2059	4	2	6	Jul	4	2
2059	4	2	7	Aug	3	3
2059	4	2	8	Sep	2	4
2059	4	2	9	Oct	1	5
2059	4	2	10	Nov	9	6
2059	4	2	11	Dec	8	7
2059	4	2	12	Jan	7	8
2060	3	3	1	Feb	6	9
2060	3	3	2	Mar	5	1
2060	3	3	3	Apr	4	2
2060	3	3	4	May	3	3
2060	3	3	5	Jun	2	4
2060	3	3	6	Jul	1	5
2060	3	3	7	Aug	9	6
2060	3	3	8	Sep	8	7
2060	3	3	9	Oct	7	8
2060	3	3	10	Nov	6	9
2060	3	3	11	Dec	5	1
2060	3	3	12	Jan	4	2
2061	2	4	1	Feb	3	3
2061	2	4	2	Mar	2	4
2061	2	4	3	Apr	1	5
2061	2	4	4	May	9	6
2061	2	4	5	Jun	8	7
2061	2	4	6	Jul	7	8
2061	2	4	7	Aug	6	9
2061	2	4	8	Sep	5	1
2061	2	4	9	Oct	4	2
2061	2	4	10	Nov	3	3
2061	2	4	11	Dec	2	4
2061	2	4	12	Jan	1	5
2062	1	5	1	Feb	9	6
2062	1	5	2	Mar	8	7
2062	1	5	3	Apr	7	8
2062	1	5	4	May	6	9
2062	1	5	5	Jun	5	1
2062	1	5	6	Jul	4	2
2062	1	5	7	Aug	3	3
2062	1	5	8	Sep	2	4
2062	1	5	9	Oct	1	5

Year	Yearly Male	Yearly Female	Adjusted Monthly Number	Month Name	Male Monthly Number	Female Monthly Number
2062	1	5	10	Nov	9	6
2062	1	5	11	Dec	8	7
2062	1	5	12	Jan	7	8
2063	9	6	1	Feb	6	9
2063	9	6	2	Mar	5	1
2063	9	6	3	Apr	4	2
2063	9	6	4	May	3	3
2063	9	6	5	Jun	2	4
2063	9	6	6	Jul	1	5
2063	9	6	7	Aug	9	6
2063	9	6	8	Sep	8	7
2063	9	6	9	Oct	7	8
2063	9	6	10	Nov	6	9
2063	9	6	11	Dec	5	1
2063	9	6	12	Jan	4	2
2064	8	7	1	Feb	3	3
2064	8	7	2	Mar	2	4
2064	8	7	3	Apr	1	5
2064	8	7	4	May	9	6
2064	8	7	5	Jun	8	7
2064	8	7	6	Jul	7	8
2064	8	7	7	Aug	6	9
2064	8	7	8	Sep	5	1
2064	8	7	9	Oct	4	2
2064	8	7	10	Nov	3	3
2064	8	7	11	Dec	2	4
2064	8	7	12	Jan	1	5
2065	7	8	1	Feb	9	6
2065	7	8	2	Mar	8	7
2065	7	8	3	Apr	7	8
2065	7	8	4	May	6	9
2065	7	8	5	Jun	5	1
2065	7	8	6	Jul	4	2
2065	7	8	7	Aug	3	3
2065	7	8	8	Sep	2	4
2065	7	8	9	Oct	1	5
2065	7	8	10	Nov	9	6
2065	7	8	11	Dec	8	7
2065	7	8	12	Jan	7	8
2066	6	9	1	Feb	6	9
2066	6	9	2	Mar	5	1
2066	6	9	3	Apr	4	2
2066	6	9	4	May	3	3
2066	6	9	5	Jun	2	4
2066	6	9	6	Jul	1	5

Year	Yearly Male	Yearly Female	Adjusted Monthly Number	Month Name	Male Monthly Number	Female Monthly Number
2066	6	9	7	Aug	9	6
2066	6	9	8	Sep	8	7
2066	6	9	9	Oct	7	8
2066	6	9	10	Nov	6	9
2066	6	9	11	Dec	5	1
2066	6	9	12	Jan	4	2
2067	5	1	1	Feb	3	3
2067	5	1	2	Mar	2	4
2067	5	1	3	Apr	1	5
2067	5	1	4	May	9	6
2067	5	1	5	Jun	8	7
2067	5	1	6	Jul	7	8
2067	5	1	7	Aug	6	9
2067	5	1	8	Sep	5	1
2067	5	1	9	Oct	4	2
2067	5	1	10	Nov	3	3
2067	5	1	11	Dec	2	4
2067	5	1	12	Jan	1	5
2068	4	2	1	Feb	9	6
2068	4	2	2	Mar	8	7
2068	4	2	3	Apr	7	8
2068	4	2	4	May	6	9
2068	4	2	5	Jun	5	1
2068	4	2	6	Jul	4	2
2068	4	2	7	Aug	3	3
2068	4	2	8	Sep	2	4
2068	4	2	9	Oct	1	5
2068	4	2	10	Nov	9	6
2068	4	2	11	Dec	8	7
2068	4	2	12	Jan	7	8
2069	3	3	1	Feb	6	9
2069	3	3	2	Mar	5	1
2069	3	3	3	Apr	4	2
2069	3	3	4	May	3	3
2069	3	3	5	Jun	2	4
2069	3	3	6	Jul	1	5
2069	3	3	7	Aug	9	6
2069	3	3	8	Sep	8	7
2069	3	3	9	Oct	7	8
2069	3	3	10	Nov	6	9
2069	3	3	11	Dec	5	1
2069	3	3	12	Jan	4	2
2070	2	4	1	Feb	3	3
2070	2	4	2	Mar	2	4
2070	2	4	3	Apr	1	5

Year	Yearly Male	Yearly Female	Adjusted Monthly Number	Month Name	Male Monthly Number	Female Monthly Number
2070	2	4	4	May	9	6
2070	2	4	5	Jun	8	7
2070	2	4	6	Jul	7	8
2070	2	4	7	Aug	6	9
2070	2	4	8	Sep	5	1
2070	2	4	9	Oct	4	2
2070	2	4	10	Nov	3	3
2070	2	4	11	Dec	2	4
2070	2	4	12	Jan	1	5
2071	1	5	1	Feb	9	6
2071	1	5	2	Mar	8	7
2071	1	5	3	Apr	7	8
2071	1	5	4	May	6	9
2071	1	5	5	Jun	5	1
2071	1	5	6	Jul	4	2
2071	1	5	7	Aug	3	3
2071	1	5	8	Sep	2	4
2071	1	5	9	Oct	1	5
2071	1	5	10	Nov	9	6
2071	1	5	11	Dec	8	7
2071	1	5	12	Jan	7	8
2072	9	6	1	Feb	6	9
2072	9	6	2	Mar	5	1
2072	9	6	3	Apr	4	2
2072	9	6	4	May	3	3
2072	9	6	5	Jun	2	4
2072	9	6	6	Jul	1	5
2072	9	6	7	Aug	9	6
2072	9	6	8	Sep	8	7
2072	9	6	9	Oct	7	8
2072	9	6	10	Nov	6	9
2072	9	6	11	Dec	5	1
2072	9	6	12	Jan	4	2
2073	8	7	1	Feb	3	3
2073	8	7	2	Mar	2	4
2073	8	7	3	Apr	1	5
2073	8	7	4	May	9	6
2073	8	7	5	Jun	8	7
2073	8	7	6	Jul	7	8
2073	8	7	7	Aug	6	9
2073	8	7	8	Sep	5	1
2073	8	7	9	Oct	4	2
2073	8	7	10	Nov	3	3
2073	8	7	11	Dec	2	4
2073	8	7	12	Jan	1	5

Year	Yearly Male	Yearly Female	Adjusted Monthly Number	Month Name	Male Monthly Number	Female Monthly Number
2074	7	8	1	Feb	9	6
2074	7	8	2	Mar	8	7
2074	7	8	3	Apr	7	8
2074	7	8	4	May	6	9
2074	7	8	5	Jun	5	1
2074	7	8	6	Jul	4	2
2074	7	8	7	Aug	3	3
2074	7	8	8	Sep	2	4
2074	7	8	9	Oct	1	5
2074	7	8	10	Nov	9	6
2074	7	8	11	Dec	8	7
2074	7	8	12	Jan	7	8
2075	6	9	1	Feb	6	9
2075	6	9	2	Mar	5	1
2075	6	9	3	Apr	4	2
2075	6	9	4	May	3	3
2075	6	9	5	Jun	2	4
2075	6	9	6	Jul	1	5
2075	6	9	7	Aug	9	6
2075	6	9	8	Sep	8	7
2075	6	9	9	Oct	7	8
2075	6	9	10	Nov	6	9
2075	6	9	11	Dec	5	1
2075	6	9	12	Jan	4	2
2076	5	1	1	Feb	3	3
2076	5	1	2	Mar	2	4
2076	5	1	3	Apr	1	5
2076	5	1	4	May	9	6
2076	5	1	5	Jun	8	7
2076	5	1	6	Jul	7	8
2076	5	1	7	Aug	6	9
2076	5	1	8	Sep	5	1
2076	5	1	9	Oct	4	2
2076	5	1	10	Nov	3	3
2076	5	1	11	Dec	2	4
2076	5	1	12	Jan	1	5
2077	4	2	1	Feb	9	6
2077	4	2	2	Mar	8	7
2077	4	2	3	Apr	7	8
2077	4	2	4	May	6	9
2077	4	2	5	Jun	5	1
2077	4	2	6	Jul	4	2
2077	4	2	7	Aug	3	3
2077	4	2	8	Sep	2	4
2077	4	2	9	Oct	1	5

Year	Yearly Male	Yearly Female	Adjusted Monthly Number	Month Name	Male Monthly Number	Female Monthly Number
2077	4	2	10	Nov	9	6
2077	4	2	11	Dec	8	7
2077	4	2	12	Jan	7	8
2078	3	3	1	Feb	6	9
2078	3	3	2	Mar	5	1
2078	3	3	3	Apr	4	2
2078	3	3	4	May	3	3
2078	3	3	5	Jun	2	4
2078	3	3	6	Jul	1	5
2078	3	3	7	Aug	9	6
2078	3	3	8	Sep	8	7
2078	3	3	9	Oct	7	8
2078	3	3	10	Nov	6	9
2078	3	3	11	Dec	5	1
2078	3	3	12	Jan	4	2
2079	2	4	1	Feb	3	3
2079	2	4	2	Mar	2	4
2079	2	4	3	Apr	1	5
2079	2	4	4	May	9	6
2079	2	4	5	Jun	8	7
2079	2	4	6	Jul	7	8
2079	2	4	7	Aug	6	9
2079	2	4	8	Sep	5	1
2079	2	4	9	Oct	4	2
2079	2	4	10	Nov	3	3
2079	2	4	11	Dec	2	4
2079	2	4	12	Jan	1	5
2080	1	5	1	Feb	9	6
2080	1	5	2	Mar	8	7
2080	1	5	3	Apr	7	8
2080	1	5	4	May	6	9
2080	1	5	5	Jun	5	1
2080	1	5	6	Jul	4	2
2080	1	5	7	Aug	3	3
2080	1	5	8	Sep	2	4
2080	1	5	9	Oct	1	5
2080	1	5	10	Nov	9	6
2080	1	5	11	Dec	8	7
2080	1	5	12	Jan	7	8
2081	9	6	1	Feb	6	9
2081	9	6	2	Mar	5	1
2081	9	6	3	Apr	4	2
2081	9	6	4	May	3	3
2081	9	6	5	Jun	2	4
2081	9	6	6	Jul	1	5

Year	Yearly Male	Yearly Female	Adjusted Monthly Number	Month Name	Male Monthly Number	Female Monthly Number
2081	9	6	7	Aug	9	6
2081	9	6	8	Sep	8	7
2081	9	6	9	Oct	7	8
2081	9	6	10	Nov	6	9
2081	9	6	11	Dec	5	1
2081	9	6	12	Jan	4	2
2082	8	7	1	Feb	3	3
2082	8	7	2	Mar	2	4
2082	8	7	3	Apr	1	5
2082	8	7	4	May	9	6
2082	8	7	5	Jun	8	7
2082	8	7	6	Jul	7	8
2082	8	7	7	Aug	6	9
2082	8	7	8	Sep	5	1
2082	8	7	9	Oct	4	2
2082	8	7	10	Nov	3	3
2082	8	7	11	Dec	2	4
2082	8	7	12	Jan	1	5
2083	7	8	1	Feb	9	6
2083	7	8	2	Mar	8	7
2083	7	8	3	Apr	7	8
2083	7	8	4	May	6	9
2083	7	8	5	Jun	5	1
2083	7	8	6	Jul	4	2
2083	7	8	7	Aug	3	3
2083	7	8	8	Sep	2	4
2083	7	8	9	Oct	1	5
2083	7	8	10	Nov	9	6
2083	7	8	11	Dec	8	7
2083	7	8	12	Jan	7	8
2084	6	9	1	Feb	6	9
2084	6	9	2	Mar	5	1
2084	6	9	3	Apr	4	2
2084	6	9	4	May	3	3
2084	6	9	5	Jun	2	4
2084	6	9	6	Jul	1	5
2084	6	9	7	Aug	9	6
2084	6	9	8	Sep	8	7
2084	6	9	9	Oct	7	8
2084	6	9	10	Nov	6	9
2084	6	9	11	Dec	5	1
2084	6	9	12	Jan	4	2
2085	5	1	1	Feb	3	3
2085	5	1	2	Mar	2	4
2085	5	1	3	Apr	1	5

Year	Yearly Male	Yearly Female	Adjusted Monthly Number	Month Name	Male Monthly Number	Female Monthly Number
2085	5	1	4	May	9	6
2085	5	1	5	Jun	8	7
2085	5	1	6	Jul	7	8
2085	5	1	7	Aug	6	9
2085	5	1	8	Sep	5	1
2085	5	1	9	Oct	4	2
2085	5	1	10	Nov	3	3
2085	5	1	11	Dec	2	4
2085	5	1	12	Jan	1	5
2086	4	2	1	Feb	9	6
2086	4	2	2	Mar	8	7
2086	4	2	3	Apr	7	8
2086	4	2	4	May	6	9
2086	4	2	5	Jun	5	1
2086	4	2	6	Jul	4	2
2086	4	2	7	Aug	3	3
2086	4	2	8	Sep	2	4
2086	4	2	9	Oct	1	5
2086	4	2	10	Nov	9	6
2086	4	2	11	Dec	8	7
2086	4	2	12	Jan	7	8
2087	3	3	1	Feb	6	9
2087	3	3	2	Mar	5	1
2087	3	3	3	Apr	4	2
2087	3	3	4	May	3	3
2087	3	3	5	Jun	2	4
2087	3	3	6	Jul	1	5
2087	3	3	7	Aug	9	6
2087	3	3	8	Sep	8	7
2087	3	3	9	Oct	7	8
2087	3	3	10	Nov	6	9
2087	3	3	11	Dec	5	1
2087	3	3	12	Jan	4	2
2088	2	4	1	Feb	3	3
2088	2	4	2	Mar	2	4
2088	2	4	3	Apr	1	5
2088	2	4	4	May	9	6
2088	2	4	5	Jun	8	7
2088	2	4	6	Jul	7	8
2088	2	4	7	Aug	6	9
2088	2	4	8	Sep	5	1
2088	2	4	9	Oct	4	2
2088	2	4	10	Nov	3	3
2088	2	4	11	Dec	2	4
2088	2	4	12	Jan	1	5

Year	Yearly Male	Yearly Female	Adjusted Monthly Number	Month Name	Male Monthly Number	Female Monthly Number
2089	1	5	1	Feb	9	6
2089	1	5	2	Mar	8	7
2089	1	5	3	Apr	7	8
2089	1	5	4	May	6	9
2089	1	5	5	Jun	5	1
2089	1	5	6	Jul	4	2
2089	1	5	7	Aug	3	3
2089	1	5	8	Sep	2	4
2089	1	5	9	Oct	1	5
2089	1	5	10	Nov	9	6
2089	1	5	11	Dec	8	7
2089	1	5	12	Jan	7	8
2090	9	6	1	Feb	6	9
2090	9	6	2	Mar	5	1
2090	9	6	3	Apr	4	2
2090	9	6	4	May	3	3
2090	9	6	5	Jun	2	4
2090	9	6	6	Jul	1	5
2090	9	6	7	Aug	9	6
2090	9	6	8	Sep	8	7
2090	9	6	9	Oct	7	8
2090	9	6	10	Nov	6	9
2090	9	6	11	Dec	5	1
2090	9	6	12	Jan	4	2
2091	8	7	1	Feb	3	3
2091	8	7	2	Mar	2	4
2091	8	7	3	Apr	1	5
2091	8	7	4	May	9	6
2091	8	7	5	Jun	8	7
2091	8	7	6	Jul	7	8
2091	8	7	7	Aug	6	9
2091	8	7	8	Sep	5	1
2091	8	7	9	Oct	4	2
2091	8	7	10	Nov	3	3
2091	8	7	11	Dec	2	4
2091	8	7	12	Jan	1	5
2092	7	8	1	Feb	9	6
2092	7	8	2	Mar	8	7
2092	7	8	3	Apr	7	8
2092	7	8	4	May	6	9
2092	7	8	5	Jun	5	1
2092	7	8	6	Jul	4	2
2092	7	8	7	Aug	3	3
2092	7	8	8	Sep	2	4
2092	7	8	9	Oct	1	5

Year	Yearly Male	Yearly Female	Adjusted Monthly Number	Month Name	Male Monthly Number	Female Monthly Number
2092	7	8	10	Nov	9	6
2092	7	8	11	Dec	8	7
2092	7	8	12	Jan	7	8
2093	6	9	1	Feb	6	9
2093	6	9	2	Mar	5	1
2093	6	9	3	Apr	4	2
2093	6	9	4	May	3	3
2093	6	9	5	Jun	2	4
2093	6	9	6	Jul	1	5
2093	6	9	7	Aug	9	6
2093	6	9	8	Sep	8	7
2093	6	9	9	Oct	7	8
2093	6	9	10	Nov	6	9
2093	6	9	11	Dec	5	1
2093	6	9	12	Jan	4	2
2094	5	1	1	Feb	3	3
2094	5	1	2	Mar	2	4
2094	5	1	3	Apr	1	5
2094	5	1	4	May	9	6
2094	5	1	5	Jun	8	7
2094	5	1	6	Jul	7	8
2094	5	1	7	Aug	6	9
2094	5	1	8	Sep	5	1
2094	5	1	9	Oct	4	2
2094	5	1	10	Nov	3	3
2094	5	1	11	Dec	2	4
2094	5	1	12	Jan	1	5
2095	4	2	1	Feb	9	6
2095	4	2	2	Mar	8	7
2095	4	2	3	Apr	7	8
2095	4	2	4	May	6	9
2095	4	2	5	Jun	5	1
2095	4	2	6	Jul	4	2
2095	4	2	7	Aug	3	3
2095	4	2	8	Sep	2	4
2095	4	2	9	Oct	1	5
2095	4	2	10	Nov	9	6
2095	4	2	11	Dec	8	7
2095	4	2	12	Jan	7	8
2096	3	3	1	Feb	6	9
2096	3	3	2	Mar	5	1
2096	3	3	3	Apr	4	2
2096	3	3	4	May	3	3
2096	3	3	5	Jun	2	4
2096	3	3	6	Jul	1	5

Year	Yearly Male	Yearly Female	Adjusted Monthly Number	Month Name	Male Monthly Number	Female Monthly Number
2096	3	3	7	Aug	9	6
2096	3	3	8	Sep	8	7
2096	3	3	9	Oct	7	8
2096	3	3	10	Nov	6	9
2096	3	3	11	Dec	5	1
2096	3	3	12	Jan	4	2
2097	2	4	1	Feb	3	3
2097	2	4	2	Mar	2	4
2097	2	4	3	Apr	1	5
2097	2	4	4	May	9	6
2097	2	4	5	Jun	8	7
2097	2	4	6	Jul	7	8
2097	2	4	7	Aug	6	9
2097	2	4	8	Sep	5	1
2097	2	4	9	Oct	4	2
2097	2	4	10	Nov	3	3
2097	2	4	11	Dec	2	4
2097	2	4	12	Jan	1	5

Lo Shu Designations

Symbolic

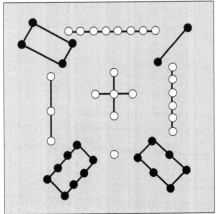

Trigrams

SUN	LI	KUN
CHEN	B5	TUI
KEN	KAN	CHIEN

Magic Square (Numbers)

4	9	2
3	5	7
8	1	6

278

Bibliography

Amen, Ra Un Nefer. The Metu Neter: Volume I. New York, NY: Kamit Corp Press 1990.

Amen, Ra Un Nefer. The Metu Neter: Volume II. New York, NY: Kamit Corp Press 1994.

Wilhelm, R. & Baynes, C., 1967. The I Ching or Book of Changes, With forward by Carl Jung. 3rd. ed., Bollingen Series XIX. Princeton NJ: Princeton University Press (1st ed. 1950).

Made in the USA
Lexington, KY
07 March 2014